"*Unceasing Worship* is a cut above the rest of the books on worship. Drawing on a lifetime of learning, artistry and leadership, Best writes with clarity, passion and deep humility about the great loves of his calling: the triune God, the Bible, churches, and music and the arts. There's encouragement, insight and challenges for every pastor and worship leader in this refreshing and inspiring book. *Unceasing Worship* is a rare gift of wisdom that combines clear thinking and warm-hearted devotion."

ROBB REDMAN, pastor, Forest Hills Presbyterian Church, Helotes, Texas, and author of *The Great Worship Awakening*

"Worship is simply the most important action in which any of us will ever engage. Harold Best tells us why. Worship is also distressingly conflicted, mired in contentious controversy and cheapened by clichés. Harold Best tells us why. But he does more, far more: in well-crafted sentences and arresting images Harold Best immerses in the deep and wide world of worship in which we receive and respond to God with 'all that is within me.'"

EUGENE H. PETERSON, Professor Emeritus of Spiritual Theology, Regent College

"In this book Harold Best has given the church a gift—the gift of understanding that worship is a poured-out offering of love to Jesus that we give him every day of our lives, with the wonderful effect that our corporate worship on Sunday is all the better for it. Along the way he exposes our fallenness as worshipers, our capacity for idolatry (especially music), and the real but limited role of art forms as conveyors of truth. Prophetic, timely, compelling—just what the Lord of the church ordered."

PAUL BASDEN, senior pastor, Preston Trail Community Church, Frisco, Texas, and author of *The Worship Maze*

"Harold Best has given us a full-field theology of worship. It is also written from the heart. Best hits the high notes and charts the pitfalls of humanity's instinctive, unceasing worship of God. Outstanding!"

PAUL F. M. ZAHL, Dean, Cathedral Church of the Advent, Birmingham, Alabama

"In a world filled with easy reads, this is a decidedly hard book. But it is exceedingly wise, and wisdom takes time and work—and love. Harold is my friend, and I know how agonizingly he labors over each word and phrase. That passion is alive on every page of this miraculous book. Like many of you, I have struggled alone all my life trying to understand what it is God wants of me when he calls me to worship. Harold Best has emerged from a din of voices to let us know we are not alone in our struggle to understand what worship demands, asks for and is. After all, this does not pretend, like so many others have pretended, to be an answer book. There is only one of those. This book is the sound of a voice, behind what was before a locked door. It invites us to struggle together to join together in unceasing worship to the One who alone deserves to be praised."

MICHAEL CARD, songwriter, musician and author of
Scribbling in the Sand and *A Fragile Stone*

"Most books on worship are filled with historical data or practical ideas. This book stands out because it is chock-full with wisdom. Every five-page segment leaves the reader with thought-provoking insights and questions to ponder, drawn from a fruitful lifetime of wrestling with how we can faithfully honor the God who created and redeemed us.

"Especially insightful is Best's insistence that worship must never be limited to what happens in a public event on Sunday morning. This theme makes this a book on worship not only for worship leaders, but for all worshipers who seek to renew their spiritual life. Consider studying this, one chapter at a time, with your church council, board, or worship leadership group."

JOHN D. WITVLIET, director, Calvin Institute of Christian Worship

UNCEASING WORSHIP

BIBLICAL PERSPECTIVES

ON WORSHIP AND THE ARTS

HAROLD M. BEST

IVP Books

An imprint of InterVarsity Press
Downers Grove, Illinois

InterVarsity Press
P.O. Box 1400, Downers Grove, IL 60515-1426
World Wide Web: www.ivpress.com
E-mail: email@ivpress.com

InterVarsity Press® is the book-publishing division of InterVarsity Christian Fellowship/USA®, a student movement active on campus at hundreds of universities, colleges and schools of nursing in the United States of America, and a member movement of the International Fellowship of Evangelical Students. For information about local and regional activities, write Public Relations Dept., InterVarsity Christian Fellowship/USA, 6400 Schroeder Rd., P.O. Box 7895, Madison, WI 53707-7895, or visit the IVCF website at <www.intervarsity.org>.

Scripture quotations, unless otherwise noted, are from the New Revised Standard Version of the Bible, *copyright 1989 by the Division of Christian Education of the National Council of the Churches of Christ in the USA. Used by permission. All rights reserved.*

Cover design: Rick Franklin

Cover image: James Maconochie/IllustrationWorks

ISBN-10: 0-8308-3229-7
ISBN-13: 978-0-8308-3229-3

Printed in the United States of America ∞

Library of Congress Cataloging-in-Publication Data

Best, Harold M.
Unceasing worship: biblical perspectives on worship and the arts/
Harold M. Best.
p. cm.
Includes bibliographical references.
ISBN 0-8308-3229-7 (pbk.: alk. paper)
1. Worship. 2. Christianity and the arts. 3. Music in churches.
I. Title.
BV10.3.B47 2003
261.5'7—dc21

2003010919

P	22	21	20	19	18	17	16	15	14	13	12	11	10	9	8	7
Y	22	21	20	19	18	17	16	15	14	13	12	11	10	09	08	

TO SAMUEL HOPE
AND JUEL MARIE WARNER

SAMUEL HOPE is a trustworthy, persevering and intellectually gifted musician. He is also the executive director of the four arts-accrediting associations in the United States: the National Association of Schools of Music, the National Association of Schools of Art and Design, the National Association of Schools of Theater, and the National Association of Schools of Dance. In this capacity he has brought unusual wisdom, stature and statesmanship to the field of accreditation, both within the arts and among the other academic disciplines. The nature of his work carries him from the arts themselves to accreditation standards and into the thickets of government policy, but always back again to the confounding variety of artistic expression. He seems able always to find light and shine it on a given agenda. But what is even more important about this gentleman is the comprehensive way he brings truth to bear on the making of art, the living of life and the particularities of his trade. He does this without superficial spiritualization or a self-referencing show of talent. He quietly glorifies God, before whom all of his work is authored and poured forth. I admire him greatly and am indebted to him for the richness he has brought to my mind and spirit.

JUEL MARIE WARNER is my wife. Her married name is, of course, Juel Marie Best. But here I choose her earlier name because in her maiden days she decided to set her love on me when I least deserved it. She saw a certain amount of good in me, so she says, and no small amount of blemish. She chose to befriend me, then to share herself with me and all too soon in our marriage—in an onset of spiritual dark and psychological gloom—she cradled me in her quiet strength, giving me comfort and cheer at no small expense to herself. Juel is a simple, uncluttered yet sophisticated and energized wife, mother, grandmother and elegant lady-at-large. Her amazing smile is interrupted only occasionally. No one is unwelcome in her company; she transmits to all a clear message of their worth and loveliness. She believes everything Jesus says. Her wisdom cuts through all the perplexing life stuff and comes to rest, time after time, smack in the middle of the truth that I so often doubt, complicate or overlook. I love her and want merely to love her all the more, so as to treat her as Jesus would, had he taken a wife to himself.

To these strikingly different neighbors, each of whom I truly love, I dedicate this book with gratitude that I have been allowed to company with them.

CONTENTS

INTRODUCTION

Why another book on worship? Who should read this particular one, and why?

As to the first question, I want first to acknowledge the value of a growing body of work on the subject. Thanks to much of it, we have an impressive store of information and perspective that should significantly enhance certain particulars of the work of both ministry and laity in corporate worship. I admire the spirit, the passion and, in some instances, the nearly encyclopedic minds that have provided us with new material and newly considered older material.

Having said this, I find that throughout most of these works the subject of worship is limited to what happens in the corporate assembly in its assigned times and places. While it is currently popular to say that all of life is worship, there seems to be little thought given to a theology of worship that makes comprehensive sense out of this statement. Thus the significance of weekly worship continues as a separate subject. This carries the implication that time-and-place worship is the primary, if not only, venue for our worship, while the remainder of our living falls into another category. And it is on behalf of this time-place emphasis that we have the abundance of symposia, workshops, books, materials, methods and options. We have gotten used to referring to this heightened interest as a worship renewal, but I want to suggest that there is a difference between a renewal of interest regarding the corporate assembly and a comprehensive renewal that issues out of a radical shift in emphasis between time and place and day-by-day continuity.

Furthermore, two other separations have quietly worked their way into prominence, both of which arise out of otherwise welcome changes in the life of the church. I refer first to what is regularly called *contemporary worship,* or *praise and worship.* Here, the separation can be seen in the way *worship* often refers primarily, if not exclusively, to the opening segment with worship as the overriding theme. The rest of the service, by implication, is something else. The second separation is even narrower than the first but derives directly out of it. I refer to music itself, which to many leaders and laypersons turns out to be "the worship." As a result, the glorious and inescapable glory of worshiping God in variegated and integrated continuity is overlooked.

If worship renewal is the real issue, then it becomes all the more important to approach the subject from the largest possible perspective—one that takes in the best of the newer practices, integrates them with a historical perspective that has regularly dealt with the tension between new and old, and enlarges the periphery to include the most far-reaching theology of which the Scriptures are capable. Doing this will open the subject up to the force of christocentric theology and will therefore summon us to consider what it means to live a life of worship of which time-and-place emphases are but a part.

This I have tried to do. The burden of this book develops the concept of continuous outpouring as the rubric for our worship. As God eternally outpours within his triune self, and as we are created in his image, it follows that we too are continuous outpourers, incurably so. The trouble with our outpouring is that it is fallen. It needs redeeming, else we spend our outpouring on false gods appearing to us in any number of guises. Salvation is the only way our continuous outpouring—our continuous worship—is set aright and urged into the fullness of Christ.

It is only in this sense that the seminal concepts in the Old (in which Spirit and truth are subject to time and place) are consummated in the New (in which time and place are subject to Spirit and truth). And it is only in this sense that the gradual unfolding toward Christ keeps enlarging the arena of worship until we discover that our worship and our continued outpouring are one and the same. Only then can we discover a new brilliance and richness in corporate worship, witnessing, preaching, praying, teaching, imagining and crafting.

Once we grasp the full implications of continuous outpouring, we can speak with authority and freedom about the arts and about the union of authentic worship and artistic action. We can be introduced to the union of God's creatorhood with human creativity (a larger subject than the arts themselves), and we can learn from the former while plying our trades in the latter. We can then approach the subject of culture—the world's view of it and the Christian view of it. We can come to clearer understanding of the difference between the things of the world and the spirit of the world. Then we are free to celebrate the riot of human creativity in its worldwide and centuries-long unfolding. We are free to understand how impoverished the church is when it limits itself to just a few ways of raising its voice to the Lord in continuing worship. And finally we can come to a better understanding of the place of quality within the whole.

These are things I have attempted to address, and I invite you to join the conversation.

Who should read this book? Worship is not a complex specialty but a wonderfully common practice. I respectfully suggest that pastors, worship leaders, ministers of worship and the arts, musicians and artists, students and professors (especially in the seminaries), traditionalists and contemporists should read it. Likewise I have faith in the ability and desire of Christian laypersons to go deeper and deeper into Christian thoughtfulness and to make their way into territory that may at first seem unfamiliar or threatening. This book is for them as well. I would like to believe that no part of this book lies beyond the hunger capacity of ardent Christians. Thus I feel that most, if not all, of the book would serve well for discussion groups interested in the relationship of worship to the arts, to work of all kinds as well as to cultural issues.

I am not the first to develop the idea of continuous worship. By all means, every thoughtful Christian should read *Engaging with God* by David Peterson. This work is what its subtitle promises: a biblical theology of worship. I cannot begin to say how much Peterson's work has meant to me, if for no other reason than for the intertestamental exegetical skills with which he goes about his task. But for decades prior to my reading Peterson, I was haunted by the idea that worship, along with every iota of Christian living, is a seamlessness, a continuity, a unity that in no way can be broken down into chronological or spatiotemporal segments. I leaned heavily on the material in Romans 12, John 4 and many of the Psalms in order to justify my convictions. Early on in my work in Christian higher education and church music practice, these beginning thoughts took on increasing life and clearer shape. They became the center of the speaking and limited writing that I was able to do and ever so gradually assisted me in reforming my aesthetic thought. In being influenced by more people than I can count, and not always knowing where their thinking and mine intertwined, a long-running theological elegance has gradually made its way into my heart and mind. Sometimes it has taken the form of an innocent phrase; other times, a long drink at a clear running spring. I confess that I sometimes feel myself to be just a basin, catching the supply from others, hoping that it does not grow stale from neglect. In putting it this way, I confess to being fascinated with the idea that truth and wisdom are in the public domain, not a dram of which is copyright. When we live in its midst, taking in its many epiphanies, the line between it and its humanly crafted dialects sometimes becomes blurred. Yet those who have been directly influential must be acknowledged.

This is where David Peterson, with his authoritative yet pastoral expertise, has confirmed and added to the convictions I have had for so long a time. My hope is that I will quietly and humbly walk alongside him, not so much to add to what he has done as perhaps to say the same things another way and to draw the arts into the conversation that he has so expertly initiated. And this is where the likes of Nicholas Wolterstorff, Karl Barth, C. S. Lewis, Jacques Ellul and Søren Kierkegaard, along with the artistic and wise force of great literature, have been crucial to my mind and heart.

In all of this, I admit to my slowness, to my more-than-occasional contrariness and prejudice. I keep uncovering camouflaged snobbery and aesthetic pride that trip me up and often prevent the development of a more biblical, in-Christ assessment of all practices, especially those that do not meet my personal expectations. Even in the earlier drafts of this book, I often found myself thinking unpleasantly, a residue of which remained even in a later version that my editor sent to a quintet of anonymous readers. Thanks to the caring candor with which most of them expressed themselves, I became more able to sort out the difference between legitimate concern and complaining—even this late. If any anger remains, I pray that it is biblical, bathed in a love for the truth and brought to naught once the sun goes down. As Paul said to Timothy, "The Lord's servant must not be quarrelsome but kindly to everyone, an apt teacher, patient" (2 Tim 2:24). Likewise, if there is anything winsome and truthful in this book, I pray that you will forget Harold Best and think on Jesus.

I say these things because I am a person still on a sojourn, not always sure where I am going, but trusting in the One who has sent me out. I say them because even the best of my inquiries and conclusions can be couched in contumely instead of prophetic wisdom. I sincerely hope that this published version contains more wheat than tares.

Writing this book has profoundly changed me, as strange as this may seem. I do not know about other authors, nor do I understand the paradox, but for me, serious inquiry has not just resulted in the filling out of thoughts but in their profound reform. Thanks be to God for his infinite patience in keeping me from writing *Unceasing Worship* until a huge assortment of issues had been further clarified.

I want to thank the InterVarsity staff for their kindness and grace. They are a family of lovely people who take good care of those whom they serve. In particular, Al Hsu, my main editor, deserves more than passing thanks. He is quick, witty, wise, far seeing and humble. His insights have been good for me even when taking me in a direction where I would rather not go. He is an author in his own right. He is one whose life shows a synthesis of brokenness and victory. I am thankful to have been put in his charge.

PART ONE

UNCEASING WORSHIP AS CONTINUOUS OUTPOURING

1

NOBODY DOES NOT WORSHIP

Worship is at once about who we are, about who or what our god is and about how we choose to live. It is about something that is quite simple but wrapped in a mystery. It is about God himself, who has but one face and whose face has been clearly shown in the person and work of his only begotten Son. It is about a world in which worship takes on a thousand faces. It is also about Satan, dressed as an angel of light, disarmingly attractive yet inherently false, whose faces are cleverly multiplied and whose one desire is to undo what has already been done from the eternities.

The thousand faces of worship contain both deadened and lively countenances. They are the lost and the found, all of whom are continuous worshipers, for as the title of this chapter states, nobody does not worship. We begin with one fundamental fact about worship: at this very moment, and for as long as this world endures, everybody inhabiting it is bowing down and serving something or someone—an artifact, a person, an institution, an idea, a spirit, or God through Christ. Everyone is being shaped thereby and is growing up toward some measure of fullness, whether of righteousness or of evil. No one is exempt and no one can wish to be. We are, every one of us, unceasing worshipers and will remain so forever, for eternity is an infinite extrapolation of one of two conditions: a surrender to the sin-

fulness of sin unto infinite loss or the commitment of personal righteousness unto infinite gain. This is the central fact of our existence, and it drives
every other fact. Within it lies the story of creation, fall, redemption and
new creation or final loss.

I have worked out a definition for worship that I believe covers every
possible human condition. It is this: *Worship is the continuous outpouring of
all that I am, all that I do and all that I can ever become in light of a chosen or
choosing god.* I want to make four preliminary observations about this definition that will feed into the many themes that this book comprises, particularly in the first six chapters.

First, the definition includes the entire human race. It is not just about
Christians, but all people everywhere who are going about their worship,
their submission to whatever masters them and their witness as to why they
live the way they do. This is why I have not yet capitalized the word "god."

Second, the words about a chosen or choosing god are meant not only
to articulate two fundamentally contrasting theological positions taken
within the body of Christ but also to depict the confused condition of lostness itself.[1] Among Christians, the debate about choosing God and being
chosen by him, as divisive as it can become, is not about two Saviors or
two atonements but about two sides of a mystery. The problem lies more
with theology than with Scripture, in that theological studies—systematics
in particular—seem always to have trouble with mysteries and paradoxes.
But with lostness, choosing a god and being "chosen" by one are con-
ducted completely in the dark and result in an infinite standoff. Lostness
is a delusion in which "choosing" a god and "being chosen" are mirror images, two opposites within a single delusion. That is, lost individuals in deluded sovereignty "choose," only to be enslaved by the choice they have
made. They can then believe the latter is the same as "being chosen." The
worship of false gods, then, is a negative condition in which sovereignty
and enslavement infinitely cancel each other out.

Third, the definition stresses the reality and foundational importance of
continuousness. That is, worship does not stop and start, despite our notions to the contrary. Once we place emphasis on specific times, places and
methods, we misunderstand worship's biblical meaning. Worship may ebb
and flow, may take on various appearances and may be unconscious or

conscious, intense and ecstatic or quiet and commonplace, but it is continuous. When we sin, worship does not stop. It changes directions and reverts back to what it once was, even if only for an instant. Repentance—the turning from and (re)turning to—is the only solution.

Fourth, although I believe every word in the above definition to have particular value, the term *continuous outpouring* particularly stands out. These two words are the only descriptors I can think of that take in both the work of God and the work of humankind as these together eventually inform a biblically complete concept of worship. Permit me to expand a bit more on them.

Continuous implies relentlessness. It is the opposite of periodic or sporadic. On the strictly physical and temporal side of things, literal continuity is impossible. I continue to breathe until I die, I continue to eat until I am full, I continue to compose a piece of music until I think I have finished. But on the spiritual side, continuity is of the essence. God is continually and unchangeably the I AM THAT I AM ; his Word abides forever; Jesus Christ is the same yesterday, today and forever. And so, over and above our physicality and temporality, we have been created to enter into God's side of continuousness. Faithfulness to one's spouse is to continue as long as life itself; we are continually to love God with heart, soul and mind; we are to love our neighbor without letup; we are to forgive endlessly; we are to continue our stewardship whether we work or rest; we are to continue in the truth whether we play or preach. At the end of all these we face a continuity of eternal life or eternal death. My choice of the term *continuous* is, therefore, solemn and deliberate.

As for *outpouring*, note that there are many words we can use to talk about the way one person relates to another: *serving, relating, giving, befriending, revealing, fellowshiping, sojourning, sacrificing, bearing up with* and the like. Any one of these relational words might have been used in place of *outpouring*. But I chose this word not only because of its scriptural force but also because it implies lavishness and generosity: when I pour something, I give it up; I let it go. Dripping is not pouring; there is space between the drops. But in pouring, the flow is organically and consistently itself. In spite of a mixed simile, pouring is seamless.

As to the scriptural importance of pouring, one need only go to a con-

cordance to discover how it pervades, explicitly or implicitly. We see the
concept of pouring in the sacrificial system of the Old Testament. We see
it in the comprehensive sense of giving, of pouring ourselves out toward a
neighbor. Most of all, we see it in Christ's own perfect sacrifice—a once-
for-all pouring out of his incarnate self on the cross. And there may be no
better final descriptor for our personal lives than in Paul's summation of
his own: "I am already being poured out as a libation, and the time of my
departure has come" (2 Tim 4:6).

Outpouring surpasses measuring out or filling quotas, even to the extent
that it does not matter if some of it spills over in gracious waste. I think of
Mary's caring carelessness when she anointed Jesus' feet. The room would
not have been filled with such abundant fragrance had she merely tithed it
out. It was the waste (both a Judas word and holy word) that was so magnificent and intoxicating. The example of this draws me even further, and I
think of Jesus, whose entire being was poured out—the world would say
wasted—for our salvation, perfume for his Father's feet. This fullness of love
is not just enough; it is infinitely enough. And when I am swept into the
infinite reach of outpouring, there are no adjectives that can increase the
value of the nouns we employ to embody it: *love, grace, favor, mercy, power,
presence.* It is the consideration of these grand qualities that makes the word
outpouring so powerful and so necessary to the definition of worship.

No one's worship can possibly be self-contained, even when it barely
dribbles out. Thus, looking ahead to chapter five, *worship* and *witness*
are two words for one comprehensive reality. Even self-worship—self-
absorbed outpouring, if you will—cannot be contained. In its perversity
it infects those who come near its self-worshiping center. Likewise, hiding one's light under a bushel is a substitute outpouring in that something is bound to show in place of what is being hidden, and those
coming in contact with it may well imitate it, joining the uncomfortably
large world of hidden light.

Finally, continuous outpouring, whatever its kind and quality, is bound
to change the outpourer, whether comprehensively or incrementally,
whether for good or for evil. Being, becoming and doing, in whatever
cause-effect configuration they may occur, are forcibly linked to who or
whatever has the mastery. Everyone, even the most fiercely self-justifying

and self-made individual, is mastered by someone or something, despite all blustering protestation to the contrary. Being mastered means obedience, willing or otherwise; obedience means service, willing or otherwise; and serving works its own changes in the servant. Even being lukewarm is still outpouring.

No discussion of worship is possible without the consideration of what worship was like before the Fall. Until recently I was hesitant to speculate about what this must have been like. I worried that I might come up with a fairy-tale version of worship, something so unattached, so conspicuously distant and hypermystical that it would be of no use. However, worry has left me because I have slowly discovered three verifiable realities to guide me both back into Eden and away from it directly to God through Christ: (1) the concept of continuous outpouring as it describes the nature of God; (2) the doctrine of *imago Dei*; (3) the sojourn of Christ on earth.

CONTINUOUS OUTPOURING AND THE NATURE OF GOD

We must begin with God, not merely because all other beginnings, continuations and endings must be explained in light of his triune Self but because continuous outpouring must above all be informed by and understood in light of his person and work. God is the uniquely Continuous Outpourer. He cannot but give of himself, reveal himself, pour himself out. Even before he chooses to create, and before he chooses to reveal himself beyond himself, he eternally pours himself out to his triune Self in unending fellowship, ceaseless conversation and immeasurable love unto an infinity of the same. Within limitless intercourse, transcendent speech and splendid work (the Father to the Son, the Son to the Spirit, the Spirit to the Father), the Godhead goes about its glorious work of being the eternal I AM THAT I ACT THAT I AM, with nothing contingent, preceding or following. This is the originating outpouring for which these mere words fail and into which our faith-not-yet-become-sight peers with intense longing.[2]

GOD'S OUTPOURING IN CREATION

But even in his satisfying completeness, God decided not to keep himself to himself. He chose to create a vastness out of nothing and to do so with infinite imagination and craft. He did not do this to satisfy an unmet need or to bring finish to something. And he did not do it to gain greater praise from the heavenly host, who must certainly have been peering into and rejoicing in the glories of eternal outpouring long before the Spirit breathed upon the waters.

God's creation is outpouring beyond himself and yet not himself. His creation comes of abounding grace and outpouring love. This creating grace—preceding, but inseparable from, sin-healing grace—is a gift of the Trinity to itself even as it is a gift to the stuff that he creates. The creation is an outpoured work, a finished work, a good work. Furthermore, it is not a work left to itself—it is not comfortless. God's outpouring toward the creation is shown in his urgent and continuing love for it, in his declaration that it has a named goodness and that it is comely and useful. His outpouring is shown in his faithful and continual involvement in its workings, for God's nature prohibits him from disengagement. He may appear to leave something alone, but this is only to show that his continuous outpouring encompasses his nearness, his distance and his withinness. Even then, his leaving alone is an action that comes of a sovereign engagement in all things, transcending our versions of sequence, spatial differences and time lapses. Thus right now, and for as long as God himself decides it to be so, creation is being held together by the outpouring Word of his Son, in whom and through whom all things come into being and consist (Col 1:16-17; Heb 1:3).

God creates; God loves. Love is not static; it cannot but pour itself outward. God's creating love and his love for the creation are not lesser loves than, say, his love for his Son, for the Spirit or for the angelic host. It is simply love at work in the doing of a different and material thing. When God creates, his outpouring love extends beyond himself without in any way diminishing the preexisting love he has for his eternal self. Creating is a certain kind of work that he sovereignly chooses to do to show that nothing that he does can possibly fall outside his love. But this is not the end of it.

CONTINUOUS OUTPOURING, *IMAGO DEI* AND UNFALLEN WORSHIP

God's grace, inexplicable generosity and immeasurable imagination brought him to create a race of beings in his own image, *imago Dei*. As complex and involved as our thinking can become about this mystery, I believe we can boil it down to this foundational idea: because God is the Continuous Outpourer, we bear his image as continuous outpourers. Being made in the image of God means that we were created to act the way God acts, having been given a nature within which such behavior is natural. The difference between God and humankind, merely and mysteriously, is one of singular infinitude and unique and multiplied finitude. Whatever character or attribute God inherently possesses and pours out, we were created finitely to show and to pour out after his manner. Otherwise, the concept of *imago Dei* would have but fractional, even precarious, significance. Being told to be holy even as the Father is holy, for example, is to understand two things at once: (1) When we were originally created, holiness was not a choice among choices; it was the only way we could be. (2) When we fell, instruction became necessary because the only way we could be was ripped from us.

We were created continuously outpouring. Note that I did not say we were created *to be* continuous outpourers. Nor can I dare imply that we were created *to* worship. This would suggest that God is an incomplete person whose need for something outside himself (worship) completes his sense of himself. It might not even be safe to say that we were created *for* worship, because the inference can be drawn that worship is a capacity that can be separated out and eventually relegated to one of several categories of being. I believe it is strategically important, therefore, to say that we were created continuously outpouring—we were created in that condition, at that instant, *imago Dei*. We did not graduate into being in the image of God; we were, by divine fiat, already in the image of God at the instant the Spirit breathed into our dust. Hence we were created continuously outpouring.

God outpours from the eternities, noncontingently; we do so because we were made so, contingently. Creator (singular infinity) and creature (unique finitude) are bound together in mutual love, communion and work. Each gives fully, the one out of endless bounty and the other out of responding stewardship. This is not an apples/oranges affair, the sovereign one always getting and the submissive one always giving. Instead it is one of reciprocity—free, full exchange between Creator and *imago Dei*, love unto continued love, giving unto continued giving, adoration unto continued adoration. It is one of outpouring willingness—the willingness of all-sufficiency bonded to the willingness of dependency, prevenient love bonded to responding love, transcendent worth in union with created worth. There can be no call to worship in this blessed condition. Continuous outpouring is of the essence, God from the eternities and humankind from the moment dust became *imago Dei*.

Now we are on safe ground in describing what it originally meant to worship, because God and humankind are knit together—the triune God continuously outpouring within himself and toward *imago Dei*, and *imago Dei* continuously outpouring toward God. Now we are free to understand the eternal and original dimension to worship; now we are free to say that we were created worshiping. Now we can say this without qualification: worship is the unique and finite side of continuous outpouring, just as lordship is the unique and infinite side of continuous outpouring. By nature, God cannot worship, even though he continuously pours out. But everything that worship is on the human side is an outpouring of what it means to be created in the image of God. Worship, in this initial and final sense, is human outpouring to the outpouring of lordship. Thus, if our theology of God and our theology of *imago Dei* are correct, our theology of worship will likewise be correct, and we can link continuous outpouring to continuous worship. But there is more.

CONTINUOUS OUTPOURING AND CHRIST ON EARTH

If our Christology is correct, we can view the entire sojourn of the incarnate God on earth as continuous outpouring of a three-in-one kind: continuous outpouring with his triune self as part of the Godhead, continuous outpouring as perfect man to his heavenly Father and continuous outpouring toward the world as the only Savior. His earthly life was thirty-three years of unrelenting worship. He is the perfect worshiper, knowing his Father uninterruptedly, submissively and completely.

In this sense Christ came to show us how Adam and Eve should have continued their worship. He came not only to take away our sin but also to show us that there was no fatal flaw, no hidden weakness in God's original creating act. And we must not forget that Christ's demonstration of the originally perfect work of his Father was set in the severe and disruptive context of a world wandering to and fro under the bidding of alien powers. His temptation in the wilderness was far more stringent and contortive than anything Adam and Eve faced. His daily sojourn was not with a perfect creation but with one set against him. He came to his own but was not received. Every action, every outpouring was sweetly contrasted with the inverted urgencies of sin swirling around him. Christ-on-earth, both God and image of God, both Creator and creature—this dearest of persons is a fully revealed picture of both how our unfallen parents should have continued to worship and how the body of Christ is eventually to worship. Furthermore, Christ's own words about worship, especially in John 4, sufficiently underscore the concept of continuous outpouring for the body of Christ. (This passage will be discussed more fully in chapter two.)

CONTINUOUS OUTPOURING AND THE FALL

With the exception of Christ's earthly sojourn, we have been discussing continuous outpouring, worship and unfallenness in the same breath: God as a perfectly whole and holy person; Adam and Eve as created perfectly, *imago Dei*; and Christ, perfect God and perfect Man. Each is a continuous outpourer—God as Lord, the human being as worshiper, Christ as both. We have patterns aplenty, but we are incapable of living them out fully. Here is where we must speak and think differently. We are fallen. We are infected hideously and need a Redeemer, else our hideousness perpetuates ad infinitum. So we turn to this crucial question: What happened to continuous outpouring in light of the Fall?

The Fall did not signal the end of worship or continuous outpouring. Something deeper happened, far down in our being, whereby our entirety was inverted and turned to ruin. We chose to believe a lie, spoken by one with whom truth is impossible but who skillfully dresses falsehood in light. We took to this reversed light and were immediately lost and undone. Our outpouring was falsified. But it continued, with one telling difference: we exchanged gods. We turned from the only One who is not creature and were left, not in a persisting vacuum (this would have been a premature hell), but with a new plethora, the universe of innumerable false gods, false religions and the religionizing of anything that catches our fancy. Heavens were invented. Evil was further falsified by making it appear to be good. Multiple salvations were enumerated, as were the systems invented to bring them about. In short, we became idolaters, for the worship of anything but God alone is idolatry.

There is no other way to explain the way our outpouring continues than to say that as an intrinsic part of our nature it remains with us and is ceaselessly at work, even as we choose death in pouring ourselves out toward false gods. As mysterious as this fact is, we can well consider it a grace, because it is a ready highway for the coming of the Redeemer. To be sure, the rough places need to be smoothed, the hills and valleys made low. The truth must be known that the Continuous Outpourer has come down among us with an enormous meaning that the prophets could only peer into. And those who see his glory, the children of a lively faith, find that slowly but surely authentic worship is reborn in their enfeebled lives.

We are not left comfortless. Christ has come.

2

WHAT IS AUTHENTIC WORSHIP?

Christ the Savior has come. He has done a work that no one else could ever do. Having come to us from the eternities, he comes again and again, yet he abides in us forever. "It is finished" runs through the fullness of the comings of Christ. Our outpouring need no longer be wasted in lostness. In him alone our new work begins and embraces the whole of our living. In Christ, *imago Dei* comes home. The prodigal son returns from pouring himself out among the swine and the husks, again and again, to the waiting Father. Continuous outpouring, of which the Savior is Author and Finisher, is made pure and is made ours.

Authentic worship can only be *in* Christ. It is not driven by a liturgy or a call to worship, a change in style or a methodology. Redemption does not signal the beginning of worship. Instead it marks its once-for-all cleansing. It is washed in the blood of the Lamb and turned into a following after of the example of Christ and into continued deliverance from the intrusions of fallen worship. Our redemption and our worship are henceforth one with the other. Our entirety, not just a narrowed spiritual corridor or mere churchgoing and ministry, is swept up in newly complete living. Work becomes worship, just as worship becomes duty and delight. Eden is not just restored; it is surpassed, for in his redemptive outpouring, God gave us the supreme gift of Christ-in-us-in-Christ. Our salvation comprises a new-found continuous outpouring of everything that we are and can become in light of all that Christ was, is and shall be—always the same, always new, yesterday, today and forever.

In this chapter I want to emphasize the importance of continuousness, saying once more that continuous worship and continuous outpouring are synonymous. As important as it was to make inquiry into unfallen worship in chapter one and the creational linkage between God and image of God, we must now apply our thinking and our biblical knowledge to our present sojourn. This means revisiting what we already know and praying that we will stop narrowing it down to a few handy tools. So we begin at the roots with the irreplaceable triad of faith, hope and love. Authentic outpouring and continuous worship are grounded in these as in nothing else.

FAITH AND AUTHENTIC WORSHIP

Living by faith means worshiping by faith, and worshiping by faith means living by faith. The two are a seamless continuum. We do not begin by faith and then, at some point of maturity, move to something higher and more effectual. Faith is its own steppingstone unto even more faith, even as continuous outpouring leads to increased outpouring.

We worship by faith. Worship is no more started up because we have pushed the faith button than our faith is started because we have pushed the worship button. Saving faith is not a different kind of faith than continuing faith. We do not step into or out of faith, nor do we step into or out of worship. Therefore, continual worship is not of a different substance than worship that takes place at a set time and in a certain place. The faith by which we live and the faithfulness of God cannot be separated. Our trust is in his trustworthiness and cannot survive on anything of our own manufacture. Karl Barth says it this way:

> Only faith survives; faith which is not a work, not even a negative work; not an achievement, not even the achievement of humility. . . . Faith is the ground, the new order, the light. . . . Faith is not . . . an atmosphere which [men] can breathe; not a system under

which they can arrange their lives. . . . There is nothing but God Himself, God only.[1]

It is important to understand the way faith, as defined in Hebrews 11:1, is coupled to Genesis 15:6. In the latter passage, we read how righteousness was accounted to Abraham because he believed God without doing one thing to start his believing. In the Hebrews passage, it is not the doing of something that is central. The verb *is* becomes pivotal: faith *is* substance and evidence. Faith needs nothing outside itself to substantiate it. Faith does not bring substance and evidence to something; faith is itself substance and evidence, even in the absence of the very things for which faith hopes. This difference between *being evidence* itself and *bringing evidence* to something cannot be overlooked. It goes to the heart of authentic worship. Forgetting this difference may indicate the beginnings of false sacramentalism, then legalism and finally idolatry.

If I am a carpenter framing out a house, as a Christian I will certainly want this work to glorify God. I will have every obligation to say that I pour my carpentry over the feet of Jesus as sweet perfume. But if I assume that faith brings a special substance or evidence to the work itself (that is, if I say that the stuff that constitutes the framing—the wood, the nails, the chalk lines, the cuts, the angles, the eventual wholeness—has become inherently special because I have put it together by faith), then I am ever so subtly slipping into darkened territory. I may even slip further by believing that calling my work worship changes me, instead of believing that because I have been radically changed, my work *is* worship. The danger is that substance and evidence begin to grow out of my work instead of remaining the property of faith alone. If I am not careful, I will slip even further by waiting for or depending on the work to make my faith effectual— God is nearer when I am carpentering than when I am not. This by no means implies that I cannot feel good (or bad) about my work or that I am not built up and confirmed by work well done. Rather, it means that the primary foundation for my life is found in the substance and evidence that faith alone *is*, not in the circumstantial comings and goings of my days.

I want to jump ahead a few chapters for a moment and apply this concept to music in corporate worship. (We could use vestments or architecture or sculpture or liturgy to make the same point.) If in making music or listening to it I assume that faith will bring substance and evidence *to* the music, so as make it more "worshipful," I am getting into real trouble. If I truly love the music—that is, if I have chosen a church that uses "my music" and I am deeply moved by it—I can make the mistake of coupling faith to musical experience by assuming that the power and effectiveness of music is what brings substance and evidence to my faith. I can then quite easily forge a connection between the power of music and the nearness of the Lord. Once this happens, I may even slip fully into the sin of *equating* the power of music and the nearness of the Lord. At that point music joins the bread and the wine in the creation of a new sacrament or even a new kind of transubstantiation.

Or let's say that I deeply love Jesus but I detest the music—it is not "my music." What am I then to do in the absence of a linkage between having faith and loving the music? Where is God in all of this? If he is in the music, I will never find him, because to me there is no substance or evidence, even though others are seemingly finding him there. Do I wait for the right kind of music so that my faith becomes effectual? Do I look for another church, hoping that my faith will be fed and my felt needs met? Or do I turn from the music to the Lord, knowing that faith remains faith and the music is merely music and not a sacramental substance that mediates between God and me? I hope that the last question becomes the only question. Otherwise, faith needs exterior scaffolding for worship to become authentic worship.

I do not think I am playing exegetical games with Hebrews 11 when I say that going to work or going to church or taking a vacation may often seem more like *not* receiving the promises than the opposite. As with the heroes of the faith, we ordinary persons might spend lengthy times, even whole lives, without receiving what we think we should have. Worship leaders may exhaust their repertoires, preachers may ply every scriptural byway and praying may go on without ceasing, and the only thing there is the substance and evidence that faith alone offers. On the other hand, our worship can be loaded with blessing after blessing; we are receiving the promises in quick succession and we bless God for every evidence sent our way. But these cannot outweigh or substitute for the kind of faith that is its own substance and evidence. Faith is not circumstantial, yet all circumstances must be gathered together and subsumed under a life of faith.

AUTHENTIC WORSHIP AND HOPE

I believe it is more difficult to get a thoroughly biblical handle on hope than on faith or love. This is partly due to the ways we downgrade this word by using it when we are not sure of an outcome or when we want to upgrade a future circumstance in relation to a present one. We cross our fingers and hope that things will get better. "I hope," "I wish," even "I pray that" are common partners in the exercise of hoping against doubt, fear and improbability. Furthermore, there is no extended treatise on hope in Scripture as there is on faith (Heb 11) or love (1 Cor 13). The Gospels hardly mention the word (Lk 6:34 may be the only instance), yet the Old Testament, particularly Job and Psalms, uses the word with some frequency. However, it is from the epistles, particularly those by Paul, Peter and the writer to the Hebrews, that the most solid picture can be drawn.

In virtually all biblical instances, hope comes across in a profoundly different way than it does in our secular usages. There is a grounding, a fixed conviction, a brightened outlook that cannot be realized without a direct linkage to the flowering of faith and the assurance of love. Thus the substance and evidence that faith inherently is, is also the final substance and evidence that hope anticipates with unclouded assurance. Love embraces the whole unconditionally and endlessly.

In this sense we can say that we worship continuously in hoping continuously. We can connect our thinking about hope to that of faith by saying first that hope is the forward joy of substance and evidence. Hope is not something we lay hold of in the absence of substance. We cannot afford to say that because there is no substance and evidence now, I will hope that it will appear sooner or later. This relegates hope to a conditional role that depends more on my quantitative concept of substance and evidence. Then I begin to interpret substance and evidence by what I observe happening around me. I become the interpreter and measurer; faith ceases to be faith and hope forsakes itself by resting in what it can see. In short, I have confined God to my spiritual backyard.

But hope that is seen is not hope (Rom 8:24). How surprising that this statement immediately follows this one: "For we were saved in this hope" (NKJV; or even "We are saved by hope," KJV). That is, even though substance and evidence may abound around me, whether of faith or of works, I cannot rest in what I can see. I must press on from hope unto continued hope, remembering that I am not guessing at something but trusting fully in that which, from the eternities, has already been substantively realized in the Lord of all hope. Our hope, then, is in Christ, just as our faith is. The substance and evidence, both realized and hoped for, are securely unified in the Savior.

Because of hope, authentic worship has a dimension to it that goes way beyond the blessing or the power or the effectiveness of circumstance. Let's return to the carpenter. His work and his worship are united before the Lord. His work, as we said earlier, does not substantiate his faith. Likewise, his work (let's assume that it is of the highest quality) turns out to be everything he hoped for. But this kind of hope is an earthly hope, a materially measurable one, related more to what his skills have made him capable of than to what he is incapable of on his own. It is similar to having faith that a hammer will drive a nail or a properly designed roof will withstand a heavy snow. But a biblical hope is in a completely different dimension: our hope is not grounded in what we are capable of; rather, we must go to Christ for hope's substantiation. Christ is, literally, our hope (1 Tim 1:1). By faith, hope sees into the magnificence of the completed work of redemption; it sees into the fullness of the wisdom of God, into the summing up of everything in the lordship of Christ. The carpenter has this hope, which reaches way beyond the hopes of his working trade. And when he joins his brothers and sisters in corporate worship, this ultimate hope does not shift in meaning or extent but continues while he sings, prays, hears and responds, even as it does when he hammers, saws and builds.

I also like to think of hope as the architectural agent of faith. By faith, I live in the substance and evidence that is of faith and not works. By hope, my living takes on a faithful shape, a spiritually transformed shape that has a holy relevance beyond the mere measurable substances and evidences that abound around me and with which my life is filled, in any combination of poverty or abundance, suffering or joy. There is a temporal shape to these circumstances, to be sure, and I can craft any number of life stories and wisdom pearls out of them. But these do not create the true shape that pleases God. The shape that he wants me to sculpt and treasure is faith-

and hope-driven, started up at the instant of new birth, derived out of the mystery of Christ-in-me-in-Christ and consummated in the sovereignty of God. All the while I am continuously at worship, continuously outpouring, by faith and in hope.

AUTHENTIC WORSHIP AND LOVE

Our continuous outpouring is to be rooted in love unto continuing love. We do not love because we worship; we worship in that we love. If faith is substance and evidence, and if hope is the architectural force that gives substance and evidence its forward shape, then love constitutes the rooting and the grounding of the whole (Eph 3:17).[2] Love raises faithful living and worshiping into a gracious, celebrative, unconditional, unfussed, giving and sharing outpouring. The description of what love is and does in 1 Corinthians 13, and especially the supremacy that Paul accords it in the final verse of that chapter, is an exact description of the way continuously worshiping people should live. And faith itself, without which the just cannot live, carries an extraordinary nuance, for it is not whole without love. Stated positively, it is love that makes faith effectual and puts it in working order (Gal 5:6). Paul is doing both in the Galatians and the Corinthians passages what Christ did when he compressed the Law, the Prophets and the Commandments into one statement in which love of God, love of neighbor and love of self are seamlessly unified. We might even say that love is the single most whole item in the triad in that it roots, grounds and makes effectual the rest. In this sense we can speak of God's love (permit this anthropomorphism) as that which drove him most to give up his Son for our salvation. We can begin to understand the enormity of love when we inquire into any doctrine or any facet of our salvation or any aspect of our living. Sooner or later, we run straight on into love, and love informs and reforms and transforms.

If I were to make God's being, his doing and his love into one name, God is I AM THAT I LOVE THAT I ACT. God's being and doing, completely at one, are love outpoured even into the infinity of itself. Since he is the Author and Finisher of our faith, we cannot but expect his outpouring love to inform, to urge and to guarantee the very faith that only he can increase in us. The intertwining of faith and love gives to the children of God (especially to us who doubt easily) a firmer hold on him. It is God's inestimable love for us, birthing our love for him, that turns faith and hope into stronger and stronger realities. I am convinced that this is why Paul is so bold as to condition faith's effectuality on love. Even as I write this, I confess to learning this truth in a new way, for it seems that faith, substance and evidence want to elude me—or I want to elude them—as I seek to press on into even the tiniest measure of the stature and fullness of Christ. But I know that the frail love I have for him is not possible without his first loving me, and I know that his love presses me upward to higher ground, further and further away from the erosive backwash of unbelief. Whatever befalls us, wherever we are in our sojourn with the Lord, we cannot escape the simple fact that our worship and our outpouring are to be continuous if for no other reason than that love is ceaseless.

I have recently come to wonder whether the Reformers paid too little attention to the wholeness of the faith-hope-love triad. I wonder, too, about what more could have happened within the body of Christ had the doctrine of love as the effectualizer of faith been pressed with the zeal that "faith alone" has been. What would it be like to imagine a "love alone" ethic from which faith springs in complete effectiveness? How many times is our faith tarnished because of a flawed, underestimated practice of love—loving one's neighbor, much less one's brother and sister, with the love that led God to send his Son?

We may separate faith, love and hope topically if we like, but only for so long, for the depth of one forces the depth of the other. We must always return to their oneness, their saving and effectualizing unity. Doing this does not leave hope in arrears. It repositions it as a living concretion, the antithesis of wishful speculation and repackaged doubt. Hope becomes strong and singular because it sets itself firmly on unassailable love, on substance, evidence and the unseen. Continuous outpouring has no other foundation. It is a condition of soul so firmly fixed that as I share a meal or kneel in prayer or work in the fields, I can at any moment turn within—not from—the doing of these to the sweetness and holiness of the Lord, without any hint of changing from work to worship or from the mundane to the eternal. Personal holiness is not an essence—some ideal out there to which I occasionally turn. It is a hungering, growing, pressing-on condition in which all things take on the peculiar fragrance of being done for Jesus' sake. Then we can say that all of our work, done in full-fledged faith, is eternally finished in Christ. Our task, therefore, is to make our way through the doneness of it, step by step, moment by moment.

The whole of Scripture verifies the principle of worship as a continuum.[3] Two words for worship—*proskynein* and *latreuein*—suggest a close relationship between worship in a given place and time and worship as an all-pervasive and ongoing condition. *Proskynein* expresses more the idea of bowing down or surrendering, whereas *latreuein* is effectively rendered as "service" or "serving." Thus, while bending low and submitting are certainly included within this idea, serving opens out into a life-wide continuum that, in turn, is driven by submission—continuous bowing down. There is no alternative to this two-in-one principle, even though of late we seem to have separated them more than is warranted. Not so with the Scriptures, even the earliest ones. But when we come to the New Testament, we find that there is no escape from the idea that worship is an undiminished outpouring, even though, curiously enough, the words for "worship" are not used much (that is, not used to refer to what we often think of as worship—the actions that take place in corporate gatherings).

There are many places from which we can take our start, but Romans 12—16 and John 4 are magnets toward which any number of other passages (including those from the Old Testament) are drawn.

CONTINUOUS OUTPOURING AND LIVING SACRIFICES

Romans 12:1 (NASB) says this: "I urge you, brethren, by the mercies of God, to present your bodies a living and holy sacrifice, acceptable to God, which is your spiritual service of worship."[4] This verse cannot be taken by itself. It has been preceded by a ruthlessly detailed inquiry into creation, fall, sin and righteousness. No stone is left unturned and no person is left without excuse or without a Savior. Above all, the first eleven chapters of Romans are about continuous outpouring—that of God in the creation, that of humanity in its fallen and inexcusable enthusiasm for evil, that of Christ in his total victory over sin and death, and that of all believers in their pressing on against sin and upward into Christ's stature and fullness. Paul finishes out this remarkable essay with an insight that, in its mystery, only the Holy Spirit could author: "God has imprisoned all in disobedience so that he may be merciful to all" (Rom 11:32). In stunning fashion Paul brings together every dimension of divine and human outpouring—eternal, fallen and redeemed—and fits them to God's sovereignty. What more could Paul do but leap into praise (v. 33) and then reach back to Isaiah and Jeremiah and tune their singing to the finished work that he has so carefully explored (vv. 34-35)?

Only then does 12:1 take on its full magnitude. Paul is really saying something like this: "On the basis of all that I have been teaching you about your condition in light of God's holiness and his Christ, about the disappearance of the old system with its continuum of dead sacrifices, and about your turning from these to the once-for-all sacrifice of Christ, you have only one thing to do: present yourself as living sacrifices, the undertaking of which constitutes your spiritual worship, or continuous outpouring."

There are at least four important ideas tucked away in this verse, each having to do with continuousness. First, we are now to be once-for-all living sacrifices on the merits of Christ's once-for-all sacrifice. There is no repetition, only continuity. The two are sealed together in the eternities and cannot be broken. Second, we remain alive even while we are sacrifices. Death, in all of its significance, even the kind of death that leads to atonement, has been done away with. Having died with Christ, we are caught up in life even as Christ himself took life back to himself, and now we place ourselves on the altar as a way of continued living and outpouring. Sacrifice is moved away from substitutes to incarnation. Third, we offer ourselves. In this we follow hard after the Savior's example with the freedom that comes only in gift giving. Fourth, there is no other way to describe this continued action but to call it worship, even if we prefer the word *service*, as many translations do. Whichever we choose, we are bound up in intertestamental accord in which bowing down, serving and worshiping are identical. We must call this kind of worship spiritual, not only because it is in Christ and of the Spirit, but also because we walk as continual worshipers by faith and not by sight.

Immediately, in verse 2, Paul says this: "Now that you know where the truth is, don't mess up. Don't rejoin the previous system against which I have been writing in the beginning part of this letter." Having struggled his way through the crafting of chapter 7, he realizes how easy it is for living sacrifices to flirt with dying ones. He makes it clear that being conformed to this world is inverted outpouring. It is not just the doing of things that vacillate among gray, white and black, depending on the church you join or the traditions that have been following you around. It is a clear-cut mindedness toward fallenness, a desire to leave the manna and go for the leeks and the garlic. Conformity to the world is conformity to a worldview that, however subtly, reverses the order of Creator and creature and once again places power in handiwork and perpetuates the confusion of master to slave.

After the warning against a reversal in mindedness (creature worship) in verse 2, Paul follows with another warning (v. 3) about self-worship, surely to keep individual living sacrifices from making too much of their individuality or their sacrifice. In other words, continuous worshipers are a vast aggregate in which inequality and disregard are abhorred. A continuous worshiper must therefore fight two battles, one against a world-driven mind, the other against self-driven mind. Verses 4-8 make it clear that individual worship carries with it corporate responsibility—the body is not healthy if its members are disintegrative. This is yet another way of remembering that faith working through love is the only effectual faith.

Being members one of another is not a mechanical arrangement, this part interlocking with another, the whole somehow greased up into smoothness. Rather, being members of one another is organic. In a love-driven community of believers, no one should be able to find the seams. No one person or gift distorts the comeliness of the whole. Individual gifts, even, when examined closely, are common property of every member. For example, if I don't have the gift of prophecy, I must prophesy anyway, because it is the duty of the body of Christ to tell forth, even though some might do this in a particularly gifted way. Continuous outpouring, then, is a totality. Every believer, pouring out to God while in the world, is doing so both in terms of specific gifting and all-encompassing responsibility. This is another way of describing what it means to be a living, not occasional, epistle.

CONTINUOUS OUTPOURING AND SPIRIT AND TRUTH

This story about the Samaritan woman in John 4 is about two things that encompass each other: salvation and authentic worship. If we were to leave out verses 15 through 22 and connect verse 14 to verse 23 (parenthesizing the first word of the latter), we would have a complete description of continuous outpouring as it should be, in Christ. Whereas Christ will always unify salvation and authentic worship, the woman (representing the generally religious world) wanted to keep them separate. From the beginning of the conversation, Jesus was talking about worship, knowing that it is either fallen or redeemed. It was only when Jesus pointed out the woman's condition and his profound remedy for it that she turned to the subject of worship (the way we often do).

Why did she do this? Perhaps she was genuinely hungry and was trying, however obliquely, to conjoin her hunger with Christ's words. She might have done this because worship talk was safe and religious, as if she and Jesus (the "prophet") could find common ground. Or she might have become downright unnerved, as Peter was on the Mount of Transfiguration when in his fear he talked religiously but irrelevantly. We should not scoff at Peter or the woman but be reminded that we too often show up at the silly end of mystery with our God talk and our overweening worship talk. God does not scoff in these times; he persists and prods, just as Jesus did both with the woman and with Peter. He continuously pours out whatever he sees fit, whether of grace and mercy or chastisement and judgment. In all instances, it is all of love.

In any case, the Samaritan woman saw worship as an occasion, a time, a place, a tradition. In one statement Jesus subsumed *without condemning* the entire history of time and place, tradition and protocol, under a singular paradigm: Spirit and truth. He prepared the way for Romans 12—16, yet he was reiterating the grand principle that went back to the creation of Adam and Eve and culminated in the perfect outpouring of the Son of Man: true worship is continuous; time and location are incidental. He was saying that salvation and authentic worship together mean always being in the Spirit and always being in the truth. There is simply no letup or alternation. Spirit and truth are to be as manifest in the workplace, the home and the school as in the corporate assembly. Jesus was talking about the kind of continuous outpouring that precedes, embraces, subordinates and validates, yet looks beyond liturgies, systems, methodologies, teamwork, preludes, postludes, dances, songs and coaxing. Grounding authentic worship the way Jesus did means that placing primary dependence on such things violates the principle of faith, hope and love, the principle of Spirit and truth, and the reality of being a sacrifice for as long as we live. Thus all the work that composes all our living is merely a symptom of the eternal reality of continuous outpouring.

Continuous Outpouring and the Beauty of Holiness

Psalm 29:2 admonishes, "Worship the LORD in the beauty of holiness" (NKJV). Here, once again, we face the reality of worship as a continuing state, because holiness itself is a continuing state to which we are called as redeemed outpourers. Furthermore, the relentless holiness of God is the only beauty that he possesses. It is not aesthetic beauty but the beauty (there is no other English word for it) that self-inhering holiness exudes. Yet when we mention the beauty of holiness in the same breath we use to speak of God as the consummate Artist, we set a trap and then fall into it. Because of our flirtation with the idea that beauty is truth and truth is beauty, and because of the tendency of many to assume that the purpose of the arts in worship is to create a sacred bridge into the holy of holies, we are prone to reverse the order of the verse like this: "Worship the Lord in the holiness of beauty." All philosophies of "the beautiful," if they are biblically grounded, must stop short of connections between aesthetics and holiness, no matter how temptingly close they might superficially appear to be.

Any concept of God as the consummate Artist is worrisome even apart from the discussion about beauty and holiness. If he is the consummate Artist, then he is also the consummate Plumber or Engineer or Farmer, but we do not usually talk this way because these activities are not perceived to reach to the mystical level that art does. The problem with hooking God up to art the way we do is that a special justification and otherness are too easily imputed to art. Because we have named God as the ultimate Artist, we imply that our artistic creativity is a cut above other kinds of human creativity.

The beauty of holiness for a continuing worshiper is nothing less than purity of heart, manifest in working out our salvation while knowing that God-through-Christ is in us, working both to will and to do his good pleasure. The Christian life is not sequential, nor is holiness the final piece in a complex redemption puzzle. It is that which is put into operation the moment we turn to Christ. It is not simply a loathing and avoiding of sin. It is, in essence, being like Christ. There is nothing vague about this. Spiritual worship and the beauty of holiness are as down-to-earth and practical as Christians can get. Presenting ourselves as living sacrifices contains no ephemera, no amorphous shivers, no disembodied inexactitudes. John puts this beautifully and simply as "walking in the light as he is in the light" (see 1 Jn 1:7). And thus two aspects of outpouring—the corporate in fellowship and the personal in privacy—are combined and sanctified in continued cleansing. How, then, can worshiping now and then or only here and there make sense? Am I saved now and then? Am I to love now and then? Am I to serve now and then?

There is nothing more real than to be in Christ and to live in Christ—to walk, run, hunger, thirst, press on, work out our salvation and be living epistles. It is not enough to bounce into a room and say, "Well, after all, all of life is worship," then bounce out, assuming that this wonderment called spiritual worship is a cover-it-all, a free ticket to everything said and done. For me to do so would be to assume that I had the power to translate my acts into worshipful acts because, after all, I am in the Spirit and I can call the shots. It is really the other way around: because continuous outpouring and personal holiness are co-integral, I had better be sure that whatever I am doing has a direct connection to truth. I had better be sure that the supreme worth of Jesus is my starting, continuing and ending value. I had better be sure that my "freedom in Christ" is not of my own manufacture, for if it is, I am still a legalist. I have simply moved from negative legalism (I don't do this; therefore, I'm okay) to affirmative legalism (I can do this; therefore, I'm okay).

So far, we have spoken of continuous authentic worship using two comprehensive triads, the first being faith, hope and love and the second being living sacrifice, Spirit and truth, and the beauty of holiness. Let's put everything together into a single thought: Authentic worship and continuous outpouring are to be undertaken by faith, driven by love, designed by hope and saturated with truth, whatever the context, time and place. Our worship is acceptable and effective by our being moment-by-moment living sacrifices, doing everything in the Spirit and according to truth, seeking out the beauty of holiness as our only walk, holding fast to God, who alone is our praise and worship.

Deuteronomy 10:12-13 and 20-21 capture these thoughts as pointedly and simply as anywhere in Scripture.

> So now, O Israel, what does the LORD your God require of you? Only to fear the LORD your God, to walk in all his ways, to love him, to serve the LORD your God with all your heart and with all your soul, and to keep the commandments of the LORD your God and his decrees that I am commanding you today, for your own well-being. (vv. 12-13)

> You shall fear the Lord your God; him alone you shall worship; to him you shall hold fast. . . . He is your praise; he is your God, who has done for you these great and awesome things that your own eyes have seen. (vv. 20-21)

There are no exceptions to these words. They are simple, uncluttered and within the reach of every wayward but forgiven believer who follows hard after the Lord of hosts.

CONTINUOUS OUTPOURING THROUGHOUT SCRIPTURE

With the foregoing in mind, we can turn to any number of Scripture passages and see how the themes of outpouring, continuous worship and personal sojourn offer extended perspective. The passages shown below are not listed according to any logical scheme, nor are they exhaustive. Rather, they reach toward each other and serve as models for additional discoveries. Consequently we could start virtually anywhere, knowing that we remain in close proximity to the theme of personal holiness, which is the singular pursuit and only outcome of continuous outpouring and authentic worship. Remember also that I am not suggesting that these passages equate with unceasing worship on a strict exegetical basis. But since unceasing worship takes in the whole of our living, the overall spirit and force of these passages align themselves easily.

Peter's first epistle is a sweetly expressed parallel to Romans 12—16. We are described as living stones coming to Christ as to a living stone (1 Pet 2:4-5). According to verse 5, we are being built up to "offer spiritual sacrifices acceptable to God through Jesus Christ"—a sure witness to Romans 12:1. In Romans 6:13, Paul prefigures 12:1-2 by contrasting two kinds of continuous outpouring: presenting ourselves as instruments of unrighteousness or presenting ourselves as alive from the dead. Furthermore, on the side of pain and sin, we are instructed to restore erring brothers and sisters "in a spirit of gentleness" and to bear each other's burdens—impossible without faith, hope and love (Gal 6:1-2).

In Hebrews 12, running a race and looking to Jesus (vv. 1-2) are coupled to the chastening of the Lord as it yields the peaceable fruiting of righteousness (v. 11), which in turn prompts us to strengthen ourselves and make straight paths (vv. 12-13) so that we can corporately pursue peace and holiness in a way that extends to shepherding those who falter (vv. 14-15). Then verse 28 says this: "Since we are receiving a kingdom that cannot be shaken, let us give thanks, by which we offer to God an acceptable worship with reverence and awe." Chapter 13 iterates the same purpose as Romans 12:9-21, namely serving God acceptably as we "continually offer the sacrifice of praise to God; that is, the fruit of lips that confess his name" (Heb 13:15). Being a sacrifice (Rom 12:1) means living continuously in love toward God, toward other people and toward oneself in a richly fitted vocabulary of work, service and obedience, knowing that with such sacrifices God is pleased (Heb 13:15-17).

In Philippians we are instructed to be confident in the work of Christ in a vivid way: the work of Christ is completed in us *until* the day of Christ (Phil 1:6). This continuing of completion, finished as soon as begun, yet being completed moment by moment, suggests that two kinds of outpouring are working together: the outpouring of Christ working in us even as we press continuously toward our completion in Christ. In Philippians 2:12-13, working out our salvation can likewise be seen as mutual outpouring: while we work in the mystery of fear and trembling, God works in us both to keep willing and keep doing for his good pleasure. In Colossians 1:9-12, Paul's intercessory prayer is directed toward the qualities that mark a life of continuous worship: being filled with wisdom and spiritual understanding, walking in a pleasing way, being fruitful in every good work, increasing in knowledge, being strengthened for the increase of joyful patience and long-suffering, giving thanks to the Father. This last—giving thanks—completes the circle: Paul's praying results in our praying. In chapter six, more will be said about prayer as continuous outpouring, but it is enough here to remember that worshiping and praying are not two separate subjects but aspects of each other.

It is also important to think of continuous worship using the analogy of isometrics, or working against something that resists. If we were to put all the isometric verbs of the Bible together, they would comprise a rich thesaurus for outpouring expressed in the isometric terms of struggle and exercise. Here are some: running, pressing on, warring, hungering, thirsting, walking, panting, withstanding, fighting and even importuning. But isometrics also bring rest to the authentic worshiper: resting in the Lord (Ps 37:7, among other passages), leading a quiet life and minding our own business (1 Thess 4:11), taking sabbath, taking calm as a weaned child on the breast (Ps 131).

We should read the Beatitudes in light of continuous outpouring, whether in poverty of spirit, mourning, meekness, hunger and thirst after righteousness, mercy, purity, peacemaking or persecution. We can go over the parables of Christ with continuous outpouring in mind: seeking the lost; praying importunately; planting and harvesting; walking the way of the Good Samaritan or the Good Shepherd; waiting for prodigals; laying up incorruptible treasures; asking, receiving, knocking and finding; fruit bearing. Read these and the outpourings of fallenness, redemption and righteousness are made manifest yet another way. Make your way through the psalms and see continuous outpouring—the worst and the best of it, in full dress.

Given these few examples, we realize that the more we contemplate the completeness of continuous worship and personal holiness, the more the whole of Scripture lights up in a new way. Everywhere we look continuous outpouring is there, implied or explicated, in numberless epiphanies. Wherever we turn—to commandments, to promises, to principles, to parables, to stories, to concepts, to warnings and rewards—we are surrounded with this freshening witness cloud, made up of truth itself, urging

~~us onward to personal holiness and continuous outpouring in and to Christ, or warning us away from~~ our futile outpouring when we are away ~~from him.~~ Each will be consummated in an eternal outpouring, the one unto perfect and unclouded joy, the other into clamoring from emptiness unto continuing emptiness. Thus, in the book of Revelation, continuous outpouring is expressed in its finality: faith becomes sight, hope is consummated in fulfillment and love breaks its earth bonds and bursts into its infinities. Continuous outpouring is fully harmonized; the darkened glass is shattered; God sings over us even as we sing to him.

One more passage comes to mind, with which this section can conclude. In 2 Peter 1:2-7 we might paraphrase as follows:

> The knowledge of God's outpouring in Christ Jesus outpouringly multiplies grace and peace directly to us. His outpouring power has given us all things that pertain to a life of outpouring godliness. This knowledge that we have of God walks alongside his call, coming to us through glory and virtue by which, in turn, we have promises of such magnitude given to [be poured out on] us that we can be continuous partakers of the outpouring divine nature. As continuous partakers, our lives must issue in an outpouring marked by diligence, faith, virtue, knowledge, self-control, perseverance, godliness, brotherly kindness and love.

It is not difficult, then, to join this paraphrase to Romans 12:1 by saying that this is exactly the kind of outpouring that living sacrifices show forth.

I have long been intrigued by the peculiar sequence of attributes in the 2 Peter passage (vv. 5-7). They appear to be out of order, even random. Or so I thought until I heard about holograms. If we were to look at a hologram under intense magnification, we would find that any given fragment functions not only as a discrete detail of the whole but also contains a complete picture of the whole. With that image in mind, this list in 2 Peter begins to make sense and the order becomes irrelevant. If, for example, I were to create a hologram of virtue, I would at once have two sets of images, the composite one (virtue) and the many fragments comprising it (love, godliness, perseverance and the like). Each of these fragments would in turn contain a picture of the whole while in its own way presenting a picture of itself, whether godliness, self-control or the like. In this way the sequence found in the 2 Peter passage can be arranged in any number of ways because whatever composite we wish to create will, holographically, contain miniature composites that can, in turn, be used to create another whole. It does not trouble me one whit to say further that the hologram is a marvelous metaphor for anything found in Scripture: the person of God, his work, our being, our comings and goings, our fallenness, our right-eousness, our choice for or against Jesus and our eternal welfare. The hol-ogram has one grand name: continuous outpouring in which composites and fragments freely participate in each other and can freely replace each other. In all cases the picture(s) will tell one grand story in a plethora of ways: Christ is all in all and we are all that can we ever become in Christ.

Too much of today's worship talk (and we may have more of it now than at any other time in church history) overlooks the comprehensive meaning of continuous worship. I believe that our overemphasis on time/place/mu-sic worship might partly come from a failure to account for the final di-mensions of worship that a New Testament theology can bring to us. Thus talking about worship renewal the way we tend to do is almost like talking about Old Testament renewal instead of Old Testament fulfillment. Here is what I mean.

A principle undergirds the whole of New Testament thought, and it comes into focus in a particular saying of Jesus that is as foundational as anything in all of Scripture. In Matthew 5 and 19 we read something like this: "It was said of old, but now I say unto you . . ." By "said of old," Christ is indicating the law of Moses. And Christ says this after he unabashedly verifies the substance of the Law and the Prophets. Only then did he take these verities and, without tearing away at them, brought them to a unique finality—a filled-to-the-fullness—of which he was and is the unique sum and substance, the final yes.

These words of Christ are of such magnitude that the entire shape of the New Testament depends on them. And it is only because of this that the Old Testament can be quoted with such force and probity throughout the Gospels, Acts and Epistles. To put it negatively, the Old Testament is quoted because it is not finished until Christ finishes it. In this sense the Old Testament reaches ahead of itself longingly and hopefully to its finality.

To put it positively, Christ is established in the Old Testament so efficiently as to make the Incarnation an inevitable reality. Abraham, Jesus said, saw his day and was glad (Jn 8:56). Therefore it is a solemn act of verification to use the Old Testament in establishing the continuity of both Testaments and, even more importantly, the summative force of the New.

But even further, the linkages between Jesus' teachings and the apostolic writings illustrate the cumulative and summative force of the New Testament. The Old Testament is fulfilled in Christ; of that we are sure. However, this fulfillment is furthered in the way parable and wisdom in Jesus' teachings look toward and unite with the propositionally structured writings of the Epistles.[5] I would go so far as to say that the teachings of Christ, as magnificent and world ordering as they are, reach beyond and remain to be expounded on, explored and applied in the propositional work of Paul, the letter to the Hebrews and the work of the other apostles. I do not believe that this statement downgrades or demeans the teachings of Jesus—God forbid! Rather, I consider it to be part of Jesus' superb way of teaching, coupled to his perfect knowledge of what was yet to take place in the disclosure of truth after the coming of the Spirit at Pentecost. After all, did he not say that those who believed in him would do greater works because he was going to the Father (Jn 14:12)?

Keeping the principle of "Moses said, but I say" in mind, we can turn back to the problem of overstressing time/place/music worship. This can best be illustrated by thinking of the relationship of Spirit and truth to time and place in each Testament. In the Old, concepts of Spirit and truth are there but hidden (*embedded* might be a better word) in time and place. Locations were often named on the spot—a rock or a heap or a hastily built altar. There is a tabernacle and eventually the temple. Wherever Yahweh puts his name, he is to be worshiped there. As the tabernacle moves, so moves the ark and so move the locations of sacrifice and worship. As the temple is built, so the worship of Yahweh is centralized and ceremonially magnified. Spirit and truth, as verities, are amply articulated in the Old Testament, but they are not directly linked to worship. Truth lies in the Law, and truthful living lies in the love of the commandments and the keeping of them. (There is no better witness to this than Psalms 19 and 119.) Worshiping in Spirit is not directly linked to God-as-Spirit. Instead it is more evident in the idea that a spirit of brokenness or of walking humbly with God is the true spirit that makes the physical offerings of the sacrificial system effectual.

But as we have already seen, the relationship between time and place and Spirit and truth is completely reversed in the New Testament, *with nothing of the former canceled out.* Time and place are not swept aside but are swept up in Spirit and truth, in continuous worship, in living sacrifice and in the verities of faith, love and hope. When we posit a theology of worship on any other concept, we might be running the risk, however unconsciously (I say this carefully), of legalizing the subject of worship and, by implication, neglecting the finish that New Testament thought puts to the Old.

Once we understand that, in Christ, authentic worship is continuous outpouring summed up in personal holiness, we must conclude that the Christian needs to hear but one call to worship and offer only one response. These come exactly coincident with new birth and, despite our wanderings and returns to the contrary, they suffice for all our living, dying and eternal outpouring. We do not go to church to worship. But as continuing worshipers, we gather ourselves together to continue our worship, but now in the company of brothers and sisters.

3

MUTUAL INDWELLING

THE FINAL GEOGRAPHY OF WORSHIP

Outside of the names of God and the specific words describing his work, there may be no more important word in the Bible than the adhesive, outgoing and ingathering word *in*. In its own fashion, this wisp of a word carries the weight of the eternities. Studied in depth and taken to its fullest, *in* would make for a series of sermons that could easily cover an entire church year. When it comes to explaining the depth and fullness with which persons, places or things can relate to another, there is no other preposition or prefix that comes near the significance of this little word.

Here are some commonplace examples to begin with. Being "*in* the know," being "*in* on" is more important than merely knowing *about* something or someone. An *in*sider is someone who enjoys special access to another person, transaction or body of information. To have *in*sight is to look *in*to the substance of a thing. To *in*tegrate is both to have *in*sight *in*to any number of things and to bring them *in*to a working synthesis. Societally, *in*tegration is the creation of a seamless community in which the integrity of each person is honored and preserved. *In*clusiveness is the norm.

Thinking *about* art is to thinking *in* art as thinking *about* love is to being *in* love. I once asked a colleague, a philosopher, if it were possible to create an aesthetic theory without going to concerts, plays and museums. Because philosophers often spend time thinking *about* things rather than thinking *in* things, his answer was "Of course." This thinking *about,* however, granted him precious little access to art as art, but rather to something about it that could be covered with words. His aesthetic appreciation, then, turned out to be more a corollary to art rather than a direct engagement in it.

On the other hand, there are those who think little about art philosophically but are good at thinking in it. I have a son, a talented guitarist, who knows almost no music theory, cannot read music (much to my admiring perplexity) and spends little time ruminating *about* musical process. Yet he thinks *in* music in ways that outrun many musicians whose training is loaded with information *about* the workings of music.

Knowing *about* the Bible does not guarantee that I can think biblically— *in* the Bible. Applying scriptural truth does not depend on scriptural memory as much as thinking and acting *in* the truth to the extent that far-reaching principles are discovered and directly applied to a complexity of life situations. Knowing theology does not necessarily guarantee that I can think theologically, that is, think *in* theology, any more than memorizing recipes means I can cook. When Christ was witnessing to the Samaritan woman (Jn 4) and redoing the entirety of worship, he was careful to speak not *of* or *about* Spirit and truth as out-there objects but to speak of them as mysteries that he expects us to be *in* even as they are *in* us.

Going even further, my knowing *about* Jesus does not necessarily mean that I am *in* Jesus. I am not even sure that *knowing* Jesus is the same as being *in* Jesus; otherwise, how can the unbelief of his earthly brothers and sisters or Iscariot be explained? Certainly one of the greatest obstacles to a sweetened and purified spread of the gospel is explained by the difference between witnessing to people from within the truth and simply stating the facts of conversion with little understanding of how radically extensive conversion is.

So we have this differentiating word *in.* It goes as far as any word in describing the richness of continuous outpouring both within the Godhead and from him, toward every particle and person in his creation. With respect to our ultimate condition, we are either in Christ or outside of him. There is no middle ground. Outsideness is not vagueness or ambiguity. A lost person is not only *outside* of Christ but also *in* Satan. Lostness is not a vacuum, nor does it imply that there is no service, no master, no hierarchy. Lostness is a choice demanding an exchange of gods as outpouring continues. The question then is, outpouring to whom? If I am to evangelize, I will do so knowing that I will be talking to a continuous outpourer, an inverted soul, whose only hope is to find his or her outpouring converted and washed clean by turning from being in Satan to being in Christ. There is only one worship war that can be properly described as such. It is the war between God and Satan, in which being in Christ or in Satan is the bedrock issue. Our petty skirmishes about worship, as ignoble, silly and demeaning as they can become, are nothing compared to the violence and tearing of the real and only war. This war is simply not ours at our dithering local level. It is the Lord's, and if we were to better understand this one splendid fact, we would be placing far less emphasis on what we do, what style we do it in, what we keep and what we throw out, and what latest poll or societal "insight" we choose to use as our template.

But we must and can move from war to peace, and we see this magnificent word *in* unfolding like a rose—God *in* Christ. Christ *in* the Spirit. The Spirit *in* Christ. Christ *in* God. The Trinity *in* itself, complete *in* itself. Every attribute of the Godhead *in* every other attribute, in the only infinite hologram we can name. God *in* the flesh. The Son of Man *in* the flesh even as he is *in* the Father. The Spirit *in*dwelling incarnate flesh even as this flesh is *in* the Spirit.

As for the authentic worshiper, this entering-and-staying word *in* assures these glories: Christ *in* us; we *in* Christ; God *in* Christ as Christ is *in* us; the Spirit *in* us *in* Christ *in* us; Christ all *in* all; we, all that we can possibly be *in* Christ. There is no division between Christ seated in the heavenlies and Christ *in* us even as we are seated in the heavenlies *in* and with him. The body of Christ is Christ *in* the whole in a God-created and Spirit-filled union of individuals. Christ is *in* us; Christ is *in* the great cloud of witnesses; Christ is the infinite tabernacling with the finite. This is the hope of glory.

Who but Brother Lawrence, that awkward and humble tenant in Christ's vineyard, could say it so sweetly: "He is within us; seek him not elsewhere"?[1] As soon as we as believers move Christ away from us, even a split of a splinter, we have dethroned him. His immensity is up for grabs; his presence, negotiable. He is no longer God. Our relation to him becomes as chancy as a lottery, and we lose the power and the stabilizing guarantees of Scripture. The nearness or distance of Christ of which Scripture often speaks is not variable or whimsical proximity, nor is it a corroboration of our feelings as to how near or far Christ is. Rather, it is a necessary way of describing the immensity and nuance of his with-ness *in* us. To walk with Christ is not to go alongside him as if we were two persons on a path, sometimes touching shoulders, sometimes ahead or behind. I walk with Christ in me, whose *in*-ness is also nearness, whose friendship is also one-with-ness. If I walk afar off, as I am prone to do, the distance between us does not disturb his *in*dwelling. It simply reminds me of how I have distanced *myself* from his constant with*in*ness. Repentance, therefore, is not an invitation for Jesus to come back in, once more or again and again, but to shrink down my self-created distance from him within me.

It is the preceding magnificence and reality of Christ in us that makes drawing near to him more profound than merely closing a distance. Drawing near is a spiritual act of faith, love, hope and grace at work in the fullness of something that we see only in part, as through a darkened glass. Growing in Christ has much more to do with faith, hope and love brightening the glass than with wanting Christ to reclarify himself. Christ-in-me is not episodic or grudging, except as I, in my frailty, take it to be so. Christ-in-me is not my looking inward to find him. Doing this is as locationally suspect as thinking of Christ proximally near me. Christ-in-me is too complete a reality for this kind of inward or outward search. It is his oneness with me that brings the preposition "in" to its fullest magnitude. In Christ, I am no longer simply *imago Dei* but an indwelt child of the Father. Christ-in-me is the most honorable thing that could ever befall me. It is a reality that comprises my entire spiritual schooling, my fullest catechism, all of my pressing on and all of my growing up into.

THE FINAL GEOGRAPHY OF WORSHIP

So what is mutual indwelling?[2] Chapter one mentioned the dwelling of the triune God within himself—his inflowing outpouring, if you will. To this, in chapter two, was added the concept of God in Christ in us, and this present chapter began with the continuing reality of Christ in us. We can now complete the circle, bringing the vertical and horizontal fully together, by discussing the union and communion of all believers.

In Christ, we are members *of* one another. We not only worship, serve and participate together, we do so *at one* with each other, even *in* each other, even as we are commonly in Christ. I do not believe it stretches the point to suggest that spiritually we participate *in* each other. But let me clarify. I am not talking about a horizontal take on incarnationalism. I do not mean that we take up residence within each other, take possession of each other, become each other or pry into each other. This would be a crass and twisted misinterpretation of what I believe to be a profound spiritual truth. Rather, because of the profound reaches of faith, hope and love, I am enabled to enter deeply into and live within—even if for a spiritual moment—the lives of brother and sister, so as to weep, to mourn, to rejoice, to identify with, to intercede for, to uphold, to support, even to correct. This cannot be done from the outside or by interpersonal comparisons. I do not mourn or rejoice simply by objectified observation but by entering into and participating in someone's or some community's grief and joy to the fullest extent possible, solely at the bidding of the Word and the Spirit. Such within-ness is profound; it is frankly mysterious, vicarious and, above all, presupposed by the overwhelming truth of Christ in and with us.

As quantitatively biased as it may first sound, mutual indwelling is a triple mystery: temples within temples within Temple. Above all, that God is our dwelling place, our eternal Sanctuary, has been known from old times. Psalm 90 admits clearly to this, even to the extent that no generation is excused from knowing it (v. 1). Christ made it clear that he was greater than the temple (Mt 12:6). David Peterson's suggestion that Jesus' cleansing of the temple (Jn 2:13-22) is both an acted-out parable and a messianic sign in which he replaces the temple makes perfect sense.[3] As to the church itself, Paul says that we are God's building (1 Cor 3:9). He said this even in the context of divisiveness and split loyalties within the assembly. Therefore the metaphor of a single spiritual building, created and owned by God, strikes hard at any attempt to disturb the unity that is born out of our redemption. Paul intensifies the argument by moving from the more neutral concept of a building to that of a corporate temple (1 Cor 3:16-17). The body of Christ is an indwelt temple, even as Christ, the eternal Temple, is the church's continual abiding place. Then Peter further deepens the mystery by talking of Christ not only as a living stone but also as the chief cornerstone of a spiritual house made up of redeemed living stones (1 Pet 2:4-8). These stones together, with Christ, make up a temple.

We have this so far: God in Christ is our eternal dwelling place, yet Christ is one of the stones, the Keystone, in a building made of redeemed stones. He is both the eternal dwelling place and the chief part of another dwelling place—the church, whose only life is to dwell in him. The church is a fellowship of mutually indwelling believers, members of one another. Finally, each member is a temple, in which Christ comes to dwell as the hope of glory. Temples within temples within a Temple—mutual indwelling, the surety of which is as fixed as the very being of God and as far removed from forsakenness and desolation as the east is from the west. How else can futile words deal with this rich truth?

But I must yet bring this grand mystery home to the often unpleasant realities of my own heart and mind, where it is the most difficult to take in. I cannot help but ask, how can this be? How can Jesus possibly tabernacle himself in me, knowing what I know about myself and, for goodness' sake, knowing what I think I know about my brother and sister (the mote and the beam always in the wrong eyes)? How can I meet the terms of mutual indwelling with brother Arnie Northcutt, who persistently dishevels my insights in deacons meetings? Or Dr. Fleming McGruff, who dislikes my music? Or sister Sylvia Kwando-Komemos, who wants a new dishwasher for the kitchen, while brother Campbell Breighlaud insists that we need more money for the youth mission trip? Or the Reverend Enoch Royal, who wants quiet when I want tongues?

But these naggings come back around and bite back at me ever so hard: How does Jesus, and how do others, put up with *my* sinfulness, including the judgments I have just passed? How do Jesus and I consort together on this mutual indwelling matter when sin crouches at the door and far too often devours me before it does my neighbor?

Here's how: infinite grace. Mutual indwelling is not for the spiritually perfected and tidied-up folks who live and breathe unapproachable piety. Christ-in-us-in-each-other is the spiritual glue by which even the most easily riven and bleeding fellowship is held together. Mutual indwelling is corrective prophecy and godly chastisement. It is sorrow for sin, even as it takes new hold on the least in the fellowship. Mutual indwelling is bearing one another's burdens in joy and sorrow, all by faith. It is the widow's mite and the hidden petition and the philanthropist's millions. It is also, more often than we would like, pain, lament, doubt, abuse, decay and disappointment.

It is also clean and clear. Mutual indwelling continuously pours itself out, but not in some mystically shapeless and random way. It is first of all authored, contained and then poured out spiritually, in Christ. It is directed by the Holy Spirit and spills out at his command in the ways he wants and in the directions he urges. It spills inwardly within the body—throughout the temples. It goes outwardly in proclamation and in deeds of mercy. It washes feet and makes breakfast. It builds each other up; it esteems another more than oneself. It is casseroles and country fried chicken and VBS. It is souls saved and marriages healed. It is sexual addiction and drug addiction whipped. It is psalms, hymns, spiritual songs, dances, banners, children's stories, revival, another New Testament translated, missionary radio and street corner preaching. Mutual indwelling leaves nothing out in the life of the body of Christ only because the continued outpouring of the believer—the sincere and the tainted—is brought to enduring cleanness in Christ.

Mutual indwelling is both centripetal and centrifugal. Centripetally, the body of Christ avidly gathers truth; it welcomes and embraces the weak, the poor, the broken, the wealthy, the famous; it takes on burdens and drinks in things that are lovely and of good report. It feasts on the Bread of Life and the Wine of Heaven, embracing him, taking him in and learning from him. It is centrifugal as well. It goes out; it hunts down the lost; it scatters the truth in witness; its feet are beautiful in the outpouring and outgoing spread of good tidings; it makes its way into the world as living epistles; it goes to the ends of the earth as if they were just around the corner.

Mutual indwelling is effective only as we see each other in Christ, and seeing each other in Christ is not effective until we understand that the only way our lives can make any sense to others—even as we offend them or they us—is for them to see us in Christ. It is only in Christ that members of this flawed and mended body called the church have any hope of indwelling each other. Believers do not indwell each other simply by shortcutting across a few moral steppingstones and into oneness with each other. They become one by looking to Jesus and by themselves staying in Christ, the center of all indwelling, even as he is its infinite circumference.

Mutual indwellers, then, are the church, the unique bride, whom Christ keeps on sanctifying and cleansing as a glorious gift to himself (Eph 5:26-27). Peter sums it up this way: "All of you, have unity of spirit, sympathy, love for one another, a tender heart, and a humble mind. Do not repay evil for evil or abuse for abuse; but, on the contrary, repay with a blessing. It is for this that you were called—that you might inherit a blessing" (1 Pet 3:8-9). John, in his first epistle, connects abiding in the Word with abiding in Christ (1 Jn 2:24-28). As each believer abides in the word as they abide in Christ-in-them, all believers abiding in Christ-in-them likewise abide in each other. In John 15 (especially vv. 1-12), Christ couples the reality of mutual abiding to the analogy of vine and branches.

In reading G. Campbell Morgan's sermon on this passage, I for the first time encountered the simple observation that the Vine and the branches are not two things but one. Christ is the Vine *and* the branches, yet we are the branches even as Christ is the Vine.[4] His abiding in us is also us abiding in him by abiding in his words (v. 7) and keeping his commandments (v. 10). Furthermore, abiding in Christ's love (v. 10) is as much a part of abiding in him as is all else. This union culminates in the attribute of joy— Christ's joy in seeing his bride, the vine, joyfully living and abiding in him. His joy remains in us, the bride, to the extent that our joy can only be full (v. 11). When I read John 14:6 and find Jesus' answer to the "How do I know the way?" question, I find that the way *is* the person—no more separation. The One who is in me directs my paths by being my Path.

We can unite these thoughts with the outpouring words of Christ in his high priestly prayer, where the little preposition "in" is understood in every possible dimension: "I ask . . . that they may all be one. *As you, Father, are in me and I am in you, may they also be in us.* . . . I in them and you in me; that they may become completely *one*" (Jn 17:20-21, 23, italics mine). Here we have nothing but the most glorious assurance that Christ's atoning work brings everything that is lovely about the love of God directly to us in the person of Christ, who is immediately within us as we are within each other. A hymn contains a magnificent line that tunes itself to Christ's prayer: "Love to the loveless shown that they might lovely be."[5]

MUTUAL INDWELLING AND THE LORD'S TABLE

Permit a brief thought about the comprehensiveness of mutual indwelling and its relationship to the Lord's Supper. I realize that the body of Christ has come upon seemingly numberless approaches, meanings and actions within which the central fact of Christ's sacrifice is remembered and celebrated. These range from the Zwinglian constraint of pure memorial to varying convictions about Christ's being with, in, around and under the bread and wine, even to the bread and wine literally becoming the body and the blood. There is even the wonderful idea held by one of the Wesleys' pastoral colleagues, Daniel Brevint, who believed that the bread and wine are like the hem of Christ's garment through which virtue and power flow, but only when touched by faith.[6]

I am not writing to urge a given position. Rather, I want, carefully and reverently, to ask these questions of all practitioners and all adherents to whatever doctrine of the Lord's Supper they are drawn: To what extent does the eternally preceding and changeless fact of Christ in us overrule and transform the particularities of the various doctrines of his table? How do we say (and what do we mean when we say) that we are taking Christ's body and blood to ourselves, when from the eternities he has decided to tabernacle himself within us? To what extent do we risk making one truth into separated, perhaps disjunct, doctrines?

I do not deny the special wonder of going forward, kneeling and taking bread and wine to my lips. I do not deny the noticeable outpourings of the Lord toward me in these moments—they have come too many times. Rather, I wonder how much more spiritual reality there would be if I were to bring the Eucharist under this one momentous fact: Christ in me even as he is in his church. If he is truly the same yesterday, today and forever, in all circumstances and in all places, how can he change his value or his intensity by reason of our doctrinal impositions, except by his own good pleasure, no matter the circumstance?

And then all Christians should further understand that the opinions or practices they hold dear are commonly subject to the care with which Scripture treats this event. There are two central points that no one can afford to ignore. First, Christ's words in the Last Supper must be taken as Christ's words even before they are run through our various practitional and doctrinal changes. Second, Paul's warning to those whose outpouring has grown dull, become displaced or become tainted cannot be ignored. Self-scrutiny, repentance and surrender are unequivocal prerequisites. Eating and drinking in a state of spiritual decay can bring severe consequence.

Sometimes I feel that the magnitude of any grand doctrine (in this case, Christ in you) is such that we often create more tangible subdoctrines to substitute and to satisfy. Perhaps we cannot grasp the truth of Christ in us sufficiently to posit our first principles of his eternal friendship on this fact. It is simply too mysterious, too real. It is so much easier to talk about his nearness as if it were a measurable reinterpretation of omnipresence, or as if our imaginations extended to verifying his presence in some distant reach of the cosmos—a much easier thing to do than to say, "He is within us; seek him not elsewhere."

Nonetheless, this singular fact, full to the bursting, remains. It is a fact grounded in infinite outpouring: Christ is in me; I am in Christ. I am crucified with the one whose body and blood I somehow take to myself in bread and wine. I am risen with Christ, whose resurrected body is the earnest of the one I shall eventually receive and never wear out. I am seated in the heavenlies with Christ who raises me up and takes me beyond the frames and structures of earth and culture. Christ in me is not some narrow, introspective, disembodied, private, even embarrassing fact, specially savored by a narrow sect within the larger Christian community. It is an all-encompassing, all-empowering fact from which no quarter of my worship can be excused.

Here, in summary, is mutual indwelling as compressed as I can get it: the triune God dwells within himself in an infinite glory and continuous outpouring. Through uncountable mercies, we are invited and authorized to say this: Christ comes to us; Christ redeems us; Christ is in us; we are in each other; God is our sanctuary; Christ is the everlasting Temple; the body of Christ is a living temple; Christ is knit into it as chief cornerstone; each believer is a living stone and yet a temple; each believer indwells all other believers; and Christ is all in all. It is with this full promise that we are to go to the place called church and to the necessary times of corporate gathering. We take these unshakable verities with us. They are ours to keep, just as they keep us sheltered within the Almighty's shadow and equipped with the full armor of God.

4

THE CORPORATE GATHERING
AND AUTHENTIC WORSHIP

In the last chapter I pressed the point of mutual indwelling in the fullness of its spiritual reality. In so doing I ran close to the edge of mysticism in which the physical and temporal might appear to have little significance. This is the last thing I want to do, and I shall take the first part of this chapter to bring the last chapter down to earth, because the earthly side of being alive in Christ is an absolute delight. In fact, there may be no better way to approach the subject of corporate worship than through the realities of the seeable and the doable.

Mutual indwelling is not only about being in the Spirit. It is about a world full of redeemed *imago Deis* individually thinking up and doing things, walking on the ground, bound to their hours and days, exulting in the richness and cleaning up the shards around them, worshiping continuously. It is about the body of Christ taking sensuous delight, seeing, smelling, tasting, touching, working, thinking things up, playing jazz, smelling leather and feeling nubby wool, eating stuffed pork chops, listening to Bach and looking at Vermeers, mowing lawns, swing-dancing, smelling a rose, kissing babies, hugging a colt, buying birthday presents and reading George Herbert. It is about the colors, the vestments, the banners, the sounds and smells, the music, the bricks and mortar of church and altar—the vigorous and often startlingly artistic signs of how little we yet know and how much we want to declare the glory of the Lord. In these we join the creation in its irrepressible witness (Ps 19).

Mutual indwelling is about countless people in shoulder-to-shoulder intimacies: church suppers, family outings, voting, barn raisings, boat rides, garage sales, Fourth of July cookouts, parades, hopscotch, town meetings, triple-A baseball, homecoming, weddings and funerals. Mutual indwelling is the body of Christ swept up in God's extraordinary cleverness, in his peculiar love for making measurable, finite things: flesh and bone, galaxies, field daisies, giant sequoias, spring rains, sparrows, giant squid, icebergs, summer savory, rain forests, caves, clouds and cougars.

I have no doubt that the deeper we go into the unseen things of faith, hope and love, the more we will revel in the temporal stuff of life, the intertwining of divine and human handiwork, the sights and sounds of earth and art. Christians should be as delighted in the things of sight and sense as God is himself, when at the instant of every creational act, he declares goodness to be observable, enjoyable and usable. Of all people, Christians should have the best noses, the best eyes and ears, the most open joy, the widest sense of delight. That the opposite is often the case is no fault of the Lord's. How interesting that God, in correcting the ruminations of Job and his three advisers, turned to his work as Imaginer and Maker rather than to his holiness. The Creator's nose has never been pinched, nor his delight in his handiwork held at arm's length because he is a Spirit. How could anyone shy away from the dance of the creation, even in its pain, when God put the highest benediction on it by giving his Son a cardiovascular system, a brain, kidneys, a digestive system, muscles, taste buds, ears, fingerprints, genitals and toes?

The moment Christians begin to be suspicious of the temporal and to withdraw into a vaporous world of ungrounded piety, they begin to miss the wholeness of spirituality and the fullness of mutual indwelling. I realize the danger in what I am saying: that all of the created and creative delights into whose company we are invited can squeeze out the unseen, the things of the Spirit. They can do this, I know. Then we have worldliness; we are *of* the world, not simply *in* it. We enter into a state of inverted begotten-ness—creature shaping creature. We slide into oneness with, and then submission to, the very things over which we are commanded to be sovereign. We are then idolaters. But this does not have to be.

So we guard against two extremes in our sojourn as continuous outpourers: hyperspirituality and hypermaterialism. These are akin to the imbalances that damage our Christology and have dogged the body of Christ ever since the Incarnation. The Docetists want to forget that Jesus could be a sexual being, and the Arians want to forget that he was the purity and essentiality of God himself. It took a group of consecrated thinkers to overcome these off-centered thoughts as, in a carefully thought-through document, the Council of Chalcedon (A.D. 451) laid a corrective on a running controversy. I think that the overall spirit of this statement is a powerful metaphor of the unity between the spiritual and the physical in our own lives. These words are particularly useful: "one and the same Christ . . . recognized in two natures, without confusion, without change, without division, without separation, the distinction of both natures being in no way annulled by the union, but rather the characteristics of each nature being preserved and coming together to form one person." Thus our physicality and our spirituality should come together to form one person, not parted or separated as two persons, but one and the same, even as in Christ Jesus complete unity companies with clear distinction.

So we come to the subject of corporate worship as a mutually indwelling people who are already at worship. And we *must* come here, because this is where continuous outpouring and mutual indwelling take on a unique identity. Here is where the pure things of the Spirit mingle with the unevenness and impermanence of temporality. Here is where the things of sight and sense are ably guided in Spirit and truth, in faith, hope and love. Here is where believers in any spiritual state are anointed together with singular Truth, are made one yet simultaneously addressed as individuals. Corporate worship can become empty—it can turn into an abstraction—outside of each individual worshiper taking on full responsibility, for each person *is* the church, and it is the church that is to be at worship, individual by individual. In corporate worship, it is not "the rest of the folks," especially the spiritual giants, who are responsible. Nor is it the leadership, the worship team or any group or individual with worship-related job descriptions on whom the responsibility falls. When we place the responsibility for worship outside ourselves and not inside, where Christ is, we miss the biblical point of ongoing worship. It might not be too much to say that unceasing worship should be of such consistency and intensity as to raise serious questions about the meaning of the corporate assembly as it is usually perceived and depended upon.

A statement in current circulation goes something like this: "When we come to worship, we should wear our crash helmets because we're going to meet God head-on." This statement, however well intentioned, misses a point. Meeting God, crash helmet or no, is a life experience, not just a church-time happening. To say things like this may hyperactivate corporate worship, but it fails to address the more important question of continuously meeting God. For that matter, how does a crash helmet prepare us to hear the still, small voice?

If we gather together fully outpouring, then nothing taking place in the gathering can ever replace the truth of Christ in us and God already with us. To an authentic worshiper, any thought about liturgical or artistic or environmental "aids" to worship should be seriously questioned. The only aid to worship is the Lord himself. As soon as we place the Lord at the center of our worship, the idea of an "aid," even as applied to him, shrivels into insignificance, for God is our worship. Assured of this, our corporate task can be turned in the right direction and we are free to say this: Everything undertaken turns from an aid to a direct, faith-driven act of worship. The burden shifts from our dependence on what is around us to our trust in the One at work within us. We now depend on the Giver instead of the gifts. And we might become more careful about how we express our thirst for God. Being "desperate for him," in the words of a current song, has precious little basis in Scripture. Longing, hungering, pleading for, crying out to God are one thing, but once we own Christ as Savior, desperation is out of the picture.

Furthermore, we will be able to better understand why the usual call to worship should be transformed into a call for continuing worship to join with corporate worship; that music itself is not "the worship"; that we will be doing something more profound than merely sensing God's presence; that leading worship can actually be transformed into a partnership between the worship leadership and the people of God, a partnership shared because of the priesthood of all continuous outpourers.

We can now go over several matters in order to understand why corporate gatherings are so important and how our continuous outpouring is curiously brightened by assembling together.

PEOPLE NEED PEOPLE

We were not created to live in compartments. People belong together. We must own up to this fact about humanity even before we consider the scriptural examples and instructions about Christians meeting together. If I go to a baseball game, I want to be with my grandchildren or my buddies or my associates. The more crowded the ballpark, the greater my delight and the more I soak up the warmth of this communal cacophony called a baseball game. There I am, caught up in the colors, the smells, the cheers and jeers. Why do we have clubs and quilting bees, cookouts and beach parties, other than to do something in each other's company?

Put the Lord Jesus and his gospel into this natural urgency for company, and we have the body of Christ eagerly seeking times and places to be together. Mutual indwelling demands company. Continuous outpouring demands fellowship. The corporate assembly is where love and mutual indwelling congregate; it is where believers have each other within eye- and earshot, within kindly embrace. If there were no such things as church buildings and regularly scheduled services, Christians would, out of necessity, seek each other out for the sheer pleasure of finding Christ in each other, hearing different stories about his work in them, enjoying the ordinary and the exceptional, and perhaps only then gathering around what we call a liturgy. In such a gathering there would be little need at some point to say, "Now let us worship," because no one would be able to locate the dividing line between "now" and "always."

Christ in us demands that each of us seek out who the rest of us are. It means realizing that we actually *have* each other, that we are already at one with each other, greeting each other, blessing each other, settling on acceptable ways to express ourselves to God's glory. Then we craft these into a liturgy, knowing that it is at best a passing reference to the one who abides from the eternities and lights our path wherever we walk. If we were

to concentrate more on the sheer joy of getting together on a Sunday—
people made holy, people yet to be made holy and people not sure of the
difference, all banded together around the Lord—we would then more
fully understand the depth and width of "the communion of the saints" in
the Apostles' Creed.

But beyond the common need for people to be together, and along with
work of the Holy Spirit pulling us into each other's company, we are given
instruction to be together (Heb 10:25), and the writers to the churches,
especially Paul, take corporate gatherings to be regular and common oc-
currences. Within these, specific activities take place: fellowship (another
meaning of *koinonia*), praise, instruction and edification. In no place in
the epistles are these gatherings described specifically as worship times,
nor is worship mentioned as the singular, all-encompassing act, much less
the reason for gathering. The one exception in 1 Corinthians 14 puts worship in a different light. It is something that an unbeliever does in ac-
knowledging the presence of God in the context of the prophetic force of
believers around him. Despite the absence of a plurality of commandments to gather together, it would be wrong to assume that the *need* to
gather is overlooked or carelessly considered in the New Testament. In
fact, one could easily make the opposite case that the strength of mutual
indwelling and the desire to be in each other's company render any commandment to do so moot.

In this respect Luke 4:16 is a breath of fresh air to those for whom
churchgoing has become a mechanical requirement or perhaps even an addiction. For Jesus, it was his *custom* to go to synagogue on the sabbath. I
like to infer from this that he had a quiet and natural habituation to doing
something eminently desirable, within its own integrity and constancy.
This is good for us to recall when going to church may be the last thing we
want to do on a Sunday or when not enough is happening in "worship" to
keep us worked up and on top of things. If the preacher seems to have lost
the knack of feeding us with enough for the coming week, perhaps we
should discover something about the difference between lively custom and
mechanical routine, between wants and needs, between continuous outpouring and merely waiting for a nice thing to ready us for another seven-
day time lapse.

The Corporate Gathering and the
Roots of True Diversity

Corporate worship presupposes the winsome diversity of a gathered assembly. I speak here of diversity in its most fundamental sense, one that supersedes what we typically call diversity. Living by faith necessitates drawing ourselves into the company of individuals, no two of whom are alike, no two of whom are in step with each other. Even though our starting and ending points can only be in the changeless Christ, it is in his very changelessness that he becomes wonderfully variable to each believer. Spiritual diversity is the deepest kind of diversity there is. It should be this kind that overcomes stylistic diversity, showing us how shortsighted and selfish we are to divide people up over something like music—mere human handiwork. If we were to pay more attention to the discipline of unity and only then spiritual diversity, and if this discipline were the primary rule for our substrategies of corporate worship, we might find out how much deeper we could go when people of all ages, bound together by something deeper than cultural preference, are found in each other's company.

Think of a symphony orchestra. Think of how dramatically different an oboe is from a violin or bass trombone. Then think of the countless possibilities in color and texture that these and other instruments offer when guided by the imagination of a skilled composer—the more kinds of instruments there are, the more exponential the possibilities become.

Turn this analogy toward corporate worship—the more diversity there is, the more spiritual color and texture there can be. Then ask yourself about the ways we have anomalized diversity in the name of diversity by separating people from each other. Secular concepts of generational preferences do not, and cannot, take account of the unseen, immeasurable and unifying work of the Holy Spirit, whose task is to draw all people to Jesus Christ. It is far too easy to forget that the Holy Spirit is good at what he does in causing the same sermon to be milk and meat at once, breaking into the hearts of any number of worshipers in numberless ways.

Corporate worship implies an even more exciting kind of diversity—gathering those in who have lost their way or have not yet found it. Every Christian should have an address book full of non-Christian friends for whom they daily intercede, with whom they joyfully break bread, swap stories, share hobbies and work. Not willing to leave it there, they bring them to corporate gatherings, where, if anything biblical is happening, these prebelievers will discover something unsettling and life changing. The very Spirit who prompts the worshiper cuts into the heart of the unbeliever, one way or another, at one time or another. This is why we can say that witness is overheard worship.[1] In a truly Spirit-filled and Spirit-led gathering, style turns out not to matter much so long as we understand that (as Calvin Miller likes to say) when the Holy Spirit puts hurt on the human spirit, style becomes curiously irrelevant.[2]

Of course, mixing believers and unbelievers together in the same gathering means that there is no such thing as the "in crowd." It means that we have to quit worrying about how to accommodate the "my style, my worship" believer while providing enough ease and comfort for the nonbeliever to slide into the rhythms and chemistries of the same event. This softens the content of a corporate gathering two ways at once by being overly sensitive to the "my style, my worship" believer and unready for the unbeliever whose need for the gospel has not only been misinformed by the coddling of the believer but softened by cover-up language for sin, atonement, shed blood, repentance and righteousness.

Being prophetic is also being evangelistic in the sense that the same Christ is the Author and Finisher of only one gospel, that of being saved unto continuing salvation. When we take the burden away from doing just the right things and place it on the Holy Spirit, free to do his convicting and convincing work, there is no Christ-centered message on earth that will fail to do its double work. Again, the 1 Corinthians passage (14:24-25) comes to mind. If our corporate gatherings were more like the one Paul cites, there would be far less difficulty in integrating evangelism, teaching and prophecy. Saving truth is also reforming truth. The cross is central to both, as are the blood of Christ, the work of the Spirit, the force of the Word and the work of the worshipers.

THE CORPORATE GATHERING AND CORPORATE LEARNING

Continuous outpouring demands continuous intaking, as long as it is not the "I wonder if I'll get fed today" type. This is not intaking but spiritualized laziness. The body of Christ will never know enough about its Savior and should never flag in its pursuit of knowledge and wisdom. The local church, therefore, is a biblical wisdom center far more than it is a worship center, and people should be drawn there if for no other reason than to learn under the guidance and care of specially trained and called servants. This teaching body is made up of both clergy and laity, all of whom are under the similar criteria of being trained and called. Only God knows how this mixture works so well, and only the Spirit and the Word can guarantee its clarity and effectiveness—and how effective it will be if spiritual hunger, intellectual seriousness and teaching skill are brought together.

Country churches and megachurches share equally in this responsibility, even though well-known preachers never seem to be called to, or to remain with, country churches. Superior training and personal charisma seem always to drift toward the big places. Yet it is just as important for a bottomland farmer to go deeply into the things of the Lord as for a university president, and in a wonderfully ironic way, many of them do. Only the Lord knows how to put the kingdom together when such disparity marks its surfaces. Perhaps this is why Ephesians 1:15-21 is so crucial. Despite sensing possible inequality in training and skill, whether in Ephesus or Peoria, Paul is quick to place emphasis on a spirit of wisdom and revelation as the precedent for knowledge. In all cases, it is necessary for the body of Christ to be catechizing itself with this curious mixture of teachers teaching the taught, who are responsible to teach the teachers, even as everybody should be studying to show himself or herself approved.

To say, "This is what I am integrating with my faith at work and at home," then to take this to church for further testing, is just as important (perhaps more so) than to say, "Here's what I learned in church, and I wonder how it applies when I get home and back to work." This suggests that all Christians should specialize in Christianity as if there were no gathering time, so that their vocational calling and general living will be under submission. This kind of specializing is not the same as that of a theologian or pastor or seminary professor, but it is close to it. Specializing in the things of the faith should be so important to laypersons that they do the kind of reading and thinking that lead to the formation of a truth-centered worldview that informs the whole of their living. No believer should say that there is no time to do this in his or her "busy schedule." Time can be carved out of the usual TV, hobby and time-off time. Carpenters, plumbers, airline pilots, coaches, doctors, driving instructors and physical therapists should fill their days and weeks with spiritual curiosity. Their minds should be alive to ideas about the Lord, to problem solving in matters of faith and practice, and to the development of their intellects. *Intellect* and *intellectual* are not snob words; they describe how any mind can be put to work in this sense: an intellectual is a person who loves ideas, asks good questions and strives toward a wisely working whole. This is just as true of a seamstress as it is of a philosopher. It is both comforting and challenging that while we live with the *intelligence* we are born with and have no right to covet a higher kind, we can regularly pray for an increase of *wisdom* and it will be given (Jas 1.5).

Another way of stating this is that Christians should be amateur theologians and Scripture specialists, but in the older meaning of the word. Amateurs are those who love something (hence the Latin *ama* at the beginning of the word) enough to study and practice it as thoroughly as possible, to become skilled in it, without the need to call it a profession or a specialized calling. The core of our being is the image of God, and the core of our spiritual being is in Christ. Saying it this way is also to say that our vocational specialties, no matter how specifically useful and time consuming, are isolates when left to themselves. They do not find their fullest fruition before the Lord until they are surrendered over to the truth, as it teaches the continuously developing mind. This does not mean, for example, that Christian musicians do only Christian music or Christian architects do only Christian architecture. But it does mean that each does music or architecture *Christianly*.

Studying and thinking to the heart of any matter, using the constructs of the faith, are of the essence for every believer. And when it comes down to an inventory of the reading and thinking we actually do, I suggest that only so many "personal experience" books and thoughts will do. As valuable as they may be, they are limited to experience, and if we are not careful, we can be caught up in trading experiences, or even coveting certain ones, without dealing with the deeper truths that inform and transform them.

Christians must be students of Christ. It is in this condition that they come to the local assembly, richly furnished, ready to grapple with depth, ready to encourage the pastoral staff onward and higher. Sunday worship time as intellectual coddle time is out of place. Pastors may be tempted to ease up, to soften the depth and width of their teaching. They may pay too much heed to pollster talk about shortened attention spans, limited cognitive styles, socio-aesthetic preferences and generational groupthink. They may be tempted to forget that preaching under the power of the Spirit and the authority of Scripture is miraculously different from producing a sitcom. But then they will find that their congregations will become more and more difficult to please, even though content is made more and more accessible.

I write these words on behalf of all ministers whose task in this shallowed-out culture is exceedingly trying. One of my fellow administrators at Wheaton College used to say this: "People want you to lead until you do." I believe this applies to the corporate life of the church and to the kind of congregation that wants to "be fed" until it is truly fed. Then the pastor is often accused of not feeding. I beg pastors to stay with the truth, no matter the cost, and to challenge the extensive-mindedness of every living image of God. There are more people interceding for you than you might know. Since God is for you, who can be against you?

THE CORPORATE GATHERING AND THE SUM OF ITS PARTS

In a synergy, the whole is greater than the sum of its parts, and in a particular way, the corporate gathering is this kind of synergy. Here, we return to the mystery of temples within temples and focus it on the peculiar strength of corporate outpouring. Even though Christ is the same in a single believer as he is in a million believers, a corporate gathering is somehow more than the sum of its individually indwelt parts, especially in this sense: no one has the same story. Everyone is diversely working out his and her salvation, and the Holy Spirit is at work making a sum of this diversity. Christ is at work with him, presenting this combined story, Sunday after Sunday, synergy after synergy, to the Father. This will not show itself visibly or measurably but authoritatively, powerfully and spiritually. The power does not lie in sheer numbers, for where two or three are gathered, the synergy is just as real. The power and the glory of this is inward, in the heart of each worshiper. If the Holy Spirit chooses to make this outwardly manifest, and should the entire assembly break into unpredicted ecstasy (whether in charged silence or Pentecostal polyphony), so be it. Our task is to be so spiritually alive that readiness for anything is as normal as lighting the candles or singing a chorus.

There is also the synergy of the church universal, across time and culture. A local assembly takes strength in a world full of local assemblies, diversified in practice, united in the Spirit. The cloud of witnesses of Hebrews 11 joins a storefront congregation in the South Bronx. The South Bronx communion unites itself, by faith and in mutual indwelling, with an underground church in China, one in Christ with the congregants in the National Presbyterian Church in Washington, D.C. Charismatics join with sacramentalists, grape juice mixes with wine, drum sets harmonize with pipe organs, formality links with informality, rich unite with poor, and so on throughout the past, present and future world of the redeemed and the assembled. In each local gathering a synergy of song goes up to God through Christ. Corporate confession, corporate prayer, corporate hearing (both of Word and homily), corporate grief, corporate praise, corporate Communion, corporate giving of gifts, corporate alleluias and corporate hush—all of these are combined into a not-to-be-repeated whole by the work of the Spirit.

The synergy comes full turn, however, when we speak of the church as the bride and the Savior as the groom. Here we enter into a tantalizing mystery, if not a paradox. Christ is all in all, having no need outside himself, yet he chooses a bride—the church—with whom he becomes one and to whom he pledges himself throughout he eternities. Once we understand what this unique marriage means, it becomes difficult to think of Christ being complete without the bride. Yet we know that Christ is all-sufficient and, in a pure theological sense, needless. Do we rob Christ of his completeness by saying that he needs his bride, or do we rest in one of those impenetrable glories that no human mind can fathom? In this case it is the mystery of an all-sufficient being choosing to need, choosing to be given over to a loved one. I can go no further with this. Hence, without any rational answer, we accept the momentous truth that Christ has taken us to himself and is wedded to us forever. This final synergy is ours at all times and in all places. It is ours most certainly in the thick and thin of our outpouring, in its flaws and repentance. It is ours when we walk through the doors of the storefront and the cathedral. This joy-ridden thought—being wedded to the Son of God and joining regularly with the company of fellow believers, each and all his bride—has far greater weight than the nearly insignificant thought of gathering together and hoping that we will worship.

THE CORPORATE GATHERING, POWER AND EXPERIENCE

Amid the complexity and force of all the foregoing, we must distinguish between two kinds of power. There is, to be sure, straightforward and undeniable power in any unified public gathering, be it athletic, political or convocational. This power is also synergistic; it can be quite legitimate, often overwhelming, even uplifting. But it is profane in the sense that its force derives horizontally, out of its own components, objectives and processes. So if we were to take Christ out of a gathering of believers and go about the business of the liturgy, we could still experience a synergy of sorts. But it would be a profane synergy because we would have crafted our strategies out of the same procedural stuff that general culture makes use of. There would be power and experience, but in the words of the Old Testament, it could be likened to "strange fire" (Lev 10:1; Num 3:4; 26:61).

The question, then, comes down to this: In our corporate gatherings can we distinguish between the horizontal power of profane synergies and Spirit-driven ones? Secularly minded critics love to point out the similarities between profane and spiritual group behavior, especially with regard to its more overt forms: hand raising, clapping, dancing, applauding and shouting. Likewise, church leadership can erroneously make use of these similarities by treating worship as if it were, in fact, behaviorally created. And so the circle between worldly and churchly practice remains unbroken. God knows the difference, and we must learn it as well, or suffer the consequences of confusing spiritual power and ordinary power, even when to us they appear similar.

Just as there is a synergy in profane power, so there is a synergy in profane experience, and the latter can easily make its way into corporate gatherings. I will be dealing with the difference between experience and experientialism again in chapter thirteen, so let a few words suffice here. We live in a culture that is given over not so much to experience as to experientialism. The difference is simple. A true experience goes beyond mere feeling. It takes in a wealth of actions in which heart and mind, filled to the full and integrated accordingly, join to bring remarkableness. Experientialism is narrow and short-lived; it can be addictive and basely profane. It thrives on feeling. It is suspicious of the mind and the intellect. As tempting as it might be to go all-out for an experience, and as prevalent as experientialism is in the contemporary church, true worshipers should turn aside from this both out of spiritual integrity and out of deep hunger for the Lord rather than the experience.

I have Christian friends who gather in a charismatic setting, in which speaking in tongues is normal and in which the presence of the Spirit seems to come as a wind. I have other Christian friends whose love for Christ and sensitivity to the work of the Spirit is undeniable, yet to whom charismatic gatherings are uninviting, even suspicious. I realize that I am not reporting anything new. Nonetheless, the distinct reality of these differences puzzles me greatly. If some speak in tongues in one gathering and others in another do not, does this mean some have found particular favor with the Lord and others have not? Is it because some have an edge on true experience and others do not? Or does the Lord somehow recognize how typologically different we are—for whatever genetic, cultural, psychological and spiritual reasons—and, in his magnificent generosity, adjust and manifest himself accordingly? Does he turn to those who are publicly and emotionally overt and to others who are quiet and private, saying to all, "Come unto me, all you who are practitionally wearied and all who are practitionally elated, and find me to be infinitely more than your practices and experiences"? Is this generosity another way in which our Lord empties himself, ever so lovely and complete and ever so eternally continuous? Is it something that some of us are not yet able to grasp, this fullness of Christ in us that rises above our doctrinal, cultural and psychological profiles? Why do we—the quiet ones and the shouting ones—create God in the image that most quickly conforms to who we are? Is Jesus so kind, even in these microidolatries, as to adjust to our psychodoctrinal patterns and to come to us anyway, allowing us to believe, even if for a moment, that the correctness of our opinions makes his presence noticeable?

I do not fully know the answers to these questions, even though in asking them I wish that all of us would stop our doubting of each other so that the practitional lions and lambs would comfortably lie down together. I could wish that the varietal glory of mutual indwelling, with Christ as the overruling indweller, would so overcome the body of Christ that, amid all the fuss and suspicion, all the worry and the gloat, he would outshine every iota of it and cause us to see him in ever so simple ways. If there is any biblical authority behind ecumenism, it lies in the fully surrendered recognition that Christ-in-us washes our competing slates clean. Oh, that we would stop creating the menus and let the Lord feed us out of the plenitude of his continuous outpouring till we entered the paradoxical condition of hungering while being filled! That nearly inexplicable hymn line "Feed me till I want no more" can have no other meaning.[3]

THE CORPORATE GATHERING AND THE SIGNIFICANCE OF LITURGY

Another value of corporate gatherings lies in the richness of liturgical action. *Liturgy* is a rich and wide word. Its meaning goes back to early secular and religious contexts, where it referred generally to the discharge of certain services. It easily transferred over into Christian practice, not so much as an order of worship, but as a description of overall service to God. Once we understand liturgical action as both individual and corporate service to God, and once we understand that the liturgy is not worship but a variable framework for local expressions of it, we can then range through a treasure trove of information and a wealth of practice that takes in the diversity of the church throughout history and across the cultures. Our task, then, is to be temperate, to be judicious and discerning, for God has no need for us to show how many ways we can put a liturgy together. Rather, he wants us to "liturgy" him—to serve him, to work for him—even as he "liturgies" within us both to will and to do of his good pleasure.

In this light it is important for church leaders to be liturgically inventive as one of the strategies for edification and as one way of showing how we worship both variously and continuously. This is the lesson we must learn before we place any liturgy in the hands of the ministry or the congregation. The beauty and effectiveness of a well-crafted liturgy will always lie in its allegiance to the Word. Just as the arts are servants of the liturgy, so is the liturgy a servant of the Word. It might even be better to say that every element in a liturgy joins with all other elements in coservanthood of the

Word. By this I mean that there is no division of purpose or scattering of intent, no virtuosic show of information, no hidden thematic puzzles to solve. The effectiveness of a liturgy lies in its humility, in the absence of self-proclamation—"I am the liturgy; notice me." The Word of God is the gathering point for all the content and all the action. If there is a high point or seasonal emphasis in a liturgy, this is to be subject to the scriptural wholeness within which all actions and emphases take place. *In* Christ means *in* the Word made flesh, and this means that the centrality of Christ guarantees the centrality of the Word, even as we sing or pray or preach or celebrate the Eucharist. It is because of this centrality that all liturgies, whether traditionally framed, denominationally created or "experimental," will stand or fall in direct proportion to the centrality of the Word of God. This applies especially to pulpit-centered churches in which the sermon may at times seem to tower over other actions.

But I do not mean that sermon-centered orders of worship deny the Word. I mean that the very centering of the sermon, as Word-centered as it might intentionally be, can ever so subtly minimize the centrality of the Word of God as the sole force in a corporate gathering. What else edifies, what else corrects, what else converts but the Word of God? As authoritative as preaching must be, and as empowered as the Lord may wish to make it, the Word goes beyond the sermon and thus carries the sermon along with it. It seems contradictory that those who would give their lives for the primacy of the Word of God often give little time to the systematic and generous public reading of it.

THE CORPORATE GATHERING AND THE LITURGICAL YEAR

So far, none of these thoughts are about the advantages of one worship system over another. Rather, they are concerned with the overriding importance of corporate gatherings in the context of continuous worship and with the superabundant reality of Christ in us, irrespective of systems and protocols. However, I offer the opinion that for all Christians there is something valuable about the theological force and architectural completeness of the liturgical year. The lectionaries that nourish it, the prayers that adorn it, the colors and sensory materials that grace it, the temporal and procedural rhythms, the confluences, recurrences and particularities made one with panoramic vista—these and more, whether partially or fully used, can intensify the way a local assembly makes its way through the systematic study of the truth.

The Christian life is not sequential but surprisingly organic, even though one topic or another may, for a time, gain prominence over something else. There is likewise something surprisingly organic about the church year, despite its various thematic and topical emphases. These can become wonderfully pivotal and doctrinally eclectic at any given time. After all, the astonishing fact that we are sinners, that Jesus saves to the uttermost and that life in Christ takes in all circumstances has no liturgical boundaries. There is no season of the church year to which any other season, in its theological meaning, is unwelcome. Anyone who assumes that a given liturgical time or season limits the preaching of the gospel to that theme only confuses the difference between emphasizing a part of the whole and isolating it. If there is a weakness in strict liturgical worship, it lies more in the lack of theological inventiveness on the part of the clergy than in the liturgy itself. In chapter two I referred to the hologram as a way of seeing parts within wholes and wholes within parts. This same metaphor applies nicely to the relationship of liturgical specifics to spiritual wholeness.

THE CORPORATE GATHERING, AGE AND STYLE GROUPINGS

The corporate gathering is, at its best, chronologically disinterested. Here is where I unequivocally take a position. To divide congregations into age groups, style groups and preference groups is to be semi- or even pseudocorporate. The body of Christ is as chronologically and stylistically whole as it is spiritually whole. It is ironic—worse, scripturally troublesome—to see local assemblies broken into groups, each doing their niche worship, for that is all it really seems to be. It is disheartening to think that church leadership has so succumbed to the secondary things about corporate gatherings that it feels constrained to go in this direction. If, for instance, a so-called traditional service and a so-called contemporary service were radically different in *every* respect, one could at least construct pro and con arguments based on internal consistency. But here's the rub: the divisions are primarily about music and musical style. This being true, worship is not really about the binding power of Jesus and his gospel but about something earthly, relative and transient.

If we took music out of worship, would we have the same problem and the same set of solutions? I do not think so. It is not pleasant to realize how much of a burden is placed on ministers of music and worship because of the dependence on style change as the core of the solution. Ironically enough, while a music minister is expected to make distinct style jumps from one worship service to the next, the preaching pastor may do nothing more from one service to another than to take off his or her robe or move from the pulpit to the chancel floor. How out of proportion! How perplexing to think of the burden we have placed on music, this fleeting human construct! The problem is not with any one style but with the reluctance of people to rub up against a multiplicity of styles, for it is the rubbing— the creative friction—that could bring about the stylistic syntheses that the body of Christ so desperately needs.

Traditionalists have much to answer for in their reluctance to understand that tradition does not mean stasis but change. In their reaction against contemporary styles, they fail to understand that what they have gotten used to was once contemporary and often objectionable. Contemporists likewise fail to understand how blunted their tastes are when only "their music" seems to do the trick and when what they are doing has, ever so quickly, frozen itself into a tradition. So we end up with two kinds of shortsightedness, one supposedly old, the other supposedly new, and both wish fulfilling. The separation of worship into preference groups is everyone's fault, in that narrow musical satisfaction has turned out to be more important than style-proof outpouring. I encourage people of all practices to become intently and intensely curious about each other's ways.

The church desperately needs an artistic reformation that accomplishes two things at once: first, it takes music out of the limelight and puts Christ and his Word back into prominence; and second, it strives creatively for a synthesis of new, old and crosscultural styles. A deep understanding of the arts, coupled to the understanding that at best the music of corporate worship is simple, humble and variegated, would bring something about that would make all churches into worshiping and witnessing churches that happen to sing.

I offer these thoughts in summary: We gather because we cannot stay away from each other. We gather because it is our joyous custom to obey all injunctions to gather. We gather to celebrate a diversity that goes beyond mere cultural groupings. We gather to learn in common and to bring our daily learning into each other's conversation. We gather as the body of Christ, his bride, and our continuing worship turns to a gathered feast. We understand that the power and experience that comes of true worship rises above the everyday and the profane. We gather to learn of the entire counsel of God through the structures and liturgies we devise. We gather as one body—young and old, feeble and strong, rich and poor—undivided by the little things of life like style and music. We gather around the unifying power of the Word and bring our praise to the King of kings and Lord of lords.

5

WORSHIP AND WITNESS

THE INDIVISIBLE TASK OF CONTINUOUS OUTPOURING

If the whole world is continuously outpouring before its plethora of gods, and if (for the Christian) personal holiness and authentic worship are one and the same, then this can only mean that Christian witness is overheard worship. The more I think about the nature of continuous outpouring, the more I become aware of how spiritually self-indulging the idea of worship (in our current sense) can be—and how evangelism and witness are separated from it. But witness is about worship, worship is about witness, and both are about the presence or absence of a quest for personal holiness. Properly understood, a theology of worship should reform, if not re-create, our often isolated ideas about evangelism and mission.

WHAT IS WITNESS?

Even so, we have this specific and necessary word *witness* to deal with. Let's try this definition. Just as worship is a continuous outpouring of all that I am, all that I do and all that I can ever become, so *witness is both a general and a specific out-toward and outpouring testimony that verifies this*. I realize that *out-toward* is an awkward term, but it rings the right changes on continuous outpouring in that neither worship nor witness can be self-contained or self-directed. Continuing worship pours out toward God, and continuing witness pours out toward humankind as to the things of God. Likewise, by examining my sojourn as a continuing worshiper and by testing it against the truth to which I have sworn myself, I am in a position to speak and act intelligibly about it, whether through ordinary day-by-day living or through specific words and deeds that directly summon another person to turn to the Savior of all outpouring.

Everybody everywhere, somehow and in some way, is giving expression to what masters them. Some do this with great clarity, uninhibited frankness and directness. Others barely let their light shine. Just as there is lukewarm Christianity and shriveled witness, so there is lukewarm fallenness and so-so testimony to it. If Satan were granted the right of handing out eternal rewards to his followers, he too would spew out those who failed to live to the full the horror of fallenness and the exceeding sinfulness of sin. Satan is the author of fallen witness, and Christ is the Author and Finisher of redeemed witness, and in a flash of decreation, Christ will finish once for all the truthless rot of inverted witness. In the meantime, the two kinds of witness continue, each about worship and outpouring and each manifest in varied ways.

In a discomfiting way, non-Christians may have an easier time witnessing about their lives than Christians do, in that fallenness and lostness are fully consistent with each other. Even the good works of an unbeliever, which are admittedly considerable and varied, fall easily in line with their evil ones, since their reasons for doing either are driven by the same underlying falsity: the works are effective in themselves. Unbelievers not only can separate their "mistakes" from their good deeds, but also they believe that a sufficient number of the latter can offset or compensate for the former. Moralizing, when it does occur, does not take account of the fact that even the most altruistic work is still sin-tinged and in need of cleansing. Evil is seen episodically and self-referenced for what it is at the time, rather than as a part of a comprehensive condition that simultaneously infects even the good works.

This construct makes fallen witness easy to articulate. Unbelievers have several options: they can deny the reality of sin; they can make it culturally and contextually relative; they can euphemize it; and they can blame others for it. If they are sincere enough to recognize good and evil in themselves or others, they can take the balance-sheet approach—good offsets evil, and if enough good is done, evil may even disappear. And this may be sufficient to prompt the most altruistic among them to work hard at making society better. In all cases lostness and fallenness harmonize completely, as do good works and "salvation"; everything is more tangibly measurable and not hidden away in the invisible stuff of faith. The world's witness about its outpouring, after all, is down-to-earth in the fullest sense, disconnected from the idea that repentance and salvation are based on an essential and radical separation from everything that makes fallenness so easy. I further believe that this fact might be among the reasons why Christians are so easily embarrassed in their witness and why it can be so difficult to create a conversational transition between the ease and the dis-ease. After all, the dis-ease has been covered over with fun, with wrong appearing as right, success appearing as justification. Come on, what's so wrong with two unmarried persons bedding down when it's the relationship that counts?

I have often pondered my own sense of discomfort in witnessing—a discomfort sometimes bordering on shame or a sense of silliness. I am coming to learn that even though I should be ashamed of my fleshly shame, I should also realize that the gospel, especially to my Romans 7 side, is silly. It is scandalous. I stumble over it. It is about something so far removed from the way the world works, so odd, so unnecessary as to bring scorn down upon its most consistent followers. And Satan knows this all too well and works hard at making the two kinds of silliness look the same.

Furthermore, authentic witness is difficult because, while the world sees its own inconsistencies as "the way it is," it sees the inconsistencies of the Christian as a condemnable disjunction between perfection and imperfection (and therefore evidence that Christianity does not work, because Christians cannot practice what they preach) rather than a radically different way of dealing with good and evil. Christianity also looks silly because you can take your pick among its hundred or so odd and rounded-down versions until you find something that fits. So if I can take my pick, what is unique about what you are trying to tell me? Likewise, since Christians and non-Christians alike may dance, drink, work for the same company, drive the same cars, go to movies together, give to the poor, listen to Amy Grant and sing Bach cantatas, and commonly agree that the world may be going to hell in a handbasket, how has accepting Christ changed all of this? What is faith when I already have faith in my girlfriend's attestations to faithfulness? What is faith when I trust in Bernoulli's law as I board a 747? Or for that matter, what is faith when I agree that Jesus is really cool and, yes, there's something special about the way Pastor Tom brings it all down to earth? And from the perspective of the local church, whose current practices can easily be split between satisfying the saints and softening the blow for the lost (and in whose corporate gatherings there appears to be confusion as to what adjustments should be made in order to do both things at once), what should be done if authentic worship and outpouring witness are, biblically speaking, one and the same?

THE CORPORATE GATHERING AND WITNESS

What happens in the corporate gathering as to witness should be no different from what happens as to worship. That is, if worship and witness are seamlessly knit, then the corporate gathering should proceed in its fullest prophetic condition, irrespective of the ratio between saints and sinners. I firmly believe that the gospel is whole, that in its wholeness it is for the whole of humanity and that becoming saved and continuing to be saved demand that the entire message of God in Christ must dominate whatever topic or theme is being emphasized at a particular time. Through the work of the Spirit, the converted hear it inherently and the unconverted hear it readily. The Holy Spirit is at hand making sure that inherent hearing leads to further growth and readied hearing leads to salvation, even when that which is inherently or readily heard may not be fully comprehended. After all, if the gospel is the power of God unto salvation, then God in his power will make sure that the readied hearer is not left in the dark and the inherent hearer will be urged into further maturity. The secret is not in talking baby talk to the unredeemed and adult talk to the converted, nor in seeking a happy medium between the two so as to conform to eased-up protocols of certain kinds of seeker sensitivity. The secret lies in the authority, the conviction, the unswerving bluntness of all truth preached, sung and written.

I have no doubt about the capability of the Lord to intrude into the heart and mind of any person at any moment to such a degree that, should we be ready and should he will it, an entire gathering will be swept up in a wave of reformation. Over and over again I refer to the foundational witness of Paul in 1 Corinthians 14:24-25 regarding the double work that truth performs—while the redeemed teach and edify each other, the unredeemed (in that same moment and under the authority of the same content) will fall down Godward in redeemed outpouring, newly washed. That this seldom happens can be explained in various ways. First, we do not bring unsaved friends to the corporate gathering because of our procrastination or our mistaken ideas that "worship" is for believers while witness and evangelism are reserved for other times and places. Second, the prayer life of the congregation is not dominated by brokenness over lostness. Third, preaching can become muddled by an overdependence on profane advice as to how to attract and hold an audience, and the advice becomes the guide. Fourth, the Word of God is superficially treated and listlessly read in all but the most enlivened liturgical gatherings. Fifth (back to preaching again), there is the possibility of personal charisma replacing biblical authority. The style of the preacher may substitute for brokenness, clarified authority and humility. In this sense personal power and Spirit power become confused, and the kind of authority with which Jesus taught is virtually overlooked (Mt 7:28-29; Mk 1:22; Tit 2:15).

What are we left with? We know all too well: witness becomes a separated specialty, and the confusion between worship and evangelism further widens. Because we are right in assuming that witnessing is every Christian's responsibility, we are furnished with witnessing tools and prompted sometimes to the point of guilt to be ready to say a word for Christ. We look for the opener, the wedge point. If it does not naturally come, we feel compelled to leverage it into being. If neither occurs and nothing happens, we wonder if we have failed God or we settle back on our theological haunches and assume that God has chosen to harden the other person. Part of the reason for this is that we have thought so narrowly about Christ and salvation that we have only formulistic ways to talk to others. We have come to think so narrowly about truth, overlooking the countless connections between Truth and everyday circumstance, that our only option is to leverage our ideas about deciding for Christ discontextually, without understanding that all conversation is embedded in living and holds numerous related ideas, any one of which can be applied to worshiping upside down or right side up. If there is no other reason for Christians to be intellectually alive and topically imaginative, this one alone suffices.

WITNESS AND EVANGELISM

In mass evangelism, as necessary and effective as such efforts have been through the centuries, the salvation message may all too easily be left to itself. It is often perceived more as an event than a process unless there is organic linkage to the gospel of continued salvation, growth up into Christ and continuous worship. But evangelists should not bear the criticism for having little time for this. Rather, the church bears the responsibility for forgetting that its task is to deal with continuous outpouring from the full extent of its inversion to that of its conversion.

If growing up into Christ in the most complete sense were the personal agenda of every Christian and the pedagogical strategy of every local assembly, there would be little need for orientation and teaching sessions by the advance team for a visiting evangelist. After all, what do these sessions teach but the very same information that should be regularly taught at the local level and put to use all the time in daily life, corporate gatherings and personal learning? Why does the coming of an evangelistic team receive such special attention, as if there were nothing momentous about the ordinary congregational life of each local parish? Why the publicity? Why a specific time in a specific city? Above all, why the exponential letdown in its aftermath—hardly a mention, hardly any stir and excitement after the original hubbub? Is it because of the separation of gospel from Gospel and the parenthesized and categorized concepts we have about the good news? Should we not be such ardent outpourers that worship and evangelism are indistinguishable? Are evangelistic crusades as much a mark of God's patient disappointment toward the church for its inability to do what is commanded, as it is his will that no one should perish? The fact that God can and does work mightily in an evangelistic crusade may be less an endorsement than an indictment. Even as the Spirit brings the many to Christ, even as a Wesley or a Graham is rightly esteemed for being an instrument of truth, the church may be being judged for making it necessary for evangelism to be so noticeably separated in the first place.

A practicing Christian is someone who is so skilled and widely competent in being Christian, and so committed to continuous outpouring, that whatever the situation, he or she speaks fluently and ardently to it. This kind of Christian possesses a comprehensive readiness into which the Lord can pour his leading as to when, where and how. This kind of Christian is always at rest, not anxious (should I witness here and now?) but peacefully prepared. Here's an analogy for what I am trying to say. Accomplished pianists practice continuously. This does not mean that they practice all the time, but they practice so fully and wisely that they can enjoy not practicing and be at rest about their readiness to perform. A witnessing Christian should be like this. He or she cannot witness twenty-four hours a day any more than a pianist can practice that long. But there should be such thoroughness to practicing the faith that at a moment's notice it can be turned to specific witness. This readiness is not particularly about a set witness-time any more than wise piano practice is about an isolated performing event. Rather, it is about being comprehensively Christian and practicing Christianity in such a way that at any moment its completeness can be shaped to fit the circumstance.

In this respect there is an interesting difference between evangelism on the mission field and crusade evangelism. The former deals with the dilemma of lostness by taking issue with false worship and strange gods. Crusade evangelism bypasses this and goes directly to sinfulness and Christ's remedy for it, without recognizing that false worship and false gods are the bedrock issue. So whether it is "Where will you be if you die in your sleep?" or the *Four Spiritual Laws,* passing out tracts or a wrenching rebirth with no one there but the Word of God, each of these must be grounded in a comprehension that the early milk and the later meat are only the roughest metaphors for growing up into Christ. Milk is not pre-meat, as if A led to B. If anything, milk is lowercase "a" and meat capital "A." Even better, it is Alpha growing into Omega, which in Christ is endlessly beginning and beginningly endless. Thus, somewhere down the line, we do not begin to talk about sanctification or witnessing or worship growing out of the salvation experience. Rather, there is but one subject: worship as salvation and salvation as worship. I go back to 1 Corinthians 14:24-25 again. If prophecy in the context of a gathered assembly leads to the conversion of a sinner, it must be true that prophecy—speaking to one another truthfully in love—contains the seed of witness unto salvation. Turn this around and we can see how witness, as a specificity, should take in more than new-birth talk.

In these comments I cannot afford to be misunderstood. I am not trying to tear down the edifices of personal witness, even the formulized kind, nor am I hitting on organized evangelism. Above all, I am under judgment for the words I write. And I am trying to be sure that every aspect and activity of the body of Christ is interconnected and answerable to the singularity of continuous outpouring and authentic worship. Perhaps the best way to do this is to link several passages of Scripture and try to show how worship and witness can never be separated topically and procedurally until they have been united theologically.

We go back to Romans 12:1 and John 4:24. A living sacrifice is a complete person, not a sacred-secular person or a worshiping-now-and-witnessing-then person. Being a living sacrifice is about being alive, and being alive is what we are at all times and in all places. This means that my way of living is not only noticeable but also noticeably different, even when I might be doing the same things at the same times as non-Christians. It is the Holy Spirit's business to work out a noticeable difference through me. If I am in Christ and continuously outpouring both toward him and toward those in my company, he will see to it that something unique emerges and is noticed. If not, it is not my fault, nor my business, but part of the Lord's timing. My only responsibility is to be hungry for the salvation of others, doing only those things I would do if Christ were my sole companion. Likewise with the instructions in John 4:24: as a living sacrifice, I am living in the Spirit and according to truth. This is a continuum. And continua are the only credible witnesses because they can be continually depended upon. Again, the Spirit is the guarantor of my integrity as I live truthfully. This kind of living is bound to be noticed and is ready to provide a Spirit-driven entrée into the oddest moments and most unlikely conversations. As God trips up the work of Satan, as the Wind blows in the face of the unbeliever and as I continue my venture in Spirit and truth by speaking directly of Jesus, my worship is overheard in this particular way.

Second Corinthians, particularly the opening chapters, is a treasure

trove of wisdom about continuous outpouring in the presence of unbelievers. Paul's thinking is knit to the spilling of perfume on Jesus' feet in John
12:3 when he says that God through Christ, in us, "spreads *in every place*
the fragrance that comes from knowing him" (2 Cor 2:14, italics mine). As
Christ and the believer mutually indwell, as each continuously pours out
to the other, there is no place and no time exempt from the fragrance. Witness is the fragrance of continuous outpouring, both to God (v. 15) and to
those being saved as well as those being lost: to the one an aroma, to the
other a stench. Only God knows how to take continuous outpouring and
use it in these two disjunctive ways. This locational richness, life unto life
and death unto death, is what we are promised if, as living sacrifices, we
pour the perfume of our lives toward God through Christ.

Then, in one of the most electrifying thoughts anywhere about the full
weight of continuous outpouring, Paul tells us that we are to go about the
business of being ambassadors as if God himself were pleading through us
(5:20). This thought carries us all the way back to the Godhead's decision,
taken in the eternities, to pour himself out in the person of Christ so that
the world, in its falsified outpouring, would be reconciled to God. Because
the Savior has found and saved us, because he has washed our sinful worship clean and turned us to himself as living sacrifices, we have no other
duty and no other joy than to make him known even as we worship him
in Spirit and truth. God's call to the unreconciled is continuous: now is the
accepted time; it is not his will that any should perish. If God's reconciling
call comes all the time, and if we are charged with speaking and living as
though God were pleading through us, then it only makes sense that our
outpouring to him, to each of our brothers and sisters, and to the world
must all be co-incident.

Christian witness is an ambassadorial action, and sometimes a blunt
confrontation, between continuous outpourers, one right side up, the
other upside down. To be a living epistle, known and read by everyone,
demands being completely furnished for every good work. The distance
between outpouring to God and witness to the world is closed by this
single fact: a living epistle is at once a prophet and an evangelist. The two
are one, just as the gospel is both prophetic and evangelistic, just as Spirit
and truth are one, just as the Spirit is both a convicting Spirit and a teach-

and just as Christ is a both saving Savior and a sanctifying Sav-
~~ ~~~ extent that corporate worship becomes the closed-in arena for
the undertaking of that which may have no connection to the more important actions of continuous outpouring, worship and witness continue
to be two separated actions, two specialties. Both the church and the
world lose out.

SEEKER SENSITIVITY AND WITNESS

I want to say a few things about seeker sensitivity and the occasional differences between a theology of worship and witness. It is wrong to assume
that seeker sensitivity is a new thing or that it is related only to something
like the current church growth movement or contemporary worship and
praise styles. Any time the church tunes its practices to the norms and expectations of a given or potential audience, it can claim to be seeker sensitive. A church can be classicist and high culture, and as soon as it banks
on certain seekers identifying with this style of worship, it will be seeker
sensitive. Style, then, need not be the issue, that is, until style gets in the
way of a more important question: Is there a biblical difference between
seeker sensitivity and sensitive seeking? I believe there is.

In terms of the gospel, sensitive seeking places the current issue of
seeker sensitivity in a secondary position, and it places primary emphasis
on what it means for believers to seek *sensitively* on the basis of the power
of the gospel and the reality of continuous outpouring. From what I can
tell from Scripture, both seeking and sensitivity are based on the character
of God and on his initiatives. These extend both to God's hatred of the exceeding sinfulness of sin and to his love toward the sinner, to the extreme
extent of sending his Son to clear up the matter once for all.

This forces the concept of sensitivity into God's arena, thus into a paradoxical combination of love and hate, of grace and brutality, wherein God
hates the sin, takes the brunt both of the sinner's hate and brutality and
overcomes the whole with righteousness, love and grace. God is the outpouring Sensitive Seeker from the eternities, and there is no picture of him
that is complete without the inclusion of the slain Lamb. The story of his
seeking begins in Genesis, not with the provision of a skin covering or even
the promise that the serpent's head would be crushed, but earlier, in the

cool of the day, with a search and a question: "Where are you?" In this way God identifies himself as the unsought Seeker of those whose sensitivities were turned to the seeking out of strange gods and to pouring themselves out on their behalf.

This history-long and culture-wide hunting story continues from the garden, to the flood, to the finding of Abraham, to the giving of the Law, and to the grieving, protesting words of the prophets. It continues clean through the years and the dark, on to the quintessential Seeker, Jesus Christ, the Author and Finisher and final Yes to the story. He is at once the Interrogator ("Where are you?"), the Judge ("You are dead and need life"), the Teacher ("Here's what you must do to find me") and the Yes-and-No Answer ("I am your life and your salvation; refusing me is death").

Through his Spirit both working freely where he will and enabling his ambassadors wherever they go, the sought are confronted radically, directly and outpouringly. They comprise the whole of humankind in its falsified outpouring, no single person of which God wants to perish. The found finally comprise those within this whole who become sensitized by the Spirit alone—one by one—to seek, repent and be turned right side up. This is the real story of the redemptive and prophetic sensitivities of all primary seekers. Thus the concept of the redemptively sensitive seeker takes precedence over that of a culturally defined seeker sensitivity.

I am by no means alone in my concern over the way the gospel has often been thinned out and the scandal of the cross made into a heartwarming romance. To be sure, the gospel is driven by love, but love is two-sided. It carries with it the incontestable and gracious fact that God is himself love, of such magnitude as to grant the gift of the Savior. But it also carries an equally powerful and unconditional hatred of the exceeding sinfulness of sin itself, even before it undertakes condemnation of sins (which most of us now prefer to call "mistakes," as if we are dealing with the equivalent of buying the wrong automobile). One can only pray that the easy-come–easy-go practices of the majority church will be stunned into reform and that all of us together will rediscover the truth that keeps staring us in the face.

There are three issues I want to address, each of which has to do with the thinning out of the gospel.

DUMBING DOWN THE *IMAGO DEI*

The first issue has to do with our neglect of *imago Dei*. *Dumbing down* is not a new term to secular thinkers or church leaders. We have heard it used time and again in the media, in educational forums and in cultural policy studies. I want to pick up on this term in another way by applying it to the *imago Dei*. The dumbing down of culture and of people in culture is the surface issue, not to be compared with the severity and dishonor accorded to the image of God in us by dumbing *it* down. Doing this not only eats away at the heart of what it means to be human; it is a direct insult to God himself, whose person is dumbed down by the way we treat his image in us. Dumbing down the image of God is tantamount to saying that God is not important, that his imprint, however wracked in the Fall, is not worth much. But it is not just that God so loved the world; it is that he loves his triune self so much, he loves his image in us so, that he gave his only Son, who was at once image of God and Son of God—both creature and Creator. The rescue, redemption, restoration and Christ-centered schooling of the *imago Dei*, in its countless human paraphrases, is as much at the core of the gospel as anything. The dumbing down of which so many speak is certainly a scandal. But if we are not careful, the scandal remains exterior and statistical, a phenomenon that can be offset by smarting things back up. Both dumbing down and smarting up can happen without redressing the dishonor done to God by treating his image in us so crassly.

Even if we go so far as Martin Luther in *The Bondage of the Will* or John Calvin in his direst portraits of our incapability of turning to God on our own, we are still left with an enormous fact: intellectually, imaginatively and creatively, there is enough in the worst of us to enable us to go to amazing depths, heights and widths. If common grace is a workable doctrine, then it follows that the heights, depths and width of which any human mind is capable are there a priori, before the gospel does its peculiar work. Why then do we do so much to cover this up with our thinned-out and smoothed-over approaches to truth? Why are we so afraid that our witnessing and our preaching will go over people's heads? Redemption is the washing clean and re-equipping of the *imago Dei* and the beginning of a lifelong process of re-tuning it to think and to imagine, not more smartly or less dumbly, but more completely, more profoundly and wisely, after the manner of truth itself.

I cannot rid myself of the thought that being created in the image of God holds, for every one of us, a richer potential than how intelligent or cultured we are. I cannot rid myself of the thought that redemption is the resurrection of the *imago Dei* and that all our teaching and preaching and parenting should be directed toward the instruction of this newly awakened and redeemed wonder. Every time I come in contact with people who seem to be intellectually disinterested or aesthetically numb or spiritually asleep, I grieve—not because they fall below some mathematical or societal norm or might not ever make it into a selective college, but because they are in the image of God and I want to do my part (God making his plea through me) to participate in the awakening and schooling of this image. I want to shake these cherished souls and say, "Do you know what you are capable of? I'll pester you until you open your eyes to your glory or turn your back for good." And when I hear someone talking *down* to the image of God, I want to stand up and ask for the theological reasoning behind such short-selling.

SATAN AND HIS DOUBLE LIE

The second issue relates to the work of Satan. We know all too well that he is incapable of telling the truth. This is eternally impossible. He can use truth upside down and is enormously skilled in making wrong appear to be right and right, wrong. Whatever he does is a lie and whatever he says is a lie, from beginning to end. But when it comes to his dealing with the church and the world, I believe he can lie in two opposing directions at once. Here is what he, coming as an angel of light, may say to the church: "The average human being is fairly slow, culturally encrusted. People like things that are palatable and light. So be palatable and light. And for goodness' sake, don't go into the primitive stuff—the blood of Christ or the realities of lostness throughout eternity." Here's what he says to the unconverted: "You're too smart for the gospel. Look at how so many of its trappings are second-rate knockoffs of the real stuff you can find around you in the theater, in deeply thought-through books, in higher education. Notice how much more of your mind is demanded even in your daily work than at church. You're ahead the way you are."

So between these two lies he goes about his business. The church buys into the simple-minded, smoothed-over approach; the world continues its assumption that there is, after all, a certain thinness to Christianity. In the middle of this gulf there stands the Savior, asking both the church and the world for entrance and holding out only one truth to each. Nearby is the Holy Spirit in his tenderness, on a holding pattern, with nowhere to alight, while we parade our artificial paracletes: methods, style, surveys, misinformed sensitivity and soft talk.

POLICY THEOLOGY AND OPERATIONS THEOLOGY

We can state the third issue with an analogy from the corporate world. In a successful business, policy and operations must harmonize or the business suffers. Policy statements, mission statements and policy-based planning must be internally consistent and overarching. When the corporation pledges itself to do something, it makes sure, operationally, that it is done in a manner consistent with the stated mission. Let's move this over into theology and its relation to our worship, growth and evangelism protocols. I believe that we often possess and apply two differing theologies, depending on the task at hand. We can call them policy theology and operations theology.

Policy theology (we might also call it a vertical theology) is classically God-centered. It acclaims the sovereignty of God, his unquenchable love, his works and his redemptive grace. It speaks of his direct control over the world. It confirms his otherness and his transcendence, knit to his sworn purpose in redemption solely through the work of his Son. It attests to not only the overpowering work of the Spirit and the magnitude of the atonement but also the irrelevance, even pettiness, of our efforts in trying to displace God while persuading people. It places its complete confidence in the authority of Scripture and pledges itself to bring every detail of life under its scrutiny and judgment. While honoring human creativity and human culture, it places them in submission. It disparages the ways of the world—its idolatries, its pride, its faithless mechanisms and manipulations. It celebrates the power of God to change people and to move them toward him, and it is sworn to the gospel as the power of God unto salvation. It engages in a profound inquiry into fallenness, the sinfulness of sin and the mystery of godlessness. It claims that faith alone saves and that the works employed in its spread are, by themselves, of no effect.

Then there is operations theology (horizontal theology). It determines if and how we interpret and apply policy theology. It observes and analyzes the contextual surroundings in order to aid in determining how the grand doctrines—the policy theology—can best be adjusted and communicated. This is the theology that determines *how* we go about our business and informs our concept of how God most probably goes about his business. So far, so good, because all theology must be circumstantially workable and culturally relevant.

But operations theology can turn in on itself. Instead of subjecting its observations and analyses to the grand doctrines, it can do the reverse. The information gathered from observation and analysis can overwhelm or actually become doctrine, to the extent that the grounding issues—the policy issues—can be diluted or wrongly prioritized. For instance, salvation may be presented as having more to do with making a decision "for" Christ than with atonement, shed blood and radical repentance. This would be an example of dilution. As an example of improper prioritization, free choice might be granted higher prominence than God's sovereignty, in which case finding and depending on the right techniques to persuade people to change might become more important than the change itself and the power of the gospel to effect it.

In the current scene our policy and operations theology may be out of sync with each other, in that the pervasive overrelevance of culture, the power of works and the techniques and devices for changing behavior seem to be the main engine. What is effective may overcome the importance of what is true. Too much attention may be focused on temporal power and the feelings and preferences of people. Policy theology can be constricted by the marketplace, the consumer, the relationally driven culture and the behavioral machineries behind it. It can therefore become almost completely descriptive rather than prescriptive as context takes priority over content. The balance can ever so subtly shift from the sovereignty of God, the power of the Spirit and the scandal of the cross to the means by which these can be palatably articulated. Allowed free reign, this shift can turn the message of salvation almost completely away from the incisive truths of sin, shed blood, repentance, radical rebirth and disciplined growth to more smoothed-out ideas about the need for a new "relationship," a word that has been overwhelmingly misshapen by secular culture while being virtually absent in Scripture.

These two models may represent extremes, I realize. I further realize that in many cases we are vacillating somewhere in the middle. I further acknowledge how easy it is to adopt a nearly pure policy theology and fail to translate this into a credible workaday procedure. The purpose of showing these two models is to raise some questions to which each of us must give an honest answer: For the sake of Christ and his gospel, to what extent are policy and operations theology of one cloth, woven by the Master Weaver? To what extent are we too contemporaneously American—pragmatic, entrepreneurial, consumerist? By contrast, to what extent are we prophetic, meek and serving in an elegant and reforming cultural way? Is the perfume that we pour on Christ's feet truly costly?

Our answers, surprisingly enough, will earn us the right to say that the worshiping church is the most ardent champion of culture, that the church is so in love with the idea of culture, in fact, that it will invade it with freshness—sing new songs courageously and old songs newly, create art that breathes the temporal air of the first day of creation and the eternal one of the new creation, preach a gospel that at once opens the door to the fullness of lostness and the glory of salvation. The church presents a Christ who loves us so much that he joined culture, worked his trade within its norms and yet preached a message that leaves no quarter of it untouched and unchallenged.

Serving Christ while participating in culture in an elegant and reforming way can mean a thousand things in as many places. It can mean shoveling muck and bringing clean water to a barrio. It can mean writing a new praise chorus for a storefront congregation. It can mean translating the Scripture one more time for one more faraway tribe. It can mean taking old hymns and old ways and breathing new life into them. It can mean preaching simply yet eloquently, fearingly yet sweetly. It can mean praise songs cavorting with hymns, and drums conversing with organ sounds. It can mean complete freedom in the Lord and stupendous discipline finding common ground. It can mean Bach, blues, Monet, street art, child dance,

ballet, homiletics, storytelling, barn raisings and homeless shelters, all
found within the normal conversation of the believing church. Elegance,
for the Christian, is simply a thousand actions washed in the blood and
carrying the sweet savor of Jesus' love. It is, above all, the seamless garment
of worship and witness.

6

WORSHIP, PRAYING AND PREACHING

As continuous outpouring encompasses all of our living, many topics could be covered in this chapter: Sunday school teaching, parenting, Bible study, vocation and the like. I have chosen only two—praying and preaching—for particular reasons.

I have chosen praying because, just as nobody does not worship, so nobody does not pray. Life is full of prayers. Religions of all kinds thrive on prayers. In times of grief, loss and trauma, prayers break out of mouths otherwise unused to praying. The same mouths might also pray obscenely without realizing it in the vomitory "O my gods" that litter our verbal landscape. But for the Christian, praying is a redeemed honor, an unqualified responsibility and a seamless part of the continuum of continuous outpouring. It is every believer's duty. As such, it must oversee all other kinds of praying.

I also want to write something about preaching because it is an action to which all Christians must pay attention. While only a few preach, all of us must hear and then decide what to do with what we hear. Just as praying is directly linked to continuous worship, so is preaching, for reasons to be discussed shortly.

PRAYING

There are long prayers and short prayers, composed and improvised prayers, but most importantly, ceaseless praying. In the eternal sense there is no particular merit or effect to quantitatively long or short praying. Instead there is simply faithful and effective praying. In this regard we can safely paraphrase 2 Peter 3:8 this way: With the Lord, a faithful prayer is as a thousand prayers and a thousand faithful prayers are as one faithful prayer. Or, with the Lord, one faithful prayer is heard throughout all eternity, just as all the prayers from all times are heard in an eternal instant.

What is praying without ceasing? As already implied, it is not necessarily protracted praying, because even that has to start and stop somewhere. Otherwise, having no time to eat and drink, work or rest, we would die of prayer. Our Savior, in his thirty-three years on earth, could not have carried out the literal meaning of ceaseless prayer, for he would have gone hungry and the gospel would not have been preached. Even so, we cannot easily slough off the word "ceaseless." It was not uttered by Paul either to frustrate us with the impossible or to exaggerate a commandment to pray that would have otherwise come across as commonplace. "Ceaseless" is there for a reason. I believe it consists of two things.

CEASELESS PRAYER AND OCCASIONAL PRAYER

First, ceaseless prayer is a condition of perpetual spiritual readiness in which specific praying of any duration is freely undertaken in the continual now-and-then-ness of God's leading us to pray. The King James talks about this condition as being "instant in prayer" (Rom 12:12). To be instant in prayer is to be ready in prayer at any time and in any place or circumstance, at a moment's notice.

Included in this is the discipline of specific set-aside prayer times. But limiting our praying to the set-aside times may not be enough. In fact, there is a certain risk in set-aside prayer, no matter how time consuming, how spiritually rich and detailed it can be. We can get so good at it, so habituated to it, so fulfilled by it that breaking spontaneously into prayer at any other time may seem too random and too patchy. Or we may think that we are repeating ourselves unnecessarily. Has not Christ himself warned us about vainly repeating ourselves and about making our praying foolish by using many words? Likewise, doesn't the once-for-all nature of God's sovereignty make now-and-then praying redundant? If we have already prayed for the salvation of a loved one earlier in the day, why should we repeat this prayer later? I am not talking here about crisis praying—medical emergencies or sudden tragedies that pop up at unexpected moments. We will get to those in a minute. Nor am I talking about additional things to pray about because they did not quite come to mind in the set-aside time. Rather, I mean praying with the same determination, the same liquidity and flow, the same readiness, intensity and faith that we employ in the set-aside times. I mean praying in the now-and-then-ness of God's leading, in a holy randomness, unforeseen yet appropriate, unpredictable yet perfectly timed. I mean repetitions of perhaps just a few moments ago, yet as if no prayer had yet been uttered. This kind of praying is really a unity of habit and spontaneity in which, in broadest terms, the burning desire of God to heal the nations likewise burns continually within us. It persists on our lips and in our minds, and we cannot help but break into prayer—to be instant in reminding God, if you will—about his own sworn desires and his own irrefutable plans. By reason of this, our most effective praying must be Scripture-bound.

I like to think of praying as a way of speech with the Lord based on the way he has spoken to us in his Word. When we pray after the manner of his speaking, we cannot but pray aright. We will find ourselves quoting God's Word back directly to him and sometimes even debating with him on the basis of his Word. After all, do we not have the mind of Christ? This kind of praying is not thinking something up that God has not yet thought of, or trying to talk him into something that goes against his own sworn purposes, for with God, there is no new burden, no new plan to undertake. So pray we must and pray we do in that ceaseless round of bringing the particularities of our lives and others' into the rhythm of God's rule.

When we hear of someone who speaks of having wrestled with God in prayer, we should not think of this as a clash of opposing wills or even of God's having to be reminded of something he forgot. Nor should we liken it to Jacob's bout with a Man from which Israel emerged limping. Instead wrestling signifies an identity with and entrance into the might of God as he does his work by the Word of his power and as he himself engages in warfare with the evil one. We, by faith, take up the cross to which we are assigned. We join the fray and pray accordingly.

I believe we need more of this kind of praying, this wrestling intercession. I often find myself praying on the frothy surface of need without entering into the warfare to which I have been assigned by following hard after the Savior. Yes, the battle is the Lord's and I should not pretend to fight it as if I were both the commanding general and the foot soldier. But if I have joined myself to him completely, it seems obvious that part of my sojourn is to follow the Lord, even if it means taking up those things that only the armor of God can protect against.

We are told that we do not wrestle against something as nameable and simple as physical powers, but against spiritual powers of the darkest kind, in the highest, lowest and most surprising places. Being instant in prayer is to be so at the ready, so in shape, so spiritually mobile that at the drop of a hat we pick up in prayer, as if in the middle of an eternal sentence. We must be people for whom praying is as natural and ongoing as breath itself is.

At the same time, this wrestling is not just about wars and strife, for there are too many things about the Lord and his work that bring on pleasure and rest. In prayer we are reminded of the grace, the mercy, the generosity of the Lord. In prayer we are released from thinking of things too high and lofty for us. In prayer we are calmed as a weaned child is calmed at her mother's breast. In prayer we understand that the Lord loves us and that grace is infinite. In prayer we understand that we are made in the image of God, united with him at the most intimate levels. To litany forth hilariously in prayer over these lofty pleasures is also to join the now-and-then-ness of God's leading us unto ceaseless prayer. And it just might be that this hilarious wrestling, this sojourn into the joy of the Lord, is nothing other than the dance of faith turned prayerward.

But what about crisis praying? To be sure, this is part of ceaseless prayer, but only in the sense that seemingly random, unexpected and urgent circumstances bring it on. Then in straitened condition we pray with a force and a passion that often surpass our usual praying. This is as it should be, but for one thing: How can one prayer be more urgent than another? What, then, is usual prayer?

Consider the usual grace before a meal. It might go something like this:

"Dear Lord, we thank you for the gift of food set before us. Please use it to strengthen our bodies, and help us to use this strength in such a way as to advance the affairs of the kingdom in whatever way you please." Study these words and the enormity of the request. This is really an urgent prayer, of the first order, or at least it should be. In these few kingdom words, we are asking God to put us into the fray and, with him working in us, to lead contrarily minded and darkened souls to find Christ. We are also asking to act boldly if, within the body of Christ, we see the creep of error and coldness. Yet this prayer can drop all too easily from our lips. But let a crisis come—the death of a baby or the discovery of a malignancy—and we shift into our urgent prayer mode. Our spirits go from calm to ardent, and we forget that perhaps a few minutes ago we blithely coupled our thanks for a good steak with a prayer for a spiritual awakening. Our spiritual breathing quickens, our minds jump back and forth between fear and doubt, between miracle and no miracle, between yes and no.

Please understand. I am not suggesting that we treat crises offhandedly, nor am I suggesting that a prayer before a meal becomes so overtly impassioned that we can no longer eat. I am suggesting instead that our so-called usual praying may include things that could spell the difference between heaven and hell and that the content of our so-called urgent praying may be no more significant. There is such a thing as being out of shape when it comes to prayer, and it is not because we do not pray or do not pray enough. It is because we consign more of our praying to nonurgency than to the opposite. We get spiritually out of breath too easily because we have not conditioned ourselves to a prayer life of ceaseless urgency. To borrow an analogy from physical conditioning, we pray anaerobically instead of aerobically. Anaerobic exercises contain work, but not steady work. Aerobic exercises contain work as well, but every second of it is steady, therefore "urgent," work. And it is this latter kind of work that keeps us from becoming too quickly winded in times of stress.

CEASELESS PRAYING AS CONTINUOUS OUTPOURING

The second kind of ceaseless praying is foundational to all other kinds. This kind of praying is truly "without ceasing" in that while it has only one beginning, there can be no stopping it for as long as we live. To understand this kind of praying is also to understand unceasing worship, for the one is a manifestation of the other. Lives of continued worship cannot but be lives of continued prayer, since continuing worship is itself a continued and continuously varied conversation with the One who lives within us. It should be an unbroken continuum, a breathing in and out, a full articulation of all that we are in Christ throughout all our days. Living in Spirit and truth, walking the course of my days in the beauty of holiness, undertaking every action as a living sacrifice is, in its way, conversation with the Almighty. So this question comes to me: As I think of the mix of things that comprise my day, can I truthfully and unashamedly say that any one of them is in itself a prayer, another way of saying, "My Lord and my God"?

All told, our life is gathered speech, a private and public text that can be known and read by anybody. It is driven by the grammars of faith and hope, graced by the poetries of lovingkindness and offered up to the Lord as incense. How winsome to think of the times and seasons of life as a Pentecost of unceasing prayer. How winsome this is, and how sobering, for we must remember that everything we do must in some way go up as conversation with the Lord, particle after particle in a stream of unbroken prayer. Sin alone disrupts this prayer because sin is counterworship, counterspeech, counterprayer. Repentance heals this ill, and once we return to the Light, the blood of Christ keeps on cleansing our ceaseless praying, delivering us from the sin of darkened worship and darkened prayer.

As I meditate on my prayer life, ever aware that my praying may be no more than a smoking flax, I must bear certain principles in mind.

Prayer is above all about who God is and what he wants. By praying in his name, we pray *for* his sake—not on his behalf, neither to rescue him nor to inform him. Rather, by being found in him in Christ, we pray *in* him, walking the paths of his completed work that we do not yet see completed. The more intense we are about faith and hope in his completed work, the more we are taken into its sweep, even though we pray on the unseen side of all his answers. Thus we pray by faith, which is the substance and the evidence of our praying. Informed fully by his Word, living by faith, rooted in love and buoyed by hope, our praying and outpouring are as indivisible as Spirit and truth. We begin with praise and continue all of our praying in thanksgiving, within which we raise our petitions and intercessions, whether of joy, longing or grief.

Within the context of praise and adoration, the praying of the body of Christ should be dominated by intercessory prayer for the spread of the gospel and the salvation of souls. There is no other reason for Jesus to have come to earth than for our salvation. There is no theme that runs more consistently through Scripture than redemption. Sin and righteousness dominate every aspect of God's revelation to us. Every one of his attributes is biased toward the astonishing reality of the Lamb slain from the eternities and the final victory this Lamb will celebrate with his ransomed bride, the church. There is no calling more important to a Christian than to be an ambassador of Christ, as if God were making his appeal directly through him or her. This appeal is about reconciliation. And reconciliation is about two things only: salvation for the lost and growth in personal holiness for the redeemed. All else falls into place once these two realities are attended to, not the least of which are the social and ethical responsibilities that the body of Christ owes the world.

There is more than a dot of truth in the saying that we could learn as much about human anatomy by attending a typical prayer meeting as by studying physiology. When we think of the usual prayer agenda, most of it is spent on the circumstances of human illness, even though we see few instances of miraculous healing. It is not that God cannot heal, nor is it that we should not be interested in his doing so; it is just that there are far more crucial matters to attend to before we get to our physical or vocational circumstances. I say these things as a cancer survivor and the spouse of a cancer survivor. I say these things in the context of a personal history of emotional illness. I needed prayer in those times, and I need it still, for who knows how long my wife and I will live cancer-free? As to my emotional weaknesses, I can say that early on in their appearance, the Lord's voice was clear in a strategic respect: ask to be made more holy before you ever ask for healing.

I am convinced that if the church were bent over double in pleading for lost people near and far, we might quickly discover how little fuss we need to make over worship styles and church growth methodology. So much of our praying is about things God would take care of anyway, especially if he saw our praying turned in the direction of his urgent desire that all should come to repentance. Even if we changed the direction of the little praying that we do and spent it on lostness and redemption, I am sure God would look back over his shoulder, turn our way again and bring both an awakening and continued revival.

There are only two other themes that should dominate our praying as continuous worshipers: sanctification and service. The first is the unavoidable follow-through to praying for lost people, namely praying for continued growth in personal holiness, to the extent that no corner of our lives is to be left unattended to. Just as I pray for continued maturity, and just as the Lord is bound by his word to bring steady answer to this prayer, so my passion for those who do not yet know Jesus increases. There is no way that these two issues can be separated, for the more we understand the sweetness of growing up into the stature and fullness of Christ, the more we long for others to come into the same condition. Thus awakening and revival, salvation and continued reformation, initial repentance and continuing forgiveness are seamless continuities. Then within this grand union we pray that our service to the world, the daily foot washings to which we are called, will not vaporize or be lost in the rush of trying to keep up in our praying for the lost. While it is God's business to redeem, it is our business to witness, and no witness is complete if saving souls is disconnected from the ambassadorial work of attending to the needs of the poor, the homeless, the orphan, the widow, the disenfranchised, the alcoholic, the AIDS victim.

This question should burn into every pastor's mind: What is the prayer life of your congregation like? What is its overriding theme? How anguished and how victorious is the praying? Continuous outpouring cannot be whole without continuous praying, and continuous praying cannot be whole without being grounded in the mind of Christ, for whom the salvation of the world is foremost.

Strong and wide-ranging praying is a powerful witness to the unbeliever. We do not know how much of the prophesying in 2 Corinthians 14:25 was given over to prayer. Nor, for that matter, can we separate Spirit-driven prophecy from Spirit-filled praying. In any case the unbeliever will not be unchanged by this. At the interpersonal and social level I believe in the witnessing power of prayer when, for instance, my wife and I invite unbelievers to our home for a meal. In fact, one of the reasons we do this is so that they can hear us pray, giving thanks for food in the larger context of mercy, grace and well-being in Christ. It is not that such praying needs to turn into a minisermon or a recitation of the plan of salvation. Rather, speaking to the Lord with a full heart and a fertile mind cannot be without its impact.

It is important to attend to the quality, the construction and the vocabulary of our praying. Worship leaders and preachers do a lot of public praying. This area of public worship can often be careless, cliché-ridden and theologically thin. It can turn into a daisy chain without much thought to overall flow, biblical precision and word beauty. Were the Scriptures themselves muddled this way, we might have a case. Public praying should not only be scriptural as to content but also scriptural as to loveliness of style, richness of expression and fullness of truth.

The crafting of eloquent and clear prayer is just as important for individuals in their private prayer life as it is in public worship. If praying is to be scriptural, then the Scriptures themselves become both content and template in every respect, from the doctrinal to the aesthetic to the comprehensive. If believers want to frame the whole of their outpouring in the best possible way, then it is no light thing to craft prayers that take in the whole of their spiritual and theological vocabularies. Each of us should take the time to study praying and to work hard at praying, to practice praying as an exercise that taxes our intellect as well as our biblical knowledge.

Above all, the prayers of Scripture should be studied and assimilated as our prayers, and we should learn to craft parallel prayers, using these as templates and using our best thought and best language. The prayers of the great liturgies should be studied, particularly the collect form in the Anglican and Episcopalian traditions. These are paragons of beauty, brevity and architectural wholeness, usually one sentence in length. It is a worthy exercise to learn to improvise single prayers or chains of them within their constraints. The form is simple and contains: (1) an opening address to God, whose person and work is described with a specific topic or liturgical theme in mind; (2) a request or requests, aligned with the topic or theme; (3) the expected result and its contribution to the kingdom; (4) an ending phrase in which, not infrequently, an echo of the main theme appears, followed by words such as "through Jesus Christ our Lord, who lives and reigns with you, in the unity of the Holy Spirit, one God, now and forever. *Amen.*" For example, from the liturgy of Good Friday, we have this collect (the parenthesized numbers refer to the above scheme):

> (1) Gracious God, the comfort of all who sorrow, the strength of all who suffer: (2) Let the cry of those in misery and need come to you, (3) that they may find your mercy present with them in all their affliction; and give us, we pray, the strength to serve them (4) for the sake of him who suffered for us, your Son Jesus Christ our Lord. *Amen.*[1]

The value of praying this way does not lie just in brevity and economy but also in thematic discipline and scriptural harmony. We find ourselves bound closely to an urgent request and we find the scriptural and theological means to follow this through to its finality in Christ. Furthermore, the scheme of the collect is so innocent and style-free that it can be used in virtually any context. The secret is precision, clarity and beauty.

If I could recommend but one book of prayers, it would be *The Private Devotions of Lancelot Andrewes.*[2] This volume is an exhaustive collection of all kinds of prayers, all written by Andrewes and used by him. The prayers are intricate, passionate and schematically ingenious. There is no subject or condition left uncovered. The editor has provided exhaustive marginal and exegetical references that key an overwhelming amount of the written material back to Scripture, the Apocrypha and a miscellany of documents and authors.

PREACHING

As a church musician, I have worked with preachers and army chaplains of virtually every kind and practitional stripe, well-known and unknown: expositors, topicalists, current event/Charlie Brown freaks, sacramentalists, Reformed, Wesleyan, Holiness, Covenant and still others more theologically eclectic. Some were not following Christ as they should. Yet the overwhelming majority were deeply in love with Jesus and faithful to his gospel.

I am also a preacher's son. I remember many times when my father, as the administrator-preacher-pastor (no staff, no secretary, no administrative budget) worked diligently through his weekly round. I watched him and a few laypersons construct a camp meeting-type tabernacle out of new and used materials in Sharon, Pennsylvania. He worked forty hours a week as a cabinetmaker in Baltimore, Maryland, while holding down a full-time call to a church so that my mother, sister and I could be fed and clothed. I saw him dog tired on weeknights in Santa Ana, California, because during the day he helped dig through foundation material, move timbers and work building jacks in moving the sanctuary from one part of town to another. I saw him, and was old enough by then to work alongside him, in Big Bear Lake, California, as he and his congregation hammered and nailed an entire sanctuary complex into being on potluck Tuesday and Thursday nights. All the while, God helping and he surrendering, he led Bible study every Wednesday night and preached two different sermons every Sunday.

I am amazed at the durability of these and countless other warriors, week after week, in ardent preparation. In the case of those truly called, truly meek and in deep communion with Jesus, I can only thank God for them and pray that their work will be constantly bathed in the power of God and protected from false light and strange fire. If I am occasionally critical, it is only because a host of excelling preachers, my father at the top of the list, have lit the way for me and set a lustrous example. Though I have occasionally preached and find myself nearly ecstatic when doing so, I know little about its full rigors. I write these few thoughts anyway, knowing that writing itself might stretch me a bit more.

Even though it is the personal responsibility of all Christians to grow up into the stature and fullness of Christ, as if there were no preachers, it remains the responsibility of the pastoral staff to preach as though there were no other way to get the full truth of the gospel across. Hence, there should be a parallel responsibility between the laity and the pastoral team: the laity is directly and personally responsible and accountable for its spiritual growth, and the pastoral team is responsible for corroborating and challenging that growth.

But even in the course of a flawed sermon, there is still the Word of God and the work of the Spirit to contend with. The Holy Spirit will see to it that the truly hungry are fed, not because of the sermon but because of the Word and because it is God's will that those who hunger and thirst after righteousness will be filled. Every preaching pastor should take comfort in this, especially in a culture in which learning about God is taken to be another form of entertainment. I am old enough to have seen churches grow or shrink on the basis of who the preacher is instead of who Jesus is. And having spent over four decades of my life in the practice of church music, observing reactions to preaching and music, I know that all too often believers choose their churches on how well everything is *managed*—there is no other word for it.

The burden that the inhabitants of contemporary culture have placed on the pastoral ministry to hold them, to feed them, to pleasure them is a near disgrace. It is an insult to the Savior, yet certainly no surprise to him, for in his brief ministry he too was under pressure to adjust his teachings to the desires of the crowds and to add pleasurable confirmation to their preconceptions. He decided against doing so, and despite much talk about how Jesus spoke in the language of the people, his way of doing this not only decreased his audiences but often mystified them.

The idea of speaking in the language of the people can become a distraction, if not an illusion. It will mean little unless it is linked to richness of content and authority of presentation. It was content, not style or language, that made the difference in Jesus' work. It was authority, that clarifying and unequivocal presentational weight, that made his teachings as incisive and provoking as they were. Christ was willing to face shrinkage, in fact, rather than to smooth out the content or forsake the authority that truth granted him. I believe he understood the fundamental difference between authority and stylistic power and, further, the difference between stylistic power and Spirit power. I am further convinced that in his kenosis, his emptying, he knew that true power was not his to impose or conjure up while he preached. He remained willing to leave the power question to his Father, whose work through the Holy Spirit brought people to decision. In this light it should become apparent to all who preach and teach that the real struggle is out of their hands. The battle is the Lord's, the power is his alone and the Spirit will be free as the wind to work his work.

All of us must remember that preachers are ordinary people. They may be called of God to preach, and this in itself is solemn and honorable, but they may not have the spiritual maturity of many people in the congregation. A preacher may be backslidden or grief stricken or physically broken or on a mountain of triumph. He or she may be fresh out of seminary or an old hand. The preacher may be brilliant or pedestrian. The preacher may even be out of God's will by being a preacher. Nobody knows these things for sure, and nobody should guess at them or allow them to stand in the way of the Word of God and the delivery of a message. All continuous outpourers—preachers and laity alike—are sinners who need the same Savior in exactly the same way. They are blood washed or they are not; they are hungry or they are not; and they worship God or they worship Satan or one of his stand-ins. In all cases something beyond mere preaching and mere listening is at stake, namely Christ-centered growth into increasing holiness for some, repentance for turning aside for others and salvation for still others. These three conditions are the only ones worth addressing. Taken together, they ultimately account for everything that the Word of God has to say about the way each one of us is to live.

Likewise, preaching is enabled by the same power that enables all believers in all walks of life who are pursuing the glory of continuous worship. God is not a divided God in the sense that he apportions himself differently to different people on the basis of their title. Being called to preach does not make a person eligible for a bigger piece of God than being called into nursing. God pours himself out on anyone for whom the articulation of truth is crucial and all-significant. The preacher is honored in preaching by this fact alone. The power that may be manifest in authoritative preaching is there because God is interested in validating his truth, in making sure that it is being preached accurately and intrusively. Even in those times when the preacher is literally swept up in the Spirit, it is not he that is powerful; it is the Spirit working his way through the gospel. The power, in fact, should hide the preacher; the greater the power, the less the preacher.

As to the relation of preaching to the rest of the liturgy, it is to be seen as an offering of worship among the many offerings of the corporate gathering. Preaching is not the high point of worship to which all prior actions are meant to point or for which they prepare. It is not a chosen oracle or an automatic apex that towers in importance over the Word, the sacrament or the simple singing of a hymn, because, in fact, truth is at stake in all of these actions. For that matter, there are no preset high points in worship, because authentic worship is not a series of points, high or low. It is an ongoing and organic call to pour out toward God through Christ. Only the Holy Spirit may choose any moment in the midst of any liturgical action to move an entire assembly or just one person to brokenness or celebration. Even then, "high point" is a rather empty expression because of our temptation to measure height in terms of highs instead of constants. Or we are more prone to think of emotional reactions instead of infusions of prophetic wisdom. Even so, preaching cannot be confined to an action within a specific time and place, but through the continuing work of the Spirit applying it over and over to the hearts and minds of the hearers, it reaches beyond time and place, persists as a part of continuous outpouring and finally comes to rest in the very Word that prompted it in the first place.

Furthermore, the preacher—not the worship team—should be the chief teacher about worship as continuous outpouring. If preaching is but one kind of continuous outpouring, and if continuous outpouring is to mark the life of every believer, then all preaching should be tuned in one way or another to this central idea. As important as it is to make authentic worship the subject of a single sermon or sermon series, it is even more important to ensure that unceasing worship becomes the guiding assumption within the gathered body.

Finally, in all preaching to all kinds of people, there is a difference between depth and complexity. Here is where the secular impulse for the quick fix and the academic impulse for density clash, making life hard for the preacher. It seems to me that the best preaching seeks out the kind of depth that holds the attention and challenges the average thinker yet leaves the sophisticated thinker with more than enough to ponder. I call this kind of preaching wisdom preaching. It subsists on, and parallels, the way the prophets spoke, the way Jesus preached and the ways of Peter and Paul and John and Stephen. It is furthered by the likes of Morgan, Bonhoeffer, the Wesleys, Luther, Thielicke, Spurgeon.

To conclude this brief section, I want to express my love for ministers of the gospel and to assure them that I—and all believers—intercede for them daily, not just that they will please us but that they will be richly imaginative and speak the truth fearlessly, lovingly, comprehensively and without regard for the praise or pleasure of humankind.

Dear preaching pastors, keep it up, stay close to the Savior, lean on the everlasting arms, quiet yourselves on the Lord's breast, feed yourselves on the Bread of Life, carry the gospel to the least likely hearts and the most fervent servants. You are unceasing worshipers even as you show us what unceasing worship is.

PART TWO

UNCEASING WORSHIP
AND THE ARTS

7

CONTINUOUS OUTPOURING
AND ARTISTIC ACTION

So far we have seen this: Authentic worship is a continuous outpouring of all that we are and can ever hope to become in light of the saving work of Christ. It reaches into every quarter of our living, informing all of our actions and safeguarding them within the arena of Spirit, truth and sacrificial living. Without this understanding, all of our work, however magnificent it might be in its own right, is misdirected.

Now I want to examine the arts as they relate to continuous outpouring. But I want to begin with the subject of artistic action before discussing the arts themselves. I have two reasons for doing this.

First, the arts cannot stand by themselves, at least not for the Christian. They are but one part of the creative ecology of our living. They do not arise on their own nor subsist on their own. Art for art's sake is a pagan idea. There is, to be sure, a peculiar individuality to the arts, as well as a Christian perspective on them, and I will be going over certain aspects of these in the next few chapters. But a Christian perspective on the arts must first of all be a *Christian* perspective that applies equally to every aspect of life long before we examine any separate aspect. It is almost always a mistake to begin with a specific subject or area of study and proceed to develop a foundational worldview with that subject primarily in mind. The danger is apparent: we may tune the worldview to the subject instead of surrendering the subject to the worldview. And if everyone does this in their respective areas of work, we can easily end up with competing worldviews, which in turn gives critics one more opportunity for saying there is no unifying force in truth.

Second, it has already been established that continuous outpouring is a falsity without continuous action. We cannot be continuous outpourers without being living sacrifices. Living sacrifices are not spiritual abstractions but living doers. Thus the full significance of an action is lost if we forget that continuous outpouring is the grounding concept for it. We act *because* we worship, not the reverse. To believe the latter is to realign with bald-faced legalism, and *legalism* is just a nicer word for idolatry. If outpouring is continuous, and if the first task for Christians is to fill their living with a continuum of offerings, then it follows that the making of art is likewise a Godward action. Christian artists, therefore, must understand from the start that their art, whatever its kind, venue or quality, is as much an act of worship as is preaching the gospel. Knowing this first of all, before they pick up brush or chisel, is of supreme importance. The more Christian artists understand that artistic action is nothing other and nothing less than pouring perfume on Jesus' feet, the more they will be refreshed and liberated in their imagining and crafting.

Here are some additional concepts that may be helpful.

AUTHENTIC WORSHIP AND CREATIVE FREEDOM

Continuous outpouring liberates Christians to discover real freedom in artistic action. I chose the word "liberates" carefully. Some people think that Christians are severely restricted because, after all, they are confronted with a whole dictionary of don'ts and perhaps-nots. Yes, but not in the way the unbeliever or fearing Christian thinks. The dictionary of dos for authentic worshipers is virtually limitless. Once they choose the narrow way, they find that its dimensions are of a different order. This road is limited to continuous outpouring, but continuous outpouring is as wide as the freedom of the Lord, as deep as we can take things and as open as the keys to the kingdom can make it. The truth-liberated imagination is the imagination that is linked to that of God himself when, in one blaze of glory after another, he made the variegated wonder called the creation.

Christian artists have true artistic freedom, not on the basis of something as simplistic as right, wrong and so-called artistic license, but on the basis of intent and direction. Here's what I mean. Christian artists first of all understand that making art is indistinguishable from worshiping Jesus. In this sense their art joins up and is made common with everything else in their daily round for which they are responsible as continuous outpourers. Their art may be their specialty, and its quality may be—should be—of the highest, but it has no greater standing before God than an honestly prepared income tax return.

Furthermore, artistic intent and direction are fully known only to God through Christ, while content is known both to God and to people. This does not mean that Christian artists must limit themselves to so-called Christian content, especially the all-too-prevalent kind that is little more than spiritualized gingerbread. It means that every aspect of life is open to aesthetic inquiry, both as to the sinfulness of sin and the grandeur of holy living. Thus, to the Christian artist, there are no off-limits subjects even though there are off-limits intentions and directions. But since the primary responsibility of Christian artists is to direct their art Godward (we can call this final authorship before God), and since these artists should have no primary intention but to offer their art as an act of worship, they will see to it that their approach to content is guided by those two solitary facts for which they are eternally responsible. Thus, no person has a right to lay an accusing hand, even if it means that the artists, along with Christ, may be accused of consorting with sinners, gluttons and winebibbers.

ARTISTIC FREEDOM AND WISDOM

Artistic freedom, however, is not artistic license. There is a twofold danger in what I have said in the preceding paragraph. First, unwise or giddy Christian artists will be tempted to take up the badge of artistic freedom in itself (a much flawed and idolatrous badge) instead of being thrust forward in the freedom that is in Christ alone. Also the public, especially the theologically pinched-up kind, will confuse artistic content and the artist's intent and arbitrarily accept or reject both art and artist on that ground. Ultimately the artist must stand before Christ and answer for every artistic action taken.

Even so, Christian artists are the freest of the free and, as said above, freedom in Christ is the narrowest kind of wideness and the widest kind of narrowness. Just as it is in the best interest of every Christian artist to place freedom in Christ above artistic freedom, so it is also in the best interest of the Christian public to trust the person of Christ who indwells the person of the Christian artist as he or she attempts to be true to artistic action, even when this takes them into forbiddingly dark or startlingly light territory. Far too often, both kinds of art—the truly dark and truly light— seem to unsettle the kind of Christian who looks for the safe, the hazy gray, the modestly risqué and the superficially familiar in all walks of art. Evangelicals in particular have done a poor service to the arts in their failure to understand the enormous responsibility that the Christian artist has in addressing all quarters of the human condition.

Second, there are some Christian artists whose view of being free is such that their approach to the human condition is no different from anyone else's. This view, ironically enough, also confuses content and intent, but from the opposite direction. It goes this way: "Since I've been told that my art glorifies God, and since I can call my art my worship, these two facts by themselves exonerate me. So let my art speak for itself. Since there is only good and bad art rather than Christian or non-Christian art, it is my responsibility to make good art. Artistic value is what finally counts, because God is a God of excellence."

I can understand why some Christians have taken this approach. On the one hand, they have been frustrated by the lack of quality in much so-called Christian art, and they want desperately to remedy this. So *quality* becomes the watchword and raising standards becomes more important than intent and direction. On the other hand, they have been equally frustrated by the blunted and shortsighted concept of content held by so many Christians. For the latter, only acceptable behavior comprises acceptable content, and if unacceptable behavior is portrayed, it is watered down to a level of acceptability that completely masks the realities being addressed. This includes spiritualized fairy-tale solutions, caricatures instead of portrayals, truncated versions of lostness and perfectionist views of redemption. For example, in the area of the visual arts, nudity is equated with pornography, and abstraction or radical stylization is equated with a fractured worldview. In dance, the body is defensively robed, redeemed sensuality is repressed, movements and gestures are severely limited. In music, consonance is equated with a healthy spirituality and dissonance with a fallen and corrupted culture.

Consequently many Christian artists react to these shrunken opinions with angered and corrective intent. Instead of continuing to make art for the simple reason that they must be true to the principle of final authorship before God, they decide that rock-'em-and-shock-'em content is the only way to shake their critics out of their lethargy. Then they overdo. But once again, content and intent are confused. Artistic intention turns toward anger and away from offering, and content becomes more of a weapon than a medium for the articulation of artistic wisdom. To compound the error, the secularly trendy idea of the artist as prophet instead of servant takes center stage, and both sides end up in isolation: the artist hides behind the prophecy mantra and the public retreats back into the ministry mantra. The public goes back to the safety of art-as-usual in the context of Christianity-as-usual, and the artist retreats to a world in which a secular welcome is far more acceptable than an ecclesiastical brush-off. The body of art done Christianly remains severely impoverished, the world finds yet another reason to ridicule Christianity, and the artist remains in the dark as to who he or she really is.

But here's where wisdom lies: for the Christian artist, his and her work is action toward God, before God and under God's protection. This splendid triple fact alone should be the guarantor of quality, excellence, ruthless inquiry, honest response and redemptive resolution, even if it means that the artist is rejected and the so-called Christian public seeks a lesser good and a foreshortened aesthetic. However, for the Christian, being an artist is not being heroic; it is not being nerdy or even being the *artiste*. It is being in Christ, in whom all faithful artistic actions cohere, before whom all artistic knees bow and with whom genuine aloneness is no new thing. As for those Christian artists who say that their action is Godward but in reality have decided that it is action toward the public, toward the market researchers, toward the agents, toward immediacy, toward the ministry-equals-excellence handwringers and before the sales charts—they have their fifteen minutes, more or less, down here and their eternity sometime hence, but they will answer, because all actions and all intentions will be passed through the fire. Then God alone, before whom intent and direction come to final answer, will be the one who decides between a reward and a purging.

BEING IN THE SPIRIT IS NOT SPIRITUALIZING

Making art Godward does not mean falsely spiritualizing it or even making it sacramental. It does not mean that art takes on a different light or is artistically better than an art piece made by a pagan. In fact, Christians have made some pretty bad art even though they have honestly made it by faith and have offered it Godward. High intent in no way guarantees better content. And only God can work through the seeming contradiction by seeing all faithfully offered work as perfect in Christ. However, saying it this way does not encourage or justify shoddiness. We reside on the temporal side of the artistic action and are fully responsible for the content and intent. Thus it does no good to say that because God sees bad art through Christ we are absolved of responsibility for quality.

Look at it this way: if I have a toothache and I go to my favorite Christian dentist, I will expect high-quality work. I will not tolerate any statement like this: "My work is ministry above all. God looks at my heart, not the tooth. Quality? I just want to minister. We do accept Visa and MasterCard. God bless." Or look at it this way: I am a publisher and someone comes to me and says, "The Lord gave me this song," as if to imply that this puts the song above criticism and guarantees its publication. I must recognize two things at once. First, the Lord gave that same person breath, but that does not save him or her from halitosis. Just as I must get my teeth cleaned and fixed, so I must clean up and fix what would might otherwise be a flawed song, God-breathed or no. Second, that same person who claims divine authorship might want to ask questions as to whether the song should be copyrighted, since it is not really his. And he might want to think carefully about who receives the royalty payments.[1]

ARTISTIC ACTION AS DIGNIFIED WORK

Artistic work is hard work and demands all-out concentration. Just because Christian artists make their art Godward, they cannot afford to assume that while their work is going on, they are to be obsessed with God thoughts or to be spiritualizing every gesture, color and texture. This would be artistically disastrous as well as theologically mistaken. Final authorship before God does not mean that God and ministry thoughts should preempt compositional, technical and aesthetic thoughts. This goes back to one of the verities of continuous outpouring, namely that from the first moment of our turning to Christ, *all* of life in all its parts, from the so-called secular to the so-called sacred, is given over to him and put to work *in* him even as he works in us. All our outpouring, and therefore all our action, is *in* him, *unto* him and *for* him. This is the only possible fact that allows us the freedom of concentrating completely on the content and process of our work without having to obsess about God while undertaking it. We can be thankful that a surgeon can make a spiritual offering of a coronary bypass without having to think about God while doing the cutting, discarding, adding, splicing and stapling. Only God can mastermind and synthesize this remarkable union of temporal work and spiritual offering, and it is his responsibility alone to unite the work—its processes, techniques, content, vocational and spiritual meanings—with his sworn purposes of leading us into deeper holiness and allowing our works to comprise a life of witness. How else did Jesus do his carpentering, and how else are we to make our art?

When we try to propagate our homemade versions of God working in us, we are too often prone to saying, "Well, it wasn't really me doing the suture; God was holding the needle for me," or "It was God singing through me." But in saying things like this, we virtually deface—no, we pervert—any biblical concept of our humanity, namely that God created us to do things fully, exhausting our capabilities as good stewards. Christ in us does not mean that he replaces us as if we no longer existed or as if he were the better half of a two-part construct. Furthermore, the more we persist in comments like this, the more we make the mistake of involving God in only the most important things we do. We never say, for instance, that God is brushing my teeth or flushing the toilet through me. We never say that while we were getting voice lessons or going to med school, God's voice was getting trained or he was the one memorizing the periodic charts. Furthermore, if I say that he is sewing up incisions or singing songs through me, I am cozying up to a combination of pantheism (God is my sewing arm; God is my voice) and puppetry (when God pulls the strings, I sew or I sing).

But this is what we can say on the biblical side of the argument: In the doing of everything, Christ in us will surely strengthen us and dignify what we do by blessing our work and bringing his power down as we work. Philippians 4:13 bears this truth out well, making it clear that our work is through Christ in the same sense that his work can be done through us. Our task is to keep this order of events straight in our minds. In so doing we will not confuse our work with Christ's work. Likewise, the overarching doctrine of Christ in us must be kept free of the thought that Christ replaces us, and herein lies one of those mysteries that we can only mention and acknowledge without being able to explain. We must rest in its purity and simplicity without splitting it up into our spiritualized or nearly pantheistic nostrums. The truth remains: while we act by faith, using every fiber of our being, he acts, not as a substitute or a proxy, but by completing (not revising or fixing up) the work *in* himself. He does not become or replace the work, but he acts above and along with it, wanting us to understand that his power bears no relationship to what we have done, that his power is his alone to manifest even in an artistic vacuum—nothing there but the Lord himself. He may use the work, but only if he wishes, to accomplish the same things that he could accomplish without it.

This fact alone constitutes the real truth behind every one of our actions. You see, if we are continuous outpourers, then no single action can be separated out as if it had enough significance for us to say, "God is using this right now." To the contrary, he might be working on the basis of a prayer somebody on the other side of the world uttered days or decades ago, a prayer of which we knew nothing but which he chooses to put to use at a totally different time. We cannot afford to say that because we did such and such, he acts. Rather, he acts as he wishes even as we do such and such, not on the basis of the action, but because he is the sovereign Lord over a plan in which, by grace alone, we participate and to which our actions contribute as offerings, not levers or on-off buttons.

CORPORATE WORSHIP AND ARTISTIC ACTION

We make and offer art *because* we worship; we should not make it to *lead us into* worship. We can carry the above concepts into the weekly corporate gathering. Since Christians come to such gatherings as continuous worshipers, it should now be obvious that it is erroneous to assume that the arts, and especially music, are to be depended on to lead to worship or that they are aids *to* worship or tools *for* worship. If we think this way, we fuel two untruths at once. The first is that worship is something that can start and stop, and worse, that music or some other artistic or human device bears the responsibility for doing the starting or the facilitating. The second is related to the first: music and the arts have a kind of power in themselves that can be falsely related to or equated with Spirit power, so much so that the presence of God seems all the more guaranteed and the worshiper sees this union of artistic power and Spirit power as normal, even anticipated. This thinking lies behind comments of this kind: "The Lord seemed so near during worship time." "Your music really helped me worship." And to the contrary: "I could not worship because of the music." These comments, however innocently spoken, are dangerous, even pagan. Senior pastors, ministers of worship and worship teams must do everything to correct them. If we are not careful, music will be added to the list of sacraments and perhaps with some Christians become another kind of transubstantiation, turned *into* the Lord's presence. Then the music, not the Holy Spirit, becomes the paraclete and advocate. God is reduced to god and music is raised to Music. Thrones are exchanged, lordship reverts to its fallen hierarchy, and conditioned reflex replaces faith.

At the same time, I want to be among the first to celebrate the power that resides in the arts. They do contain enormous power of their own kind, not just expressively emotional power, but intellectual and architectural power. When I speak of art's power this way, I go beyond the currently pervasive obsession that expressiveness is limited to having an emotional experience, brought on quickly and kept on high burn for as long as possible. But if we were to understand experience as a vast synthesis of all that heart and mind are together capable of—what I like to call the thinking heart and the expressive mind—we would be approaching the subject of artistic power and artistic action far more comprehensively.[2]

But such is not the case in our massified culture and in the ways many Christians have narrowed experience down to "how it feels to worship."

There is a further aspect to the feeling-power issue, and we need to understand this fact in the context of the contemporary scene. We live in a culture in which power of all kinds—media power, political power, economic power, corporate power, celebrity power, personal power, but especially spiritual power, coming from all directions, mixing dark with light—is as common as smog and as sought after as fast food. We are not only a culture that overlooks the difference between a complete experience and mere experientialism; we are also prone to ignore the difference between temporal power and the power of the Lord. This is a culture in which strange fire blends in with Pentecostal fire, a culture in which behavioral mechanisms are disguised as prophetic actions. It is a culture that subsists on leveraging and manipulation, and it makes rampant use of technique and exaggeration to convince and convert, from selling tacos to voting for the next president to (unfortunately) aiding worship.

And music, especially that of mass culture, is right at the center. It might not be too much to say that we are a musically addicted culture, just as prone to shoot up on this substance as we are on others. No wonder the church is tempted to come alongside and impute its own definition of spiritual power to the things that addict, using them almost exactly the way they are used in the world. It seems that all that is needed is to change the words or the liturgical instructions, and the internal power mechanisms will then spool up and do the rest. Perhaps I speak too harshly. But I do so because I am convinced that real wrong is at work, having often found myself in the midst of it, not in borrowing art and music from the world (this is quite normal and often rewarding) but borrowing its worldview: *why* the world uses what it makes and *how* it depends on what it makes to accomplish a given task.

Content, direction and intent are completely different chemistries to the world: content is completely relative, direction is horizontal and intent is diverted away from Creator and turned toward creature. The creature's legitimate power is elevated to prominence over the ones who are meant to be sovereign over it. Action toward God is diluted, even turned aside, and worshipers can come to depend on humanly made things. For the authentic worshiper, action toward God is prior and all-consuming. For the world, being acted *upon* in order to act *toward* assumes preeminence. And this difference spells out several things at once: works precede faith, works produce righteousness, artifactual power overtakes Spirit power, creature is enthroned over Creator, and idolatry is hosted in its many epiphanies.

We have to remind ourselves continually that even though the arts have power, their power is of a lesser order. The arts are less than their makers and users, who are, in turn, instructed to be sovereign over them. Only fallenness, in its inverted and confused behaviors, holds to the opposite. Idolatry is, at base, the act of shaping something and then falling under the assumption that it can shape us. If we are not careful, then, music and the arts will be acting on us instead of us acting on and with them. However, coming to Christ and being found in him provide us with the right view of these lesser powers. The Christian, as a continuous outpourer, acts toward God, not on the basis of the power of the art, but by faith. We trust in the power of the Lord, before whose transcendent glory and holiness, the arts—even the greatest of them—are but a lisp and educated stammer. We worship in the power of the Lord while the power of the artifact finds its humble place among all lesser powers over which we have been granted sovereignty and from which we are completely free. Therefore, God forbid that we call these powers "ministry" and hide behind them while we watch them go to work.

In chapter two the difference between faith *bringing* substance and evidence and actually *being* substance and evidence was discussed. That singular difference applies here as well, for we must guard against the temptation to think that the power of art enlivens—brings substance to— our faith. As powerful and wonderful as the arts are, faith alone, not art, is substance and evidence, and it is by this kind of faith that we offer the arts to the Lord even as we continue our worship. This is what is meant by artistic action. Even when I am listening to an anthem or a solo, it is not enough for me to say that the choir or the soloist makes the offering while I listen in. I also have the responsibility of making an offering of my listening, just as much as the musicians make one out of their performing. I cannot escape the principle that all of my actions toward God are faith based and not content based.

Furthermore, making art by faith does not substantively change the art. Rather, it spells the difference as to whether God receives it or rejects it. We must go so far as to say that a work of art—beautiful in every respect—made by a faithless person will be cast away by God. The same work can be offered by a faithful person and God will receive it hands down. The art remains unchanged. Substance and evidence remains the province of faith alone.

ARTISTIC ACTION AND THE CELEBRATION OF POWER

We can now come to the final juncture. To repeat, we have the wonderful truth that art does have power, for we know it and we feel it, even if it is a lesser power. As a person who has been trained to perform, to compose and to celebrate the arts, I would be the last one to refute this glory, to imprison my emotions and to revert to a cold, hyperintellectualized approach to the arts. But if I did so, I would be denying the mind of God, who filled his universe with such wonder and delight that more often than not the only thing that will suffice is a shout or a dance or a doxology.

So what do we do with this power? Do we suppress it or act as if it is not there? Not at all. Rather, we celebrate the power both in its inherency and in its subordination to God and to us. We must keep the strength of our responses and feelings intact. We must be thankful that our faith—our continuous outpouring—is a thing of perpetual joy, of richness of sense, deep feeling and especially fullness of faithful response. The key lies in these last four words: "fullness of faithful response." It is in this fullness that the final secret lies: The power of the arts and our faithful response to them are together to be offered up to the Lord, who is infinitely beyond them, as a part of our continuous worship. *Instead of depending on the power of the arts to enhance their worship or bring it about, faithful worshipers can actually enhance the power of the arts by the faith-driven force of their worship.*

In other words, when I sing or listen to my favorite song and a flood of feeling washes over me, instead of thinking that Jesus is nearer because I am filled with such feeling, I come to understand that it is because the Lord and I love each other so much that I feel this way. This is right-side-up worship, and this is the way it must be. Then everything falls into place: the power of the song is there, but the power of the Lord is all the more fully there and more fully real. The glory of the Lord, not the song, takes preeminence. I continue in my continuous outpouring; I sing with all my might; I feel deeply; and if I am really connected to my faith, I engage my deepest thinking with my deepest feeling, for as Paul would say it here, when I pray or when I sing, my spirit and my mind are locked in union. This reality finally spells the difference between faith-full worship and worldly worship.

Artistic Action: Bringing the Walls Down

I can finish this chapter by asking a question based on a story from the Old Testament: What can we learn from Jericho? The story of the defeat of that contrary city cannot be fully understood without reference to the music that was made as the people marched around its walls. The story is so familiar that it need not be repeated here, except to say that music making was among the actions that God told Joshua and his people to undertake, even to the extent that the walls were not to fall down until they were finished (Josh 6:1-22).

There are two ways to interpret the musical part of this story, one biblical, the other pseudobiblical, and I fear that the latter often takes precedence over the former in our worship. The unbiblical interpretation goes this way: people blew their trumpets and brought the walls down. Simple, isn't it? It was the music that did it, by golly. It was music that caused the crash. Isn't this what many of us say, or at least hint at, about the role of music in worship? Bring the music on and great things will be done. Bring it on and people will worship. Bring it on and the church will grow. Bring it on and God will be brought on, for without it, God might be hobbled.

The biblical interpretation goes this way: as people blew their trumpets to God in obedience to him, *he* knocked the walls down. For it is God and God alone who does the work that he wants done as we take action with our art and act toward God in faith, love and hope. He can do whatever he pleases, and we can take no credit for what he has done. If he works mightily when the music is made, let's be sure that we do not create a presupposition out of this, for if we do, we are bound to expect music to repeat the glory, when it is God's business never to repeat any glory but to bring on new and greater glory, music or no music.

So let the music come. Let art break in on us. Let all of it break its boundaries and in Godward action speak powerful things. Let a thousand tongues say a million things. Let it all come in corrected and rightful newness. Let it all come, not to alert God to make his presence with us, but because he is already here from the eternities, before we can ever tune our instruments, pitch our songs or weave our tapestries. Let it all come deep from within our outpouring, impatiently pressing into the next time and then the next, as if we cannot wait to lift our art to the One who is Author and Finisher, Alpha and Omega, Sin-bearer, Redeemer and Lord.

Music cannot help or prevent worship. If it does, it becomes an idol.

8

WHAT CREATIVE PEOPLE
CAN LEARN FROM GOD'S CREATION

We can now discuss some of the workings of art, why we make art and how we should relate it both to the work of God in creation and to the varied work of everybody around us. But before going further, I want to insist that this chapter is for everybody, not just artists, because it deals with the relationship of the way God creates to how each of us should do our own daily work, whatever its kind. God is a singularly consistent Creator. He does not divide the creation into art pieces to be studied by artists and other pieces for scientists, mechanics and engineers. His creation is of one piece, and in its completeness it contains lessons—really, commandments—for everybody.

ART IN CONTEXT

If art holds a special place in the annals of human creativity, it is only because God has created certain people with special abilities to shape the stuff around them into works of such noticeable aesthetic significance that, if so desired, they can be called art and be set apart and enjoyed for what they are in themselves. But setting art apart as significant work should not mean separating it away from other work, since all work is significant. If there were no such separating words as *art* and *artist* and no intellectual reason, for example, to call a skyscraper a structure and a statue an artwork, it might just be that the artistic and structural qualities of everything made—from toothbrush holders to sonatas—would be accountable to similar criteria. Do not misread this sentence. I am not implying that a toothbrush holder is equal to a sonata. What I am saying is that both the toothbrush holder and the sonata should be imagined and made with the same eye (or ear) for aesthetic beauty and structural integrity. Then, if someone decides that the toothbrush holder is really an art piece and the sonata a mere acoustic fill-in at a wine tasting, this just means that by switching labels the status of something can be raised or lowered. But despite this all-too-frequent game, the status of the toothbrush holder would not have been elevated had it originally lacked a certain aesthetic quality and structural integrity. And it is the "certain aesthetic quality and structural integrity" issue about human work that interests me most. So even though an artwork may have special significance and a toothbrush holder lesser significance, the two should share similar responsibilities in their making.

As the above implies, I shall not attempt to define art, because we always have to cope with the distance between any of its definitions and how we apply them to this or that object. The same goes for definitions of beauty. The problem lies not only in agreeing to a definition but also in applying it to objects that have no equivalent in the words comprising the definition. Just as it is possible for me to say that someone (not an artist) or something (not an art piece) is artistic, so I can also say that a Porsche 911 or my wife or a lightning storm is beautiful, even though this does not mean they become art pieces.

So I would say this: art and artistry have broadly to do with the mingling of imagination, skill, style, intellect and aesthetic value whenever these are at work specifically (in the making of an art object) or generally (in anything imagined and made). I like this assumption much better because it obligates everybody everywhere to pursue quality and aesthetic grace in their work. There is no hiding from the call of beauty and richness for any of us. There is no theological escape hatch from the call to excellence, and there is no practice of excellence that can rest on its laurels, even for the best artists. For all of us, there is always the next step; there is always something out beyond that should be taken on, worked through and mastered.

Creative people, then, should never see the end of the road, because a healthy creativity is like everything else in a healthy life—it demands newness, change and growing excellence.

There is, however, one broad constraint as to how we use the words *art* and *artistic*. For example, when somebody says that throwing a cut fastball or landing a Boeing 777 in the fog is an art, I would disagree. These are consummate skills, but skill itself is not art, even though art demands skill. But if I were to add criteria about pitching and piloting that included the aesthetic grace and style of the pitcher's wind-up and delivery or the smoothness and style of the pilot in bringing the 777 to a safe touchdown, then I would be closer to the idea that pitching and piloting may parallel the making of art. But as soon as I do this, I leave the finality of objective measurement (Was it a ball or a strike? Did the plane land safely?) and enter the arena of opinion and counteropinion.

Consequently we cannot afford to talk about quality and beauty as if they were the responsibility only of artists. Likewise, the development of "taste" is not a separate item, to be activated when it is time to go to a classical concert or an art museum. Our lives should not be split up this way. Life is whole, and our lives must be commonly graced with the wholeness of doing everything with an eye to quality. Christians, of all people, should know this best, but it is often we who practice it worst.

We should be careful in what we mean by saying, "Well, after all, God just looks at the heart." It is like saying that attitude (my narrow, spiritualized definition of it) is everything, that attitude is a secret, untouchable thing instead of a clear and unequivocal summary of the way I articulate my entire worldview at any given time. Again I am drawn to 2 Corinthians 5:20: we are ambassadors, forth-telling outpourers in everything we do, as if God himself is making his appeal through us. Yes, he uses the lowly things of this world to bring honor to him. But "lowly" has a deeper meaning than "mediocre" or even "untrained." "Lowly" means meek, humble, quiet, whole and perhaps small, whereas "mediocre" means tawdry, poorly structured, wasteful, irrespective of size, training or talent. If God chooses to work in the presence of mediocrity, especially when it is meek and unknowing, so be it. For there is an innocent kind of mediocrity that, in its own way, is often touching, because the larger circumstance in which it is offered breathes a quality higher than the work itself, and that circumstance becomes the primary witness.

In spite of these questions and issues, I end up with the unshakable conviction that art truly exists, that a large portion of it is transcendently significant and that I need to partake of it regularly, to let it magnify and refine what I see minutely and coarsely and to challenge me to do everything as beautifully as I can. This means that I must exercise an active faith in the long stream of artistic action that has graced this and other civilizations for millennia. I must trust the trustworthiness of artists who, over and over, have provided me with examples of rare worth, whose work in turn is modeled on the integrity and imagination of their predecessors and contemporaries, generation after generation. The trust I have for this stream of goodness, and for the grace and depth that mark it, is such that I am impoverished without it. Even though the world is often a messy place, and even though many outstanding artists are moral grotesqueries, I can look to God and thank him for enabling both just and unjust people to create beautiful artworks. This grand wonder, flowing out of God's commonly strewn grace, relieves me of the awkward and impossible situation of having to decide on the worth of art on the basis of the condition of the artist. Just as I am free to worship in a church building that may have been designed by an atheist, so I can listen to the music of Richard Wagner even though he was a libertine and an anti-Semite.

And behind any discussion about art, we need to remember that, as images of God, we were created to do things the way God does and to work the way he works. God is Creator. We are creative. *Creating* and *creativity* are not exclusively artistic words. They are comprehensive words in that neither God nor we lack the twinned abilities of thinking something up and making it. Despite talk about God being the supreme Artist, this not only denigrates him but it also falsely elevates artists themselves. God is above being an artist and above our definitions of art. Within his creation, what we may call beautiful or ugly, he calls good. Maybe this is a better way of saying it: God's creatorhood entails much more than making *things*; it includes salvation, which is a unique kind of creating work, drawn from the wells of a triune imagination, the extent and purity of which escapes us. Salvation is not an artwork even though it took singular imagination and singular work; it is infinite and transcendent, soaring above any earth-bound definitions of quality, quantity, effort, expressiveness and beauty.

In spite of the degree to which the image of God in us was tarnished and twisted in the Fall, and in spite of the way the entire creation shows the ravages of Satan in ways that go deeper than murders, hurricanes and pestilence, we are created in God's image and the creation continues to declare his glory. No one, not even a Shakespeare, a Bach or a Monet, can ever out-imagine, outcraft or outwork the Creator of heaven and earth, who through the Word of his power continues to spin wonder after wonder in endless variety. This stream of loveliness will stop only when an even lovelier creation, unscarred by sin and Satan, will unroll in an eternity of glory and beauty. But for now I revel even in the scars and gashes of this creation, for surrounding them and shining through them is a work that could only have been authored by the uncreated Creator and the unimagined Imaginer. The fact that we were created *imago Dei*, and through Christ have become both image of God and children of God, means that there is an unavoidable and continually better way for each one of us, whatever our aesthetic condition and however we use artworks in our living and worshiping.

No two people can be expected to go about this created and redeemed glory the same way. Some of us are fast; others, slow. Some are highly talented; others, only average. But this single fact faces us all: we are created to do God's work the way he does his work, and we are to love our work with his kind of love. And because no two of us will show equal progress, and because only God knows the truth about the relation of our inside capabilities to our outside work, it is God's business alone to check us out as to how our growing faith informs the growth of our creative stewardship. None of us is capable of this judgment, despite years of training, evaluating and working in the ecclesiastical vineyard. It is the responsibility of all Christians, irrespective of the observed quality of their work, to purpose inwardly before God, in spite of contrary comment or cost. In other words, we are to imagine and to make while being like our Savior.

LESSONS FROM GOD'S CREATORHOOD

What can we learn from the way God imagines and makes, and how must we change our ways of imagining and making because of what we observe in his ways? Here are a few things to think about.[1]

1. What we call strange or abstract art may be closer to God's way of creating. We need to learn that the kind of art that does not copy or represent anything may be the wellspring of all art, including representational art. I think this is why: When God created the first giraffe, he did not have one to imitate or to copy. It came out of his imagination and, in the finest sense of the word, was abstract, because it did not look like anything else; it had no exterior reference point.

If we could entertain the idea that God has faith—that is, self-trust—we could put it to work right here. When God imagined something out of nothing, he trusted himself; he had faith in the unsettling workings of his imagination. He did not need a conference call or a quick huddle with his Son to gain the assurance that, after all, it is okay for a giraffe or a cockatoo to look the way it does. He believed in himself, and that was enough to authorize him to call everything—in an amazing spectrum of size, shape, color, movement, sound and habit—good.

When people grouse about a painting that does not look like anything, kindly refer them to God and what he did in starting up the creation. Ask them to take a microscope or a telescope and note the countless oddities, dazzlements, flashes and sublimities—abstractions all, nothing imitating anything else. Let them divest themselves of silly romanticist notions that God is an artist because a pretty sunset tells them so, and let them launch into the genuine mystery and unsettlement of Genesis, when God was out on one limb after another. In our standard way of reacting to strangeness, we might imagine Michael nudging Gabriel at the time of creation and saying, "I wonder if the everlasting Father understands aesthetics?"

2. With God, there is a difference between replication and continuation. Here is where we might get hung up in our preference for representational art over abstract art or locked up in suspicion about the experimental, way-out stuff. Our reasoning might go this way: "Yes, I can agree that God was the first abstract artist, but he acted this way only once, to start things up. After the first giraffe, there were billions of giraffes, and I know they are giraffes because they look like each other. So why should we not continue the parade by drawing giraffes that look like giraffes?" There is a simple answer: even though God may repeat an action, he does not replicate the object of his action. The genius, if you will, of God's repeated creational acts lies in the deeper fact that giraffes dramatically vary from each other in ways that go beyond their seeming similarities. And it is the variation that not only brings delight but also allows us to tell one from the other. All giraffes have spots. These, in themselves, are uniquely varied—without precedent. If we looked closely at these, not taking "giraffeness" for granted, and if we truly reveled in the endless variety of this single detail (and remember, spots are but one detail), we will begin to understand how extraordinarily singular, how abstracted, each giraffe is. We will realize how little they resemble the others and how superficial we are when "giraffeness" is the only thing we take account of.

Let's push further. Let's assume that we anticipate the countless ways that artists paint giraffes, even to the point where there are almost no "giraffe clues" left in the painting and we have to ask the artist what the painting "looks like." If he is wise and wants to do more than smirk at my naiveté, he might say first that the painting looks like itself; second, that it looks like yet another version of the giraffe; third, that it looks like what he had in mind about giraffes all along. This last "looks like" is crucial because it validates the theological truism that the creative mind is related to God's mind, in that God might have created the first giraffe knowing how any number of artists would paint it. That is, there were no preexisting rules about giraffes that God had to obey to know how the first giraffe had to look. God had the prerogative to imagine freely, and so does the artist as *imago Dei*. Despite the chicaneries that exist in human creativity (and there are no more in the arts than in practicing law or selling lettuce), it is exciting to come to know and trust the seemingly limitless stretch of the human imagination.

Let's push further yet. Let's say that I no longer care about painting giraffes—or for that matter, barns, apples or birds. I am really going to paint "abstractly." And I do so with every bit as much integrity and imaginative gusto as when I painted giraffes. My intellect labors even as my brush runs freely, and one shape after another appears in an astonishing variety of color, shape, texture and flow. But then I pick up a book filled with images of highly magnified cells, pictures from the Hubble deep field, the interior of a wood burl, images of crystals and gaseous and liquid formations. And suddenly I am humbled. There is nothing, not even in the most remote places of my abstract lexicon, that God did not venture into first. All I can do is bow down before the unimagined Imaginer and thank him that he has allowed me to imagine and make after the originating manner of just a few of his thoughts. And as I kneel in my humble station, as I place the fruit of my imagination at the Creator's feet, I can at least say this: "Honored Creator, whatever I have tried to see, you saw it first. But thank you for allowing me to suggest just one more way of seeing it." Then I rise from my knees and give witness to the world that God's greatness outshines anything I can do.

What do these ideas suggest to all continuous outpourers? Simply this: Do not stop pushing ideas, images, textures, compositions, shapes, contours, colors and gestures. Take them to their furthest possible reach. Do not rest with the idea that if something is familiar, it is valid, and if something is strange, it is suspect. Combine the first day of creation, when everything was startlingly new, with the seemingly endless days of continued creation, when nothing repeats itself, when the amazement over shifting nuance is coupled to a hunger for the familiar made strange and the strange made familiar. Remember that being *in* Christ is being one with the unimagined Imaginer and the uncreated Creator, who was just as comfortable in the first glorious creational flash as he is in the ever-changing, never-repeated strange variations that we foolishly call repetitions. Of all people who face the wonder of the unleashed and originating imagination, Christians should be the most comfortable, the most celebrative. That they are often not is sad witness to their lack of identity with the complete Creator and the complete Son of God. How delightful our lives would become if, in experiencing unsettling creativity, we would celebrate another person's ability to do something we cannot do, instead of grousing because it does not do what we would like it to do. Let's do more trusting and less complaining.

3. God's inside workmanship is as exquisite as his outside workmanship. When God makes something, it is marked by structural integrity and impeccable craftsmanship through and through. There is no such thing as rough work and finish work with God. The joints and marrow of our bodies are just as finely wrought as our teeth and faces. More than that, the elemental particles that comprise the joints and marrow are just as finely made as the galaxies. No wonder the universe holds together so well.

However, when we make things, we want them above all to look good or sound good on the outside, often with little regard to the inside craftsmanship. Exterior show and interior work often turn out to be two different things, and this is why things fall apart so easily in our culture. It may also partly be why we tire of them so soon and why we need so much surface variety. What is the quality of our work when the surface is scraped away and we can look down into its inner workings? What is God's opinion about the contradictions between the inside and the outside?

4. God's idea of quality is the same whether he makes something for quick or for long-lasting use. When God makes something, he does not pay less attention to it or make it less carefully if he knows that it will be quickly used up. Likewise, he does not augment his integrity or increase the quality of his workmanship if it is to last a billion or so years. Look at a mango or a mayfly; notice the wholeness and the loveliness. After all, the mango is just nourishment, part of a soon-to-pass meal. The mayfly lives mere hours, yet look at the gossamer, the near translucence, the grace. Why take so much trouble, God, when death is just around the corner or when with a few succulent snaps and chews, the mango is turned into nutritional slurry? Because God is honest and does everything well.

How about us? Does a praise chorus on a Wednesday night extract the same kind of integrity as a full-scale production of Brahms's *Requiem* on a festal Sunday? If not, we are not behaving the way God does.

5. God's handiwork is not divided between doing great things for magnificent display and doing average things for ordinary circumstances. Do we have a concept of creativity that is divided between a museum mentality and a workplace mentality—great art for the ages and so-so art for the worship place? This is where studio artists and commercial artists often have it out with each other. This is where church musicians and concert musicians often come to loggerheads. They often divide artistic action into two kinds, one that scoffs at putting art to work alongside other kinds of work and one that places more value on putting it to work than on its inherent quality. Where does God come into this? Look at a rose or look once again at the lowly, eatable mango, and you will see inherent beauty at the same time you notice that each has work to do. The mango does nourishing work: I can eat it and benefit from its nutriments. If it falls to the ground and rots, it nourishes the ground, feeds the insects and the worms, and contains the seed for its replacement. The rose is a feast to the eyes and nose. It also is nourishment; it makes a good medicinal tea; it feeds the land; it nourishes the insect world and adds its pollen to that of other flowers, giving us stimulating, eye-brightening honey.

God saw to it, in his ways of putting things together, that inherent worth, intrinsic beauty and usefulness quietly and humbly merge. What must we learn from this? That just as function and worth go hand in hand with God, so they should with us. Everything that we imagine and make should be put to some kind of work, and everything that is put to work should have inherent comeliness.

6. *The Creator is not the creation, and the artist is not the art.* God is superior to what he makes, sovereign over it and separate from it. He is everywhere at once, at the bottom of the deepest sea and in the midst of a primrose. But he is none of these, nor can he be. He made the creation; he did not beget it. By the same token, we are not what we make. We are superior to it; we are sovereign over it and separate from it. A potter no more begets a piece of pottery than God begets a salamander. This is the truth, in spite of the currently self-centered, thin-headed, pseudo-incarnational talk about "I gave birth to my art. The two of us are of a piece. Touch it and you're touching me."

If there is such a thing as pantheism, there is also such a thing as panthropism. Both are pagan; both are evil; both are to be avoided, especially in this present culture where virtually everything we do is "me" or "mine," an extension of us. When lit up with God talk, "mine" becomes "God's" to the extent that no one can question its use or suggest that it be replaced or improved, because doing so is tantamount to questioning God. It is important for Christians to lead the way in declaring their separation from any kind of handiwork, in declaring their sovereignty over it and in maintaining that truth alone has saving power.

There is a double value in this. First, the Christians who have freed themselves from any untoward attachment to what they make are freer to imagine wildly and craft wholeheartedly because there is no identity crisis, no need to find or perfectly portray the "real me" factor in what they make and no need for them to assume that when people condemn or praise their work, it is they themselves who are being crushed down or idolized. Second, when Christians understand that what they make is powerless over them, they will be able to avoid the pagan notion that art has inherent power over other people to make them better or worse. No longer should anybody say, "The music made me do it," whether in a worship service or a mosh pit, any more than someone else can say, "The god I carved causes me to worship it."

7. God is not especially interested in straight lines, perfect circles and geometric tidiness; his work is more chaotic than symmetrical. A statement like this flies in the face of our neatly packaged, superficial and often spiritualized ideas about order, symmetry, harmony and balance in the creation. I say superficial because of the way we talk about order and symmetry in the creation and then develop our own ideas of what order and symmetry are: straight lines, equally divided entities, replicative patterns, geometrical abstractions and such. But walk into a meadow and see if you can locate a straight line of buttercups all exactly the same height, each with exactly replicated petals. Or try to find a strictly triangular stand of perfectly symmetrical trees foregrounding a mountain range the left side of which is a mirror image of the right side. There is no landscape in which we can find any semblance of order, no storm at sea in which the waves are the same shape, height, creaminess or momentum. Swing a pendulum in a vacuum and you will soon discover that it leaves its regular pattern of oscillation and begins to move randomly, and if you repeat the experiment endlessly, you will observe an endless set of variations on the random oscillations. Nothing repeats and nothing is predictable. But here's the odd twist on it all: underlying the asymmetry and the randomness, there are governing laws that do not randomly fluctuate, even though the outward workings of the laws allow unpredictability and fluctuation.

This seeming paradox has given rise to a branch of scientific inquiry popularly known as *chaos theory*. We should take time to read up on it, for it is one of the most scintillating exercises we can put our minds to.[2] I do not profess to understand it in its mathematical details, but its basic premise is theologically exciting, and its implications reach into every quarter of existence, from meteorology to population dynamics to engineering to weather forecasting to pork futures. Chaos theory essentially says that randomness, asymmetry, unpredictability and endless variety mark the way the cosmos goes about its work down to the tiniest particles. At the same time, this theory harmonizes with the operation of immutable laws that undergird and are not shaken by the existence of continuous shifts and changes.

I mention chaos theory here not only because of the fact that only God could pull off a synthesis in which unpredictability answers to immutable laws, but also because chaos theory has everything to do with our creativity. Chaos theory helps us understand why no two simple melodies are alike even though we have but twelve pitches to work with. It helps explain why we can generate a virtually infinite palette of hues out of a set number of primary colors. It helps explain why a painting as profound as *The Last Supper* can be as unified as it is even though the hundreds upon hundreds of brush strokes that make it up could in no way have been completely controlled by the artist. Why is it that, try as I might, I cannot exactly duplicate my signature? Or why is that, try as I might, I cannot draw two exactly parallel lines, let alone making either one exactly straight? Why is it, for that matter, that a straight line is so frankly boring? Carry this further: If I look at an "exact" straight line, drawn by the best ruler and the sharpest instrument, through an electron microscope, I will find that it is hugely irregular because the pencil lost part of its sharpness during the drawing and because the surface of the paper is a chaos of peaks and valleys. In reality, then, the straight line is only an idea or an abstraction. Reality turns it into a nonrepeatable asymmetry.

I would urge everyone who is serious about human creativity to think deeply about the wonder that lies in the synthesis of changeless principle and flexible variation. I would urge everyone to understand that even the work of the Spirit, blowing where he will, lies at the divine and holy edge of chaos. And thinking of chaos with God in charge of every nuance, variation and mutation causes us to forsake the older meaning of the word *chaos*. With God, "chaos theory" is nothing other than infinitely varied rightness.

8. God has the jump on anyone who thinks that cultural diversity is the greatest thing since the automobile. For that matter, the current version of multiculturalism is a poor example of what intercultural love and artistic exchange should be. It has often been soiled with political rhetoric, tainted with new versions of racism and marked by strange examples of exclusivism. It is also wrongly linked with postmodernist relativism. With the latter, there is no center, no absolute to which everything need answer or relate. Moral relativity and artifactual relativity are placed on the same level. If you are truly multicultural under these terms, you must buy into the idea that belief systems are relative just as artifactual systems are. This goes completely contrary to the Christian worldview, in which absolutes are separate from legitimate relativities.

For instance, I must be willing to die for the absolute truth that Jesus is the Christ, the Son of the living God, but I can live comfortably with the belief that a Beethoven symphony is but one song among many songs, no one of which is the true song. The biblical defense for cultural diversity lies in the way God speaks, the way he creates and especially the way he clarifies the fundamental difference between his Word and what he creates. For the moment, I shall limit the discussion to the domain of handiwork and wait for chapter nine to complete the full relation of God's creation to his truth and the relation of our work both to truth and to our condition.

God is the most complete diversifier we know of. His handiwork is endlessly varied; all of it is good and each particle fits easily into its ordained place. Bullfrogs are not inferior to peacocks. Eucalyptus trees do not hang their heads in a forest of giant sequoias. The tiniest wisp of a water bug has its own place among the planets and supernovae. Gold may be worth a mint in Fort Knox, but it cannot equal or match propane for fueling a stove in permafrost country. Furthermore, while everything has its own worth, nothing exists independently of the other, for the entire creation is a community of subsistence and interchange.

I am not naive about all of this. I know of snakebites, tiger kills and bacterial virulence. I cannot fully account for these other than to say that God recognizes the anomalies and promises a complete remaking of things. So when I laud the handiwork and praise the communal beauty of the creation, I strain, along with all other created beings brought under the pain of drought and pestilence, and I peer by faith into a new completion. Even so, there is already enough beauty, example and wonder to tell me that if I want to understand artistic and cultural diversity, I must first look at God's way of diversifying. But above and beyond the diversity of God's handiwork, I can turn to the wonder of redemption by which two contrasting realities are preserved and harmonized: first, the continued diversity and worth of races, ethnicities and cultures, and second, the unity they enjoy in Christ.

One of the most important issues facing the body of Christ today is the issue of artistic diversity and stylistic pluralism. We theologize and rhapsodize about how awesome God's imagination is, how manifestly varied human creativity is, how exciting the music, the art pieces, the cultural ways of the entire world are.

America is, without a doubt, the most diverse country in the history of civilization. Think of music alone. Within these shores we have jazz, classical, opera, folk, ethnic folk, ethnic pop, blues, bluegrass, country, Appalachian, Cajun, rock, hip-hop, gospel (white and black), rap, Broadway, adult contemporary, on and on and on in an explosion of styles, substyles and fusions. As Christians we talk about this, glassy-eyed and bedazzled.

But here's an embarrassing and saddening truth: we are locked in a dilemma over two minuscule and static practices, traditional and contemporary, and when we really get adventurous, we blend the two. We are discarding hymnbooks, organs and notational literacy, and we are buying up sound systems and mixing boards. We are rearranging seating, as if circles of folding chairs do more than lines of pews. We are seemingly afraid of anything that smacks of the past, yet just as afraid of anything truly contemporary and truly diverse. We are doing this before the face of the only One who understands that diversity takes faith, trust, love, courage, imagination and belief in the power of God over the power of handiwork. Offering but two general stylistic options and then separating them into group preferences is not real diversity. It is more akin to a choice between two kinds of vanilla. It makes little sense to embrace a theology of diversity and then decide that church growth, spiritual growth and unity within the body should rest on such a shallow understanding of it.

Earlier on, I said that *both* traditional and contemporary practices are static. Most believe that this is true only of the traditional. I think otherwise. It has taken but twenty or so years for the contemporary worship movement to freeze into an established repertoire that, in the average congregation, might depend at best on three or four dozen songs that circle around a similarly limited textual core. This hurts the real meaning of *contemporary*. Literally taken, this word should at least mean keeping up with the times, and to seriously imaginative artists, it means leading the times, if not going beyond them. At the same time I fully acknowledge that a great many traditionalists are at fault, both for narrowing their own practices down to less than what valid traditionalism would call for and reacting ever so stubbornly against the contemporary efforts. I am quite sure that the body of Christ could be on a more peaceable practitional road if traditionalists understood tradition as a dynamic, ever-changing phenomenon and if the contemporists would understand that a tradition is ready to begin as soon a new song is repeated even once.

Allow me these thoughts about the praise and worship repertoire. Admittedly there are hundreds of songs that go beyond the basic core I spoke of above. But numbers alone will not suffice until the textual content of this repertoire takes in every aspect of God's work and every human condition imaginable, from lament to questioning to an issue-by-issue affirmation of the sovereignty of the Lord over the life of the church and victory over the powers of evil. I would encourage all contemporary songwriters to go beyond the usual worship-related constraints and to explore the whole counsel of God, the extreme width and depth of the human condition, to leave no doctrinal stone unturned and to make sure that the body of Christ is fully equipped to sing its way through the entire catechism of the work of God. This is what the tradition of hymnody has done for the church and what, so far, the contemporary music movement has failed to undertake.[3] Were this to be accomplished in the latter, a fresh and remarkable synthesis and a freshened recasting of the entire potential in congregational song would emerge. I say synthesis because it implies dependence on creative interchange and forward vision. Then we could enter into a radically new era of diversified song, where stylistic self-centeredness surrenders to the single truth that Christians, of all people, will leap to the chance for the thousand tongues. Blending and convergence, as initially appealing as they might seem, are not enough, because they are more concerned with stylistic balancing than with newness.

I know that some of these words imply my disappointment, even anger, over the intransigence that hurts both sides, and I feel no little concern that I might be grieving the Lord or hurting his people as I write. I realize that the body of Christ is debate-ridden, and I do not want to make the debate any more divisive. I only want God to be right, even if it means that my thinking will be forgotten and more thoughtful people will set things in order. In the introductory comments to this book I stated that I would not be pushing or attacking any particular style. In the above remarks, I am remaining true to that promise for this simple reason: it is not only a new synthesis for which I long, or a set style that I might criticize, but the exclusiveness with which style is being treated and the provincialism that keeps the styles separated. I am saying these things out of love for the Lord, out of respect for his rich imagination and out of love for people, including what even the most average of them is capable of. I am grieved over the richness and depth that Christians are being deprived of. I know there are exceptions; I know there are passionate and Christ-honoring people on each side of the style issue, and I have been spiritually deepened by the quality, sincerity and deep-felt hunger for the Lord in any number of traditional and contemporary settings. As I have said several times before, I know that God is gracious enough to break through and bless in ways that make any style of no consequence. As much as I love music—many, many kinds of it—and as much as I realize that we are commanded to make music, I will say over and again that we have placed far too much faith in it and not nearly enough in the power of the Word, the authority and sweep of fearless prophecy and earnest, yet hope-filled, intercessory prayer.

I have often wondered what would happen if we got music out of the way, especially in its upfront dress, and spent abundant time in interceding prayer, reading and searching the Scriptures, sitting in silence, prophesying and perhaps only then singing and making music. Stated another way, I wonder if Christians would be able to enter into such personal and experientially ecstatic praise of God—corporately or privately—without music, with just the Word, words about the Word and sheer silence within which the work of the Spirit cannot be related to or equated with anything we craft or shape.

But the stylistic split, stylistic colorlessness and theological thinness are not the end of the problem. The real problem lies not only in the poverty of what we are doing for people but also in what we are *not* doing for them. Whether unsaved people or Christian, they are, from their first breath, images of God. I refer back to the chapter on mutual indwelling and ask this question: What does it mean for us to take the glory of little children, young people and older people and to perpetuate the secular assumption that they have no God-centered reason to continue their outpouring in each other's presence? Somehow we have concluded that there might not be enough strength in the gospel to create a body of practitioners who can transcend the usual cultural naysaying about style and age gaps and forge their way into corporate union. This used to be done regularly among evangelicals. I grew up with it—hymns, gospel songs, Negro spirituals, youth choruses in popular styles, pianos, organs, church orchestras, trumpet trios, gospel duets, trios, quartets. Of course eyebrows were raised, but they were raised in community. Kids, teenagers, young marrieds, senior citizens—all had their ideas and personal preferences, but they joined in with it all, as one group, in the morning worship service and the evening evangelistic service.

What is so different now? It might lie in this idea: we have two different views of secular culture but adhere to only one. One view deals with the work side of culture and the other with the leisure and entertainment side. The work side recognizes that truly successful people in any vocational walk must push hard, learn the unique languages of the trade, expect slow growth and subject themselves to frequent and rigorous evaluation. The leisure side has to do with recognizing that the multiplicity of consumer expectations, style preferences, entertainment options and pleasure-giving wants and needs of an increasing subdivision of generational types demand that a set of markets be developed that cater to the various niches and accommodate transient shifts. Unfortunately it is the second perception, the safer and more attractive one, that appears to be driving the way the church beckons to the world. So instead of basing our approaches on secular notions of rigor, perseverance, discipline, hard work and interior authenticity, we have chosen only the market-based, feel-good approach. If we are going to imitate the world, we should at least imitate that part of it that most closely resembles the way the body of Christ should face the rigors of living and worshiping

I began this chapter with the suggestion that God's handiwork contains a set of lessons for us as to how we should go about imagining and making things in all of our work and all of our living. It ends with a plea for a commonsense, courageous effort on the part of the body of Christ to go beyond the usual, the static and the overly simplistic approaches to artistic diversity in the worship of the gathered assembly. This is a call to creative diversity of the most fearless sort, in which the way God goes about his creating work is to be our model, even as we place the burden on the Giver instead of our few paltry gifts.

9

THE PECULIARITY OF MUSIC
AND ITS UNIQUE ROLE

It is fruitless and damaging to assume the superiority of any art form over another. The peculiarity of music lies in its nature and not its "superiority." Even though I am a trained musician and can speak more knowledgeably about music than other art forms, I want the reader to realize two things. First, as much as I love music and as much as I revel in a multiplicity of musical styles and dialects, I am deeply concerned about the way music has taken over the debate and has led to so much division in the contemporary church. This is wrong and desperately needs reform and repentance. Second, I love the other art forms immensely and am likewise concerned over their neglect, their frequent cheapening and their misuse in so many churches.

So why is music peculiar and why is its role in our worship gatherings unlike that of the other arts? By the same token, why does its peculiarity make it prone to misuse in certain kinds of worship? In answer to the first question, the following thoughts might help.

THE UNIQUENESS OF THE HUMAN VOICE

The human voice is the only musical instrument that God has directly created. By doing so, he has provided equal access to music and singing for

everybody. Song is the music of the human voice. Its relation to speech is
not only physiological, in that our vocal chords can produce both speech
and music, but also inflectional, in that any steadily sustained vocal sound
is the same as a pitch. Furthermore, a succession of pitches, arranged according to an acceptable cultural norm, can be called a tune or a song. The
implications are enormous. Song, almost without exception, is the main
musical identifier in any culture. Where instruments are used (and hardly
any culture is without them), song has probably preceded and extensively
influenced it. True, musical instruments are capable of surpassing the human voice in certain matters of technique and range, but this in no way
undercuts the importance of song and the beauty of a well-trained voice,
a naturally fluent untrained voice or an unforced child's voice.

LACK OF TRAINING DOES NOT PREVENT ATTRACTIVE SINGING

Untrained singers of all kinds and qualities can join together and produce thrilling music, unique in its unschooled color and moving in its
intensity. This alone can verify the importance, if not preeminence, of
song in the body of Christ. In fact, the center of all church music—whatever the style, the size of the assembly or the training of any leaders,
choirs, ensembles or instrumental groups—is congregational song.
There should be no attempt in any music program to undo, cover over
or compromise this primary musical action. It is imperative that organ-
ists, pianists, choirs, song leaders, worship leaders and plugged-in worship teams understand that it is the congregation that is to be heard
above all. If it is not, then one of two things is wrong: either the congregation is not singing to the Lord with all its might or some other musical
body or activity is keeping this from happening. In the first case, a spiritual revival is the answer, and in the second, a thoroughly disciplined
and acoustically humbled reworking of what it means to take the role of
a servant in collaborating with corporate song is needed. That is, the congregation must increase and the leaders decrease. It could easily be argued that, no matter the style, overwhelming the congregation with
sheer musical dazzlement, unwarranted physical movement and plain-
old loudness turns most congregations into a mixture of observers and
competitors. But back to basics: the human voice, given over to Jesus,

and found in company with other voices given over similarly, produces a dignified and worthy song from storefront church to cathedral.

THE IMPORTANCE OF SCRIPTURAL INSTRUCTION ABOUT SONG

Music's capability for union with words is unparalleled in any other art form. This means that the most exact form of communicating truth (words) can be coupled to the most inexact (music) in a completely natural way. This fact holds over the entire range of pitch and word, from chant to oratorio, from a child's singsong to the most sophisticated art song and from simple Scripture songs to the most artfully composed hymn. The Scriptures accord a special task to music making, especially singing. Among countless references, two in particular deserve extended attention, as they sum up the rest.

The first is short and simple: "Sing to the LORD a new song" (Ps 96:1, among many others). This is really a four-in-one commandment. The first commandment is contained in one word: "Sing." Singing is not an option for the Christian; no one is excused. Vocal skill is not a criterion.

The second command is directional: we are to sing "to the LORD." These three simple words, especially the first, make it clear that singing is above all an act of worship, an offering to the Lord and not to people. We sing first to the Lord and only then to each other. This goes for concert artists as well as for choirs. Performers should understand that their performance is directed to God while people listen in, not the opposite. Those listening must understand that they are not being sung to but are overhearing an offering and continue the offering by faithful hearing.

Third, we are to sing "a new song." It is important for all Christians to understand that biblical newness is first of all a newness that arises out of a life of faith. This is what I mean: whether the song is borrowed, repeated or upsettingly different, faith alone makes it new. Only then can we press for the stylistic side of newness as originating newness, and only God knows how little of it there is in the musical practices of the body of Christ.

The fourth commandment is not immediately obvious, but changing one word from an adjective to an adverb brings it to light (I do not think I am stretching the point too far here): Sing to the Lord a song *newly*. This is what I mean: We can sing a truly new song only once, and thereafter we repeat it.

Some hymns and praise songs have stayed around for so long that it would not be an exaggeration to say that a single Christian may have sung those songs hundreds, maybe thousands, of times. Singing a song newly means that we must sing the thousandth repetition *as if for the first time*. Otherwise, we are as guilty of vain repetition in our singing as Christ spoke about in some people's praying (Mt 6:7). Only the Lord can make all things new. Only faith expedites newness by keeping us from vainly repeating. It could be argued that there might be as much profanity in church on a Sunday as there is on the street, unless we are sure that we say and sing everything newly by faith. This becomes especially important in praise singing, where repetition is carried more by musical and rhythmic forces than by a simple desire to repeat lyrics, *as if for the first time and as if there were no music*.

TEACHING, ADMONISHING AND SINGING TO THE LORD

The second Scripture passage is a fascinating one and constitutes the one fundamental segment of musical instruction in the New Testament. As such it brings finish to the conceptual and narrative stories of music making throughout the Old Testament. It appears with only slight variation in two different epistles:

> [Speak] to one another in psalms and hymns and spiritual songs, singing and making melody in your heart to the Lord. (Eph 5:19 NKJV)

> [Teach] and [admonish] one another in psalms and hymns and spiritual songs, singing with grace in your hearts to the Lord. (Col 3:16 NKJV)

Commentators have spent too much time speculating on the differences among psalms, hymns and spiritual songs, and this may have caused us to overlook more strategically important information. Since we have little idea of what early Christians used for texts and for music, we can only guess at the differences, and guesswork gives precious little direction, although it allows for remarkable freedom. For this we should be thankful. I firmly believe that Paul was possessed of remarkable intellectual thoroughness and conceptual accuracy in everything he wrote. This passage is no exception, and under close scrutiny, it offers subtle advice.

The importance of this passage is twofold, one having to do with the role of text, the other with the role of music, as two completely separate but coordinated actions, fulfilling two functions and going in two separate directions. First, we are told that we are to teach and admonish with psalms, hymns and spiritual songs. What do we teach? We teach truth, and music cannot teach truth. Only truth can teach truth. Therefore, we can assume that it is the text, the Word, that teaches and admonishes. In this respect the textual direction is horizontal. It goes back and forth among continuous outpourers as edification and instruction.

Second, we are instructed to sing and make melody *in our hearts to the Lord.* As we prophesy to one another with divinely revealed truth, we sing to the Lord with humanly crafted handiwork, music. This is the direction, always, of music: vertical, to the Lord, first and foremost.[1] Music is not truth telling, and God does not need truth; he is the Truth. But he wants to hear us use his truth prophetically even while we make music to him lovingly and praisefully. Lest any of us think that music is strictly emotional and primarily spiritual, we have but to listen again to Paul, who struggled mightily in all his writings, but especially in the twelfth through the fourteenth chapters of 1 Corinthians, for a balance between the intellectual and the spiritual. He concludes this way: "I will pray with the spirit, and I will also pray with the understanding. I will sing with the spirit, and I will sing with the understanding" (1 Cor 14:15 NKJV).

We must remember that Paul lived in a pagan culture that believed in the causal force of mere things, the arts among them. It is important to understand that the sum and substance of Paul's theology about human handiwork, from the literal existence of idols to ordinary work to the various art forms, was that these are nothing when it comes down to the fundamental relationship between the alleged power of handiwork and the personal responsibilities of the user to rise above and to be in charge of whatever is being used. In this light we should notice the impeccable consistency in Paul's thought in these passages. From them we can infer that music is of a different order than text, and the two cannot be taken as co-equally empowered in the life of the believer.

Yet some teach that music empowers text, or that text without music has less emotional significance. A question emerges: do the words of songs such as "Lord, I Lift Your Name on High" or "He Is Exalted" or "Shine, Jesus, Shine" have the same spiritual and emotional carrying power when taken without the music? If we were to look at the flow-chart concept used by a number of worship leaders, in which certain emotional effects can be brought about by combinations of tempo, rhythm, key structures and changes, and so on, we must conclude that the strength of the text per se is at the beck and call of the music. Various schemes called "progressions" (for instance, the "classic progression," the "earthquake progression," the "mild progression") can be set up to give a particular emotional contour to the worship set. These are musical and not textual constructs. There are even arguments about the relationship of the flow of endorphins to feelings of well-being about the Lord, his presence and the joy that comes during or at the conclusion of the set.[2]

Several questions and concerns arise immediately. The first is about text, the Word itself. Do we expect the stand-alone power of truth, read authoritatively and by faith, to generate the same endorphin-based response? Why is it that a body of believers, supposedly moved by the Lord and the joy he alone can bring, do not emote, raise their hands, clap and shout during an authoritative reading of the Word of God? Why is music needed to do this, and why does our behavior seem to depend so much on particular kinds of human handiwork?

Second, why is a worship set—and it can be called by an assortment of names—so self-enclosed, as if there were no other "set" in the corporate gathering called by the same name and full of the same energy? Should not a worship set (assuming the legitimacy of this term) be a complete way of life, not a parenthesis within it?

Third, if it is true that music has such force in the context of worship, it must have similar force in the context of worldly gatherings. If intimacy with the Lord is expedited by music, then why not sexual intimacy or drug intake in a mosh pit? Since some argue that music is morally and spiritually causal, it would follow that the music producing worship would have to be radically different from music producing immorality. If this is true, then why is so much praise and worship music based on rock music? If the argument is that the Holy Spirit makes the difference, then why is he so quiet during other "sets" than the worship set or in the use of traditional music?

Fourth, could it be that the role of music in much of our worship is the contemporary equivalent of holding on to the high places in biblical times? We repeatedly read of Old Testament kings turning back to God with all of their hearts, yet the high places were allowed to remain. They just did not want to let go of humanly constructed devices that seemingly mediated the presence of God. Might music be one of these for us?

Someone might identify a flaw in my reasoning and say, "Okay, I admit there is an attempt to guide emotional response in a worship set, and I admit that emotional response to the same style of music may induce immoral behavior in one gathering and a sense of worship in another. But doesn't this difference in behavior depend on what's inside the person? Isn't it true that it is not what goes into a person that corrupts him or leads him into purer things, but what comes out? And since believers who gather together want with all their hearts to worship God, can they not rightly turn the emotional power of music into a time of adoration and joy?" The answer is yes, except for one crucial question.

Why then do so many leaders consider music a tool of influence for worship?[3] If it is a tool, this must mean that people come to corporate worship unprepared for worship, or at least neutral, expecting worship to be initiated, and the music segment becomes the tool for this. If music is a tool *for* worship, it defies logic to say that it is an act *of* worship, yet who would disagree with the latter? As harsh as it sounds, an analogy would be that if an unbeliever went to a rock concert unprepared to misbehave sexually or take drugs, the music would be the tool of influence in these directions. Then we are back to square one: music has power over people in spite of themselves. The argument doesn't wash, then, that "God made music and he's smart enough to understand its power over us." That's like saying that God made stars and trees and he is smart enough to understand their power over us.[4]

Even though a good part of the foregoing refers to certain practices in praise and worship, I want the reader to know I am not criticizing one segment alone. Above all, I want to be fair to sincere and dedicated leaders, my brothers and sisters in Christ. One of these, Andy Park, says this: "So let's not falsely label our high emotions as a visitation of God's power. Emotion in worship is good, and the presence of God is good, but they are two different things that are not always experienced simultaneously."[5]

But if this is true, why is so much time spent in the design of worship sets that are meant to produce behavioral results, and why so little on the danger of confusing them with God's presence? It seems that the two issues should be reversed and that a theology of the presence of God and a theology of artistic action should be so carefully explored as the primary issue that the secondary, behavioral issue would naturally flow out of, and be subordinated to, the primary one. Perhaps it would need no mention at all.

In all of this, traditionalists are likewise theologically at risk, for many of them make beauty into a spiritually causal issue and assume that tradition offers an emotional assurance of the presence of God. I have had more than one discussion with serious and sincere Christian musicians from the classical and traditional side who insist that beauty is equivalent to truth and that, by consequence, mediocrity is the equivalent of untruth. Taste, then, becomes the spiritual arbiter (good taste equals vivid faith), and a concept of beauty is based almost exclusively on Western classical art. In this case aesthetics becomes sacramental.

TESTING FOR BALANCE

So what do we do when we hear from one side that we need to get our emotions back into the worship picture and from another side that only the best art should be used because of the power of beauty and tradition?

First, each of us needs to be sure that, in every event, God is supreme above all. We are in his charge and under his authority, subject to the work of the Spirit.

Second, we must not only understand, but also act on, the creational principle that just as God is above his handiwork, so are we. Just as God cannot be subject to the power of his handiwork, neither can we be subject to the power of ours. And because we are sovereign over what we make, we can celebrate it more completely than when we assume ourselves to be subject to it.

Third, we must understand that joy, pleasure and adoration are neither valid nor complete unless they can be shown and lived out in a variety of circumstances. Then, if a certain activity in a certain place—say, worship music—works its spell upon us, we need to be sure that this experience in no way substitutes for the experience we have by being in Christ as continuous outpourers when there is no music.

Fourth, in a culture of addiction (and music can be a form of addiction), we must dissociate ourselves from music as the primary social glue in the secular world and spiritual glue in the ecclesiastical world. We must realize that, if we are to be a biblical church, not simply a culturally relevant church, we must discount such heavy dependence on our limited and provincialized inventory of works and get down to the business of depending on the power of the Word and the force of the unleashed gospel. We must look to the Spirit, not to our humanly contrived proxies, as the only Paraclete.

As I have said before, then, but only then, and by all means, let the music come. Traditional, contemporary, avant-garde, ethnic, jazz, rock and chant—name it and pour your heart and mind into it. Rejoice in it. Dance with David in it. Let Taizé ring the changes on the glory of God, and let "Jesus Loves Me" done in a thousand styles become everybody's invocation and benediction. Let the emotions roll and the endorphins break their dikes. But for Jesus Christ's sake, let's get music back where it belongs—as a lisping sign and not a glittering cause, as the response to a commandment and not just a set of tools for influencing people.

10

THE ARTS IN CONTRAST

ALLOWING ART TO BE ART

At one time or another in its history, the church has been in the middle of artistic action of virtually every kind. We need only refer to what we can call classical sacred art, and our eyes, ears and minds are filled with examples of the highest artistic achievements imaginable. In fact, it is safe to say that until recently sacred classical art has influenced artistic action in general culture in ways that should shame the contemporary church. For this reason alone, no one should play games with traditionalism, especially when it comes to shutting the door on it in the name of relevance. I can understand why thinking Christians would question the way in which sacred art has often been given undue spiritual prominence and contextual force and has become a form of idolatry. I can also understand why nobody should be expected to embrace every style and call it their own. Respecting tradition does not mean using all of it. It means, rather, understanding that human creativity is a huge stream. It is impossible, therefore, to turn away from tradition, no matter how new, daring or different you want to be, and start something up from scratch. This has never been done, even with the so-called avant-garde. Even if it could be shown that the avant-garde starts up everything strictly on its own, once started, it begins a tradition of one kind or another.

THE LOCAL CHURCH AND ARTISTIC CHOICES

I can also understand that local congregations vary greatly in aesthetic understanding and local talent and often lack the material resources to sponsor the making of truly fine art or to branch out into all the arts at once. But this is merely a local and understandable condition. It turns into a serious problem—really, a theological problem—when the local assembly creates an aesthetic sense based exclusively on what it is locally capable of, then remains content with it and closes itself down to the riches of what surrounds it. If this kind of closing down becomes too connected to spirituality, it becomes easy to say that as long as the art honors God, it need not press on further. But this eliminates a central truth in any kind of human action, namely that we do not exist as secure creative islands but are part of a vast community through the achievements of which we are enriched and further stretched. Think, for instance, of where technology would be today if, after the invention of the steam engine, a group of people decided that as long as they could thresh wheat faster than they used to by hand, they would look no further into advancing technology, even though another group had found out about the internal combustion engine.

But something is changing in the contemporary church. There is a resurgence of interest in other art forms, such as sacred drama and sacred dance. All Christians should rejoice in this, regardless of the quality of the art being practiced in any local gathering. Assuming that the church keeps its theology straight about the relationship of artistic action to continuous outpouring, and assuming that every congregation couples continuous excelling to a fearless desire to imagine and craft after the manner in which God imagines and crafts, it might just be that culture will once again turn its attention toward the church instead of the opposite. There are several versions of a saying attributed to G. K. Chesterton. This one can suffice: "If a thing is worth doing, it's worth doing poorly." However, we cannot afford to leave it there. I would rather it be said this way: "If a thing is worth doing, it is worth doing poorly, but only as a start."

Churches that are considering expanding their use of the arts in worship should observe two cautions. First, they should avoid the mistake of leaning on sophisticated artistic labels to give luster or prestige to what are otherwise basic activities. This is what I call *verbal legalism* (a more candid word is *exaggeration*): the act of changing something into what it is not, or barely is, by giving it a name with a higher meaning than it deserves. Here is an example. When the responsive reading of a Scripture portion or a poem or a literary fragment between two desig-nated people is called a dramatic reading, we should flinch. A dramatic reading is more than a name given to an ordinary activity to which a modest amount of vocal inflection is added. Going a bit further, a sacred drama is more than what in other circumstances would simply be called a skit. Using high-sounding labels is not a good example of a church branching out into the dramatic arts, or if it is, it is worth doing poorly but only for a short time.

Second, churches should avoid expanding their artistic horizons simply to show how with-it they are or to try to keep up with the church down the street. If we go about the arts this way, we run the risk of doing our work poorly before the Lord because our reasons are not faithful ones. There is such a thing as church growth by envy, and I fear that in our growth-addicted culture, we can easily put growth ahead of principle. We need to be sure that our choices are based on one clear fact: we humbly love God and are convinced that the addition of the arts cannot change this or add to his passion. We want to show our love by enlarging the highways of our outpouring toward him, knowing that a thousand tongues will never be enough.

Different Art Forms, Different Functions

But I am going to assume that the arts are being explored for the right rea-son and that, throughout this process, the local congregation is doing its best to do better. What I want to do in the following remarks is to lay out a conceptual scheme that allows for maximum artistic freedom and min-imum friction or overlap among the arts. This scheme will also include thinking about the relationship of artistic content to its role or nonrole in articulating truth. It is important from the outset to avoid lumping the arts together as if they were a single substance, then expecting them to act similarly because they are all called by the same name, art. Also, there is a great difference between developing a theology *of* the arts and deriving theology *from* the arts. These two issues are often carelessly linked, and if they are not clarified, they can lead to mistaken concepts about the true role of the arts in corporate worship. Two simple statements will launch us into these issues:

1. When it comes to proclaiming truth, words are the most accurate form of communication we possess. When it comes to showing truth, words and deeds must harmonize.

2. Not all the arts use words or portray deeds; consequently, they vary greatly as to what they "say" and as to what kinds of messages they give out. They should not be expected to do the same things or be used the same way in corporate worship.

THE ARTS, THE WORD AND WORDS

Christians have a driving passion for the truth to be told at all costs. One of the most assuring facts that they have is that the truth has already been told by God, who made sure that the Scriptures contain everything we need to know about faith and practice. This gracious act of self-revelation was supremely essentialized in person by the Son of God. As the Word made flesh, he once for all and forever sealed the truth in a perfect union and continuous outpouring of Word and deed. Therefore, the task of each Christian is to be sure that, in Christ, the Word of God is thoroughly learned, lived out and told forth.

How does this apply to the discussion at hand? I firmly believe that in corporate gatherings, the Word is to be preeminent. This Word "rightly proclaimed must always outdistance other words."[1] The authoritative reading of an abundance of Scripture (not merely a fragment of it in order to introduce the sermon), the authoritative and Spirit-driven preaching of the truth, the Word-driven force of the sacraments, the Word-authorized content of ceaseless prayer and the congregational singing of fully developed truth are far and away the most important actions that can take place. Then come the arts. Once we give priority to the Word in corporate worship, we can assume a priority among the arts as to their ability to articulate truth. As for this task, dramatic presentations come first and music last.[2] Here is why this order is so important.

MISDIRECTING THE WORD

Many Christians are more than Word-centered; they are word-and-message obsessed and have a tendency to expect everything in the arts to act like the Word acts and to give out messages the same way the Word does. To them, every artistic action should clearly make some sort of witness point. If it does not, its content is manipulated until it does. This obsession connects directly to the idea mentioned in the last chapter that the visual arts are suspect if they do not replicate something: a house or a tree or a horse. When this is taken too far, the nonverbal arts are expected to perform a function of which they are incapable. Dancers are expected somehow to dance propositional truth. But how do you dance John 3:16 in a way that makes it propositionally clear that believing gives eternal life? The dancer might manage certain gestures and choreographic movements that suggest love or acceptance, but this does not mean that the fullness of truth is being articulated. Furthermore, there are only so many gestures that approximate love and acceptance or joy. Then what? I believe this is why so much sacred dance is the same from performance to performance and theme to theme. People are afraid to let go of the idea that dance must preach a truth. They are afraid of allowing dance to simply be dance and allowing the body to celebrate its physical, sensuous self, as if God was embarrassed when he gifted us with physicality and gave us the desire to make our gestures aesthetic.

So when we try to make certain art forms do what they are incapable of, or undertake what other art forms more easily do, we commit two errors at once. First (believe it or not), we denigrate the Word. Unwittingly, we are giving the impression that the Word needs help from every quarter possible, when it is actually the other way around—everything we know of needs help from, and is informed by, the Word. The irony of this is that this error is most often committed by those who are the most outspoken in their belief in the accuracy, power and self-sufficiency of the Word. This belief, furthermore, may be perpetuated by two related assumptions. First, we can become so obsessed with words that we end up worshiping them and then making everything after their image, instead of simply trusting in them for what they are: treasures in earthen vessels paying full service to the revealed Word. Second, the ghost of pagan philosophies about divinely and humanly created things still haunts the Christian mind. We too quickly assume that we can insert our beliefs into what we shape so that it actually transmits the same message to the observer or listener. I want to deal with this in some detail further on, but only after mentioning the second major error, as follows.

MISDIRECTING ART

In trying to make certain art forms speak the truth, we not only denigrate the power of the Word but also weaken the art form itself. Each art form has its own propositional mechanisms, its own particular kinds of language and vocabulary, and its own ways of holding together in a final shape. It is important, therefore, for everyone to become conversant with these individuated processes. Some art forms use words alone (literature and poetry); some use words, gestures and deeds (the dramatic and cinematic arts); some utilize only stylized gestures that may or may not suggest an outside meaning (dance and mime); others, while wordless and deedless, contain recognizable objects (landscape and seascape art, abstract sculptures or ceramic objects and jewelry); some contain deeds and gestures but are frozen in space (paintings, drawings and engravings of battles, family outings, love scenes and the like). And there is one art form that contains no words, no deeds, no gestures and virtually no exterior referential devices. Music alone falls into this category and consequently is the most abstract of all the art forms, the least capable of "saying" anything outside itself, therefore the most open to associational meaning. It may accompany speech, as in a hymn or an opera or a jazz ballad, but it cannot replace or equal it. At the same time, music is the most ubiquitously expressive of all art forms because it soaks up meaning from around itself more quickly than any other art form. As soon as we attempt to front-load an art form with a truth task of which it is incapable, we immediately call into question the mechanisms and expressive worth of the art forms themselves. Before we know it, the art form has begun to collapse, to cease being its inherent self, as it struggles to carry an illegitimate burden.

Even in the various speech forms themselves—for example, legal briefs, scientific treatises, documentary prose, literary prose, drama and poetry—words are expected to act differently in one form than in the other. As I move from left to right in this list, I move from speech forms in which words are expected *to mean one thing only* to forms in which words are expected *to mean and refer to many things at once*. The Scriptures work this way as well, with Leviticus, for instance, at the "legal brief" end, the Pauline and Petrine epistles somewhere in the middle, John's epistles slightly right of the middle, and the Psalms, prophetic poetry and the Song of Solomon at the other end. This fact is part of what makes the Scriptures so exceedingly rich and delightful. It also contributes to making certain passages more difficult to interpret than others.

The Scriptures provide us with a complete methodology about how widely we can express ourselves in the use of language and the articulation of truth. There is no doubt in my mind but that God intended this wide spectrum of expression to be included in his revelation to us. If anybody understands multiple meanings within the same thing, it is God. Nonetheless, I firmly believe that the best preaching, as poetic and elegant as it can become, cannot afford to drift too far into meaning many things at once. As important to the human soul as the Psalms and the poetic utterances of the prophets are, the preaching that issues out of them should lead back into the firmness and direct applicability of propositional truth.

Once we look at the various art forms this way, seeing how some of them do certain things extremely well and others do them poorly or not at all, we should strike a balance and celebrate each art form for what it does uniquely well. This is enough.

This issue is not limited to the church. As irritating as it might sound, totalitarian regimes often use art the same way, though with an evil motive. Please understand that I am not trying to create a linkage between the church and totalitarianism. I am merely saying that a passion to make a message consistently clear, whether this passion is holy or wholly evil, can lead to a flawed methodology. In the case of totalitarianism, the artist is coerced into being a messenger of the state, and any art that fails to speak the message clearly is destroyed and the artist is prosecuted. Any art that encourages people to think on their own is suspect, because thinking on one's own might undermine the prerogatives of the state. In spite of the evil of this approach to art, the church can make this parallel assumption: whatever art is done, it must align itself with truth. If it does not do this clearly, the artist is suspect or is expected to manipulate the art until it does.

LET ART BE ART

What does this mean for the arts in the church? Simply this: instead of pushing art forms beyond their limits, we must allow art to be art. We must allow each art form to be its own form of praise to God. It then becomes the responsibility of every member of the local gathering to join the particular language of the art form and to offer it directly to the Lord for what it is instead of looking for a substitute language. Even though all art forms carry equal aesthetic responsibility, each one has a different task and a unique quality, and all are equal as aesthetic acts of worship. The arts should never take the place of direct proclamation. Rather, they should be used in worship as themselves, ultimately pointing away from themselves to the truth, but never giving the impression that they can do what truth alone can do. We must allow each art form, with its particular vocabularies and structures and contours to go directly to God in their purest form, uncluttered by our weak and untrusting spirits that get nervous if everything that we do does not shout John 3:16.

At the same time we must be careful lest we turn sacred drama into the equivalent of the typical sitcom, with its formulaic approaches to human realities. If we force drama too hard, we end up with unreal, falsely idealistic dialogue, mechanical changes of attitude and fairy-tale endings. Real drama takes time; it is complex, and there are no easy answers, because life itself is a mysterious interweave. I wish that liturgical drama would reflect the best secular drama and would content itself with portraying situations that often remain unresolved or in tension in the drama itself. Then let preaching take over. Let it unwind the truth carefully and clearly, allowing the Spirit to make application appropriate to each heart.

God knows what art is about. He knows why we have art. He understands that just as his handiwork cannot say "Jesus saves," so a good bit of ours cannot either. He knows that his handiwork is capable only of pointing back to him and that its only words are "We are not the truth. We have our limited ways of declaring the Maker's glory, but when it comes to telling the real truth, our lips are sealed. Yet we point to the only One capable of telling the truth, the Creator himself in his revealed Word and in his Son, the incarnate Word. Don't come to us for truth; go directly and urgently to him, and he will save you through his Word."

Our task is to make art as honestly and freely as we can and then offer it to him, and when we do, he will do his work in a way that will validate both his power apart from the arts and the arts themselves as given over to him. He alone can free us from the worrisome thought that the arts are a failure unless they "preach."

THE ARTS AND THEOLOGY

Two final issues need to be clarified. The first was mentioned at the beginning of the chapter, namely that there is a difference between articulating a theology *of* the arts and attempting to derive theology *out of* the arts. It should be apparent by now that the former is preferable and the latter is often risky and theologically uninformative. Theological thought should provide mechanisms that validate the arts, distinguish among them, inform their use and direct them, according to their kind, in the continuing worship of God. We have established that each art form is unique as to its materials and mechanisms. The vast differences among images, gestures, words, pitches, colors, syntactical and architectural processes, and space/time relationships make it virtually impossible to derive theological principles or ideas *out* of them, with the possible exception of the speech-driven art forms. Any attempt to do this with nonverbal art forms plays into the hands of belief systems in which artificial equations and relationships are inferred from, and moral and morally causal power are imputed to, speechless and deedless things. At the same time, I grant that Christians who are trying to do this want very much to see truth clarified and proclaimed everywhere. Also, I must own up to the fact that there are manifestations, proportions, attributes and syntheses in mute handiwork that may suggest certain things theological, such as a major triad implying something about the Trinity, or the universality of the golden mean suggesting something about a common, perhaps divine, influence on human creativity. But these findings are pliable and often culturally biased.

The second issue is about the word *truth*. When I say that music, for instance, is incapable of proclaiming truth, I do not mean that music does not have its own kind of truthfulness. All art forms have an inherent obligation to be true to themselves in the minutest detail as to their interior workings. This kind of truth, or lack of it, is bound to show exteriorly. The best art—simple or complex, Western or non-Western, popular or classical—is the art that shows its procedural, intellectual and architectural truthfulness. The pursuit of this kind of truth should burn into the hearts and minds of Christians, and no art form prepared for the gathered congregation should duck this responsibility or spiritualize it into nonexistence. Amazingly, this kind of truth is brought under judgment by Truth itself, because all artists have an ethical obligation before God to be truthful in their reasons for making art as well as for bringing the interior truthfulness of all of their art to magnificent conclusion.

words = message
truth

art = says things

11

"YOU SHALL NOT WORSHIP ME THIS WAY"

Worship, Art and Incipient Idolatry

In this chapter I want to bring together comments I have made here and there regarding idolatry in the life of the worshiper, developing them more thoroughly in order to prompt each of us to examine our worship and artistic action. The subject of idolatry is not something from which Christians are excused once they come to Jesus and begin to worship authentically. Authentic worship is not perfect worship. It stands in continual need of examination, repentance, increased depth and humility as well as outpouring meekness and humility.

The lordship of Christ will be tested over and over again. Other gods and other lords are hard at work, clamoring for attention. Sometimes they sing sweetly; other times, aggressively. The accuser of the brothers and sisters not only tempts with despair and ugliness; he comes also as a serenading angel bringing a version of good news that goes deep in its attractiveness long before it is unmasked in its falsity. I do not wish to call undue attention to the work of the evil one, for he loves to get believers to credit him with more effectiveness than he has. Nonetheless, we need to be as realistic as possible about his intrusion into the flaws and low spots in our common sojourn.

THE ESSENCE OF IDOLATRY

In chapter one I said that idolatry is the condition of self-deluded sovereignty by which we choose a god, assume it to be self-originating, craft a life system over which it is enthroned and then surrender to it, forgetting that its mastery is a figment of our imagination. In short, creature chooses creature and then deifies it. As foolish as idolatry is, it can range all the way from a complex religious system to hidden, private and seemingly harmless trivia in an otherwise unspotted life. While it is not very ecumenical to say it this way, all worship outside the worship of God through Christ Jesus is idolatrous. Likewise, idolatry is the chief enemy of the most fervently worshiping Christians, even to the extent that some of us may end up worshiping worship.

Most of us would not willingly (that is, rationally) choose to be idolaters. It is too . . . well, too heathen. It smacks of carvings and castings, spells and shamans. It is alien and scandalous. After all, were we not saved from idols, and are we not aligned wholeheartedly with the true God? On those rare occasions when we own up to our personal idolatry, we can easily become satisfied with merely owning up to it, as if this were the cure instead of the first step in a continuous striving against every sin and growing up into the stature of the fullness of the Savior.

But if we seriously examine the most insightfully clever, sarcastic and conceptually whole depiction of idolatry in Scripture, Isaiah 44:9-20, we understand why idolatry can be so intellectually obvious yet so confoundedly subtle and so insidiously prevalent. To be sure, Isaiah is castigating the religious systems of his day, including the more obvious kinds of idolatry. But he makes two broad points that go beyond the obvious and into the heart of our common condition. The first has already been alluded to: idolatry is the act of shaping something that we then allow to shape us. We craft our own destiny and then act as if it were supernaturally revealed. The second is that we are blinded by a simple contradiction: what we serve is made out of the same stuff that in other circumstances serves us. When idolatry is reduced to these simple concepts, we begin to understand that there is something far more fundamental at work than crafting a deity out of a piece of timber and creating a life system around it. Instead we are confronted with a subtlety that, like water, will find the slightest crack in an otherwise solid wall and leech through.

Isaiah's insights become all the more clear when we move from the Old Testament to the New. Even though Isaiah both lashed out at false deities and argued a concept that probed more deeply than that, the Old Testament is generally concerned more with the physicality of idolatry. When we come to the writings of the New Testament, however, we learn that idolatry takes in everything that stands in the way of a direct, faith-substantiated life of continuous worship. Consequently we are confronted with a pantheon of false gods that can range from something as quickly identifiable as the religions of the Greco-Roman culture to something as subtle and immeasurable as spiritual pride. When the apostle John warned his brothers and sisters to keep themselves from idols (1 Jn 5:21), he surely had more in mind than carvings and castings. Likewise, when Paul in Romans 12:2 warned against being conformed to the world, he knew that such conformity, especially when overlaid with a form of spirituality, is the practitional equivalent of idolatry.

THE EXTENT OF IDOLATRY

The range of idolatrous practice can be broken down into three categories. The first is the most obvious: the forsaking of the worship of the one true God in favor of false gods and religious systems. The second is an emulsive incongruity in which the centralities of one religion are folded into the most acceptable components of another system. This is called syncretism. I call it an emulsion because the two systems are incompatibly alien, yet through continued practice and activation, they appear to be homogenous. The third category might at first seem to derive out of the second, but its subtlety differentiates it, and it is the one I wish to concentrate on for the remainder of this chapter.

When we compare Deuteronomy 12:4 and 12:31 with other passages on idolatry (especially Deut 13), we see a curious shift in the way it is mentioned and condemned. In 12:4 and 12:31, neither apostasy nor syncretism seems to be the issue. Instead it is one of worshiping God idolatrously. As we read these two passages, we see God's grace at work even before his judgment, for he is careful to acknowledge that even though the Israelites have introduced alien substances, they are still worshiping him. This is a crucial point to recognize because of the way it applies to all of us as we work out our salvation. In Christ there is a vast difference between false worship and falsity within authentic worship. Otherwise, why would Paul, in Romans 7, be so detailed in his description of his persistent wretchedness? And why would he, in chapter 8, flood us with such comfort and joy?

Here are two translations of the Deuteronomy 12 passages (emphases in all cases are mine):

> You shall not worship the LORD your God *with such things*. (Deut 12:4 NKJV)

> You must not worship the LORD your God *in their way.* (Deut 12:4 NIV)

> You shall not worship the LORD your God *in that way.* (Deut 12:31 NKJV)

> You must not worship the LORD your God *in their way.* (Deut 12:31 NIV)

The first of these seems to suggest that the Israelites might actually use objects in their worship from a false system (something close to syncretism), whereas the remaining three suggest something subtler by speaking of *the way* other people worship. I do not believe that I am tearing away at the exegetical skin of these passages by suggesting that "with such things" implies that objects near at hand are used to bring tangibility, shape and substance to an unseeable, untouchable God. We can correctly call this golden calf–ism because the statement found in Exodus 32:4 ("These are your gods . . . who brought you up out of the land of Egypt"), coupled to Aaron's statement in the next verse that the idols would be used as part of a feast *to the Lord,* makes it clear that the Israelites were not so much turning away from God as introducing things that would represent his presence and conform him to preconceived notions. The idols would reduce God to a recognizable size and make him referentially familiar, thus attempting to bring substance and evidence to that which faith alone should apprehend.

On the other hand, "In that (their) way" may refer less to a particular concretion than to the worldview that calls for it, that is, why idols come about in the first place and why it becomes so easy to revert to them. In all these thoughts I continue to take my signal from Isaiah's conceptual model (chapter 44) and the New Testament's insistence that idolatry goes beyond the worship of a crafted thing and into the conduct of an inner condition that may call it forth. In this respect idolatry is the difference between walking in the light and creating our own light to walk in. This can happen in four ways. First, instead of faith being its own substance and evidence, faith is misconstrued as leverage for bringing to, or enhancing the substance and evidence of, things that simply are what they are. Second, our works are expected to enhance our faith, in which case legalism and idolatry join forces. Third, perfectly legitimate pursuits can interpose themselves between us and the Lord. Fourth, sin in all its forms is idolatry. Let me make some practical applications to the arts from these four points, particularly the first three.

Whenever we assume that art mediates God's presence or causes him to be tangible, we have begun the trek into idol territory. Our present-day use of music as the major up-front device for worship is a case in point. We need to ask ourselves if we, as worship leaders, are giving the impression that we draw near to God through music or that God draws near because of it. Is music our golden calf? Have we come to a place in our practices where God must say to us, "You cannot worship me in *that way*," meaning that music has moved from a place of offering to one of lordship, from servanthood to sovereignty? Or might he be saying, "You shall not worship me in *their way*," meaning that we have adopted a pagan worldview that imputes a causal force to music that it does not properly have? We need to discover the critical theological difference between being merely moved by music and being spiritually changed by it. Yes, music might bring pleasure and change our pulse rates or blood pressure, but so does taking a simple walk in the park.

I know from personal experience how easy it is to draw people into my confidence with music, using it as a means for creating a bridge between them and me, between God and me and between them and God. When we are told by fellow worshipers that our music is actually making God more real, our repentance must be followed by corrective teaching.

Beauty and quality can become idols. I need to be fully understood here. All Christians everywhere should seek to make, to do and to articulate things as beautifully as possible. Christians who play down the importance of beauty and quality as if they were idols in themselves do not understand that nothing is an idol until we make it into one. Furthermore, the neglect of beauty and high quality in many Christian circles is deplorable and can itself be a form of idolatry. Thus when it comes to exemplary artistic stewardship, the body of Christ can leave an all-too-sloppy trail for the world to follow.

We have to realize that our human love for beauty did not come into being just because we are "cultured" or civilized. It is not too much to say that God makes things beautifully, not because he took art appreciation or studied aesthetics but because it is his way of doing things. We freely choose the same word, *beautiful,* both to describe his handiwork as well as to describe what we think is the best of ours. Why? Because this deep-down search for our versions of beauty is a fundamental part of being created in his image. It is this link, no matter how scarred and confused, that counts, from the cave drawings of millennia past to Renaissance motets and on to Grandma Moses, jazz and ballet. Even though God did not create us to be slaves of his ideas and opinions, he did create us loving what he loves and calling beautiful what he calls good. Even if we say that beauty is in the eye of the beholder, we still have a world of beholders who in countless ways want to take the next step, even though it may be barely noticeable or prompt catcalls from someone supposedly more sophisticated.

In other words, beauty and quality are not static states or final conditions. In the Christian view of things, they are graduations in a long journey. As such, things of true greatness and nobility are bonded to the lesser, coarser things, and the practitioners of each are one with each other as images of God. Except for the sordid minority of aesthetic sluggards—the artistic Laodiceans of any culture or any age—quality and beauty are commonly desirable. And it is precisely because they are so desirable, even in the least of us, that they can become idols.

Beauty and quality become idols when they become intermediaries and spiritual screening devices, things that interpose themselves in the act of worshiping God through Christ, as if God were more interested in showing himself in a performance of Bach's B Minor Mass than the singing of "Majesty." For us to assume that our versions of beauty, per se, afford quicker access to God is to commit a fatal error. As mentioned in chapter two, the beauty of holiness is not aesthetic beauty, nor is aesthetic ugliness a sign of ungodliness. God sees every believer, irrespective of personal taste, exactly the same way: in Christ. It is his cleansing, rather than the quality of our art, that makes us presentable. For us to assume that raising standards is directly connected to growing up into personal holiness is to put beauty and truth back into a cause-effect relationship. But the mysterious thing about truth is that it can be deeply understood and radically applied in an aesthetically bumbling way. Likewise, falsehood can be dressed in glorious aesthetic finesse and still be falsehood.

I am slowly discovering how irrelevant artistic choice is as an interpreter of people's standing with Christ. This does not mean love for beauty has been taken from me. Rather, it means I am learning that the pursuit of holiness is of a completely different order than the pursuit of beauty, even though the latter should not be forsaken in pursuit of the former. I am always driven back to this question: is the perfume that I pour over the feet of Jesus the best I can knowingly procure, or is it something less than I am knowingly capable of offering? Notice the word "knowingly," for here is where the secret of pursuing quality lies for the authentic worshiper. When I know the artistic difference between excellence and tawdriness and I refuse this difference for one reason or another, the refusal itself is idolatrous, because it, rather than beauty, has come between me and the Savior.

We can easily make an idol out of the results we want our art to produce. Here is where artistic action and thinned-out versions of evangelization and seeker sensitivity can be such comfortable bedfellows. But I quickly add that popular art forms and careless versions of seeker sensitivity are not the only culprits. Many "fine arts Christians," the classicists, wag their fingers at the seeker-sensitive popularists without realizing that the kind of seeker sensitivity that depends on Bach and Rembrandt rather than Graham Kendrick and Thomas Kinkade is just as flawed. Why? Because in either case, effectiveness is the intermediary. The point I am trying to make is that anyone using any kind of art can compromise the gospel by choosing art primarily for the results it produces, rather than to glorify God. The final dilemma with choosing art on the basis of the audiences it draws is that once the audience is drawn they will assume an equation between what draws them and what keeps them. In this condition change of virtually any kind is impossible. Then we find another idol, that of stasis and sleepy continuity, joining up with the idol of immediacy and results. The body of Christ then finds itself incapable of undaunted creativity and faith-driven change.

Style can be a golden calf. Addiction to a style inevitably leads to a fear of variety. Are we afraid to assume that God is the Lord of continuous variety and first-day newness? "Not in my style, therefore I cannot worship" represents this particular idol. I realize that style is important. I realize further that each local assembly must make conscience-based choices about style. And I ultimately realize that no style can begin to capture the grace and glory of the Subject and Object of its expression. The foolishness of style-centered worship is exposed by the nature of God's creatorhood, namely that he does not confine himself to one vocabulary or one language. If it is true that faithful adventurousness should mark our outpouring, and if it is further true that witness is overheard worship leading to radical decisiveness, why should the Christian be so nervous about style and so obsessed with the idea that it is a crucial door opener and closer?

All the above can be boiled down into a three-part artistic dilemma that has faced the church for centuries. First, if art is beautiful, it has to be used whether it is effective or not. This is the idol of quality. Second, if art is effective, it must be used, irrespective of quality. This is the idol of effectiveness. Third, if art has worked well, don't change it. This is the idol of stasis. There is no church, large or small, rich or poor, ethnically diverse or homogeneous, that will not face one, two or all three of these dilemmas. But it usually works out that the high-culture/high-taste artists face the first idol; the church-growth/seeker-sensitivity leadership, the second; and the traditionalists, the third.

But we can ring the changes on these three dilemmas in another way. We can take the third, the idol of stasis, and apply it to any situation. When something works well and is frozen into its own continuity, we have entered idol territory through an ecclesiastically acceptable door, because we can point to this or that church and say, "Look how God is blessing. Let's change our ways to match theirs so we can expect the same." Here the idol can be described in Pauline terms as the gospel being preached in envy (Phil 1:15). Church growth by envy is only a little better than church growth by compromise, which is only a little better than church shrinkage through snobbery or stasis, because all are idols going by different names.

IDOLATRY, BABEL AND PENTECOST

Sometimes I cannot help but think that in the present confusion we face—the so-called style and culture wars—the Lord may be reintroducing us to the story of Babel. Here's what I mean. The theological dilemma of Babel lay in human beings trying to reach the heavens by themselves, through artifactual efforts and *in their way.* God knew how dangerous this was and how blind the people were to the dangers. His solution, for that time, was to confuse and scatter them. Likewise today, when we spend so much time in our ecclesiastical efforts to do the construction from culture upward instead of from kingdom downward, we too can become scattered and irreparably confused. We try this and we try that; we copy here and we "innovate" there. All the while, the Holy Spirit is in a holding pattern until we are willing to re-own the triune God as Author and Finisher.

But Babel did not last forever, nor need it persist with us. It remained for Pentecost to set things right, for Babel is inverted Pentecost and Pentecost is Babel turned right side up. It is so because God takes the initiative and does his building from his throne, at whose right hand the risen and ascended Christ is seated. I think it safe to say that at Pentecost stylistic singularity went out the window and a thousand tongues turned out not to suffice.

"Little children, keep yourselves from idols," says the sweet apostle John (1 Jn 5:21). Carved and crafted things like music and dance? Yes, sometimes. Behaviors like covetousness and pride? Yes, more than we want to admit. Legitimacies, like beauty and quality and results? Yes and yes again, for we seem to have found our own brand of holy water to bless these.

I am not bent on polemics or finger-pointing in any of these observations and questions. The subject must be, for all Christians, deeply personal and thus open only to the probing of the Holy Spirit. It is, in short, a conscience search for everyone in leadership, and no one can do another's work or take another's place in this respect. It is all too easy to look at a particular practice from the outside and form a judgment. I know from experience that when I fall into this behavior, it is about a practice that I do not personally or aesthetically approve of, rather than about the condition of heart, mind and soul with which those practices are being pursued, much less God's own way of accepting us all through Christ. For this I must repent. Yet I must continue to ask the questions and pose the dilemmas, trusting God to work mightily in each continuously outpouring heart, pleading with him to root out the idols, especially those that would cause God to say, "You cannot worship me that way or with such things."

The glorious thing about God's grace is that he can take an idol and, without destroying it, turn it into nothing in order that it can be changed into merely something to be offered back to him through Christ. If music is an idol, God can burn it clean and turn it into a faith-driven offering. If quality is an idol, he can put it in its place, thus stripping it of improper prerogative while preserving its integrity and elegance. If results are the idol, God can show us how he grows a church irrespective of the methodological and stylistic intermediaries we interpose on his behalf. In all cases the Alpha and Omega is the Lord, who is also Means and End. He alone authors and finishes, if we would just throw our idols down at his feet so that he could purge us of our deluded ideas about them and so that he could return them to their place of subordination to his sworn purpose. In this way the arts, along with beauty, quality, variety, results and even continuity, would become one in a radical newness that is always at the ready when God is enthroned over the gods.

There is a fine but absolutely clarified line between authentic and idolatrous worship. The line is not drawn by the things that we use but by what our mind and heart choose to make of them. Our prayer should always be "Search *me,* not the artifact." There is no need for God to search an artifact, for as Paul says, it is nothing, and there is no truth or falsehood in it (1 Cor 8:4; 10:19). These lie with us, and it is for us to sort them out under the guidance of the Spirit.

Before I leave this chapter, I want to be sure that I do not give the impression that there is something suspect about the love for and use of religious icons. This rich storehouse of aesthetic, tactile, visual, symbolic and catechetical objects is to be celebrated, used and continuously added to by everyone who comes to know the difference between, yet the relationship of, the uniqueness of the Savior and the artistic symbols used in his praise. I cannot begin to describe the wealth of the world of religious icons, nor do I pretend to articulate for anyone else but myself the mysterious significance that icons have. However, I do realize that a significant portion of the body of Christ remains suspicious, even condemnatory, of the world of icons. I also realize that icons can be misused.

In light of this I want to celebrate and encourage their presence and to defend and join those who craft, use and celebrate their existence. Also, I want to say that there is a difference between iconology (the making, study and faithful use of icons) and iconolatry (the dependence on and worship of them). This difference follows the spirit of this entire chapter in the distinguishing of things made and offered from things made and then worshiped. When a humanly crafted object is kept in its place as a mysterious and faithful offering (less than the One to whom it is offered, less than the truth it symbolizes and less than the one making, using and offering it), there is nothing ahead but celebration, mystery and the aesthetic imagination. But when the same thing or the same ideal gains preeminence to the point that it mediates, stands in the place of or actualizes the invisible God, then we can speak of, and must prophesy against, idolatry.

The bottom line is this: what interposes itself between the Savior and the believer? Whatever does is an idol, and I am forced back to this simple and blunt word: "You must not worship me this way." Are we wrestling ourselves free of idols? And can we pray the following words in unqualified openness?

> Search me, O God, and know my heart;
>   test me and know my thoughts.
> See if there is any wicked way in me,
>   and lead me in the way everlasting. (Ps 139:23-24)

12

THE CULTURAL EXPANSE, PART 1

REALITIES AND UNITIES

I have two objectives in this chapter. I want first to spend some time out-
lining an idea about culture that will be as uncomplicated and theologically centered as possible. In a second section, I want to think about
human creativity in a way that may help us understand a deeper unity
among what are often called high, low, classical, popular, ethnic and folk
cultures.[1] These two sections will prepare for the next chapter, in which I
want to think about contemporary culture in light of an overlooked distinction between popular culture and mass culture, along with certain
warning signs it posts to the church.

TO BE HUMAN IS TO BE CULTURAL

At base, culture is an interweaving of what people believe, what they
think up and make, and how they work through possible relationships
and distinctions between believing and making. Even if there were just
one human being, there would be a unique signature that we could call
cultural. Where there are two humans, we would have the first appearances of culture-as-community as well as the beginning trickles of diversity.[2] Then, the more the culture grows in numbers, the more it will
exhibit variety within communicable and acceptable norms. Depending

on the amount of freedom and divergence allowed, the culture-community will show its understanding of convergence and divergence, unity and variety, continuity and change. Members of different culture-communities will visit their uniqueness on one another, doing business, exchanging views, trading artifacts, intermarrying and competing, even to the point where open conflict may break out. If enough of these communities—these cultures and subcultures—align themselves under a comprehensive ethos, the result will most likely be identified as a civilization. In all cases belief and unbelief, peace and war, civility and incivility, crime and punishment, beauty and ugliness will be variously present and variously defined. All or part of the civilization might continue relatively unchanged. It might continue to mature or decay, collapse from within or be assimilated or obliterated from without. Within this vast complexity, everybody believes, everybody imagines and everybody crafts. They were created to do so. As observed in chapter one, outpouring is everywhere; it continues unabated, whether fallen or redeemed.

The fact, then, is pure: to be human is to be cultural. On this basis alone it is impossible for the body of Christ to ignore culture or to assume that to be Christian is to be above, separate from or against culture. Narrowing the discussion down a bit, the arts are not, by themselves, culture; they are simply part of its vast panorama. There is no such thing as being "cultured" or "uncultured," especially in the sense that to be "cultured" is to enjoy the higher and better things and to be "uncultured" is to grovel somewhere lower or to have no culture at all.

When I moved to the Idaho panhandle a few years ago, well-meaning friends asked me what I would do "out there for culture." I swallowed my answer for fear of being sarcastic or getting needlessly involved in a discussion as to whether culture is simply an aesthetic process or a comprehensively human reality. I knew what my friends meant: Wheaton College, suburban DuPage County and the Chicago metroplex offered me more of their kind of "culture" than Idaho would. But they were overlooking both the cultural patterns already settled within in me (which I would certainly carry to my new home) as well as the fascinating prospect of joining with the cultural differences in the inland Northwest.

In a certain respect I have come to a fuller awareness of culture in my new home than in my former digs because I am now in a place where people do not create a culture out of theories *about* culture; they simply ply their days *in* it and leave a humble but telling imprint *on* it.[3] They may know little about the Chicago Symphony Orchestra or the C. S. Lewis Collection, but their depth goes another way. They know the ways of nature, mechanisms, tools, odds and ends, and improvisation so well that cobbling something out of what lies around them is as natural as the wild grasses and daisies in their meadows. Furthermore, I now know more than ever how impoverished we can become when we fail to cross over into and learn from the ways of the others.

Above all, we cannot forget that down through the ages and within countless cultures the church has engaged in more kinds of thought and creativity and more kinds of art than any other body. That we often forget this, especially in our current folly of making artistic mountains out of creative molehills and separating styles that are siblings and common friends, is a scandal that eats into the heart of what it means to be comprehensively human and authentically Christian. It is not enough for the church to applaud cultural diversity, link arms every so often and sing about how Jesus loves all the children of the world—not when a local congregation gets agitated over something as integrative as a hymnbook and a projection screen or a praise band and a pipe organ. How can the body of Christ ever link up with the interlinguistic mystery of Pentecost, and the sovereignly aggressive work of the Holy Spirit, when we set our separated worship tables ever so blandly and monochromatically?

Being created in the image of God, then, gives us the urge to believe, the ability to think up and make, and the ability to decide how believing in and making ultimately relate to each other. These abilities must have been perfectly and grandly evident in Eden. Even so, as much as they were smeared and misdirected in the Fall, God graciously allowed something quite remarkable to remain in us. Otherwise, we would not have the stream of systems, technologies and artistic delights that come to us from every quarter of the globe. But as we saw in chapter one, our ability to believe was turned toward and surrendered to a creature, issuing in the further delusion that making something and then believing in it could be compatible. All cultures, therefore, face the question of confusing things believed and things made. Christianity, as a teacher and shepherd within any culture, offers the only solution to this confusion by restoring the distinction between revelation and creation (God's side of the issue), between truth and artifact, thus between absolutes and relativities (our side of the issue).[4] It is the singular distinction between absolutes and relativities that lends added intensity to Christ's words "Heaven and earth will pass away, but my words will never pass away" (Mt 24:35; Mk 13:31; Lk 21:33), to the psalmist's statement "Your word is firmly fixed" (Ps 119:89) and to Paul's thoughts when he showed the way out of the falsely imputed strength of idol handiwork and its bitter equation of things made and things believed (1 Cor 8). Thus the difference between a system driven by paganism and one driven by Christianity does not consist primarily in rightness or wrongness of many of the things that pass away, but in the value and power assigned (or denied) to them by that system. Even when things believed and things made appear superficially to merge or be coordinate, the Christian mind will locate the separation point and articulate it accordingly.

For example, the capitalist system is a human artifact in which an economic construct and certain ethical values can be coordinated without being equated. There is no way that capitalism can be called Christian any more than, say, an ethically driven socialist system can be called non-Christian. The alert Christian mind will not succumb to the idea that capitalism is *the* Christian system and all others sub- or anti-Christian, but will forge a biblically derived distinction between *any* such system and what is believed and trusted in. It will verify the system only when its workings conjoin with ethical uprightness. It will (or should) prophesy against it when it is practiced at the expense of the well-being of a single human soul or the violation of the smallest particle of truth. By contrast, those who applaud capitalism as a Christian system have paganized their thought because they have forged an artificial link between things believed and things made.

So we begin with the omnipresence of culture and its multiplied children. And invigorated by the biblical authority to keep belief and artifact separate, we continue with the assurance that artifacts that come from alien systems may be freely used, appreciated and turned to the glory of God. We posit this on his commonly meted grace that allows those who do not believe in him to make beautiful and useful things. Just as God's handiwork is an inexhaustible storehouse of variety, so is ours. And just as it remains beautiful while hurting and groaning, so does ours. Earthquakes, famines and inexpressibly beautiful creatures rub shoulders in his created domain as do wars, rapes and Taj Mahals in ours. It is within culture that we live and move, even as we have our being in the Creator of heaven and earth. Just as he exults and weeps over his handiwork—his "culture," if you will—so do we in our broken yet cherished state.

What then does all this say to the church? As stated earlier, it means that the church is a cultural body in a unique sense of the word. As to artistic action, it means one Christ and thousands of artistic tongues, each of which can be given over to his praise. It means that they can be kept as they are or changed, merged and transformed. It also means its art can take on a vocabulary so noticeably different that it quite literally comes to belong to the church. Gothic architecture, whether found in Chartres or Manhattan, belongs to the church. Taizé chant, whether sung in Lyons or Des Moines, belongs to the church. Anglican chant, chorale preludes, black and white gospel, liturgical vestments and praise and worship music have come to belong to the church. The list could go on, but only to extend the point that throughout church history, artifacts and beliefs have so consistently and faithfully companied with each other *in the environments of worship* that the first response is "These are of the church."

This next point is crucial. The question for the church is not one of culture or no culture but one of a liberated and authoritative *engagement* with culture, in what it means to be human, to be redeemed and to think up and make art *that would not have otherwise come to being in that way.* The italicized words are important because they support two realities at once. First, making things differently is a normal outcome of all creative people everywhere. Second, when making things differently occurs consistently in the same context(s) and settles into an identifiable body of work, the work will take on the identity of that context. It is this wonder of *things that would not have otherwise happened there in that way* that marks the artistic imprint of a vigorous Christianity on culture. And making this kind of difference is far more significant than trying to conjure up a definition of Christian art.

The near paradox of having a Christian worldview and making art on that basis, yet understanding that the art on its own is incapable of fully communicating that worldview, is of such magnitude as to call every Christian artist to fearless and liberated creativity. Only then can the church engage with culture, making use of its best efforts even while turning these into a new song. It is in this way that the church and general culture can engage in direct artistic conversation on the simple basis of differentiated creativity, even while in profound conflict over the lordship of Christ and the distinction between things believed (in) and things made. The church separates itself out to God alone by faith alone, while both serving him and enriching the world with its best efforts. Thus, while the body of Christ is pouring perfume over the feet of the Savior, it simultaneously washes the feet, feeds the mouths and enriches the minds of a soiled and ravaged culture.

Of course, there are those who say that Western art would not be what it is without Christianity. And this is true, but only up to a point. What we might too quickly attribute to Christianity in a special-grace sense might just as easily be attributed to or combined with a generous outflow of common grace. Thus, instead of creating a too-direct linkage between Christianity and the flowering of Western culture, we could say that God's goodness in allowing it to flourish should have led to even more excellence and uprightness than has been the case. Should this be true, Western culture is even more accountable to God for having refused the fullness of this open provision than for having taken advantage of it. In any case, it is presumptuous to assume, for instance, that as Westerners communicate the gospel to another culture, they should insist that Western art forms be imposed on the receiving culture as an inseparable part of the gospel.

Once a culture is transformed by Christ, its artistic dialects and processes can remain as they are even while bearing new fruit. The changes that might occur—radical or ordinary—will then come from within. No one should expect another culture to change its art into "our art" but instead to continue to generate its own authentic "heart song." This is because a culture's creative signature is unique and inherently dignified. "You shall love your neighbor as yourself" is the dayspring for engaging in and appreciating anything about the artifacts of another culture. Unfortunately there is a dark side to cultural diversity—loving a people's artifacts more than the people themselves, or rejecting them because we are prejudiced against the people who make them. But those who see clearly and cleanly should not be troubled in the least by new Christians in a remote African tribe, for example, making full use of their indigenous musical signatures to craft new songs to the Savior.

This is how Christians must understand culture. We need the analysts, the theorists, the ethnomusicologists, the anthropologists and the philosophers. They must do their research; they must think through immensely complex interrelationships and create appropriate taxonomies. But those who think Christianly will eventually intuit some kind of deep structure by which human creativity relentlessly knits to itself, and in spite of remarkable differences, they will admit to an undimmed beacon that lights up the God-authored union that only theology can explain: *imago Dei*. At this point—this anthropological big bang—all human science confesses to its finitude, signs off and gives itself over to faith.

I want to look at the role of the Christian artist in church and culture one more way before going to the next section. Amid all the variety and rich artistic opportunity that exist both in the church and in general culture, there are only two ways Christian artists can make art. The first is in the context of corporate worship. Here the arts are to be sworn to humble service. They are to be hidden behind the Word and the sacraments and are to be dedicated to function on behalf of their increase. I think of the parallel between this and the words of John the Baptist in relating his work to the Savior's: "He must increase, but I must decrease" (Jn 3:30). This principle of submission and self-emptying must likewise mark all artistic action in corporate worship. To be sure, there may be times in the life of the local assembly when the arts can be celebrated more noticeably and separately, but these are the exception, not the rule. Christian artists in direct service to the corporate assembly must understand from the start that the arts must function differently here than in any other circumstance, and this takes an enormous amount of creative humility, skill and wisdom.[5] It is in this sense that all churches—small or large, rich or poor, highly talented or less talented—cannot afford to see themselves as fine arts organizations.

The second role of Christian artists lies in the wide world of general culture. Here it is their responsibility to engage culture in a no-holds-barred continuum of creative action. I like to think of the Christian artist in general culture as a redeemed invader or (more gently) as artist-in-residence, a citizen of heaven and a continuous outpourer visiting the archives of culture, calling to account and influencing every artistic protocol. This should mean that among the best of them, the work of certain ones will shatter current boundaries and be radically path-breaking. It may mean that others will take up the strain of a current style and bring it to finer flower. And among those of us with lesser talents (there is no shame in this), it may mean that they will perform their art almost anonymously, making their way in life through the common vocabularies of commerce and trade. In all cases there is but one spiritual task: making sure that there are no tainted drops in the artistic perfume poured on Jesus' feet. "All of my art is Christian" is a far less important statement than "All of my art is offered up because I am a Christian."

All artistic action for the Christian can be summed up in these two ways. However, as distinct as they might be, they are unified by a common theological thread that must be articulated by everyone in leadership. It is this: authentic Christianity means authentic worship. Christians are living epistles, whatever their calling and trade. Christians who make art must therefore make it Christianly, wherever they make it, from the most artistically impoverished assembly to the most richly appointed venue. Artistic action is first of all authored before God by faith and joins all actions in authentic worship. It can have no higher value than this. Whatever its station or condition, it strives to become better than it was, to be fearless in its newness and humble in its service.

THE CREATIVE SPECTRUM

Artistic culture is a vast expanse. Deep within its workings, it is also seamless, even in the face of vivid differences between, say, grunge rock and Renaissance motets or street rap and Milton's poetry. It is especially important for Christians to see it this way, because this is surely the way God sees it. Just as he is no respecter of persons, so he is no respecter of styles. He does not love the Baroque artifactual signature any more than that of the South Pacific Rim. Nor would he prefer, if he were a dancer, the polka over the hora. He is Lord of diversity, Creator of the human imagination and Master of every one of its artistic ways. His lines of demarcation are based on faith or its absence, authentic worship or inauthentic worship. His call to excellence is based on how we are becoming better than we were yesterday more than how we place in a static aesthetic hierarchy. A Bach cantata is no more a musical password into his favor than a Zulu harvest song or an Indian raga. When the Scriptures call out to the nations to rejoice, they do not call for an artistic Esperanto, a colorless and hypothetical language, a test-tube Pentecost. Nor do they call out to a panel of artistic experts to determine what might please the King of kings. They call out to the many cultures to use their instruments, their tongues, their shapes, textures and gestures, their vivid twists and turns. God is happy with the plethora. He loves its faith-driven clamor and hilarious tintinnabulation. It comes to him from everywhere and from all times, translated into eternal speech by the blessed Paraclete, in whom groans, mutterings, silence, singing, dancing, shaping, masterpieces and pastiches make up a transfigured jubilee.

It is only a secular or paganized culture that chooses to divide people on the basis of their artistic preferences and choices. It is a spiritually connected culture that takes cultural differences, works through the tensions that they may create and comes to the blessed condition of mixing and reconciling them and of stewarding their increase and growth. It is therefore not amusing to hear about how we are to embrace the poor, eat and drink with sinners and cross racial and ethnic lines, only to find out that leadership, back home in the safety of the local fortress, is afraid to do the analogous kind of embracing when it comes to the arts and to the commingling of their styles. "Not in my style" may really and truly mean "Not my kind of people," except when it comes time for the yearly youth group trip to Mexico or the occasional spade turnings for another habitat. Why do we go outside the church to diversify when we fail to do so within it?

So let us assume that we can find other analytical paths. Let us agree, at least for the remainder of this chapter, that it is every Christian's responsibility to participate in the cultural tapestry as widely as possible and to use the full extent of our minds, our hearts and our intentions. Let us further agree that different kinds of art "work" for us in different ways and that, as we make our way through the tapestry, we can perceive and react one way to one kind of art and another way to another and be fully satisfied with the fact that our neighbor may see it the other way around.

Thus, instead of the somewhat divisive classifications like popular and classical, high culture and low culture, we can engage with artistic content—all of it—as a series of pairings: shallow to deep, simple to complex, strange to familiar, ornamental/variational to developmental, and entertaining to engaging. We must see every term in these classifications as neutral, each a point in a seamless continuity. Each is flexible and easily capable of crossing from one grouping to another. We can now look briefly at each pairing.

Shallow to deep. Water can run both shallow and deep. At any level it can be clean; it can quench thirst, wash and nurture life around it. It is always water. Similarly, some art is shallow and some is deep and either kind can be of extremely high quality. There is a lot of classical music that is of the highest quality but is shallow; it is not meant to take us down to intellectual or emotional depth but to engage us lightly, even whimsically. Deep art, whatever its medium or style, works differently; it takes us into the furthest reaches of soul and intellect and causes us to engage in the wonder of existence with comprehensive perception and understanding. A Haydn fast movement is shallow in its intended effect on the listener, yet Haydn may have had to think deeply to pull its lightness off. In another respect, I might emote deeply over a shallow painting, or I may react shallowly to a deep one. A piece of art can be intellectually shallow yet deeply moving, or it can be emotionally shallow but intellectually complex. It is easy to confuse emotional depth with complete depth, especially when the emotion is sorrowful and grave. But this is but half the picture. Deep joy becomes nearly inexpressible compared to the shallowness of a time of laughter or fun. To repeat the point again, the spectrum of shallow to deep in its many artistic iterations is a healthy spectrum, to be engaged in fully if we want to experience artistic action to the full.

Simple to complex. Paul McCartney's tune "Yesterday" is eloquently simple, and the last movement of Beethoven's Ninth Symphony is complex, yet both are fine works of art. The pyramids are simple, while the Taj Mahal is complex, but each has a quality and thoroughness that cannot be denied. A Vermeer canvas is exceedingly complex, but a Grandma

Moses painting is simple. Shaker furniture is simple and Baroque cabinetry is complex. Pennsylvania Dutch hex signs are simple and Islamic design patterns are complex. And so on. In each case the simplicity or complexity is not a measure of quality. And there is one more aspect to the simple-complex spectrum: complexity is not just a busier version of simplicity but a deepening of it. The solar system, in this sense, is simple; the Milky Way, complex.

But here's where things get wonderfully tangled. Even though complexity is a deepening of simplicity, true simplicity is often the most difficult thing to explain. "Yesterday" is mysteriously simple. In a way that surpasses analysis, this tune cannot be explained. How do I explain a buttercup? How do physicists explain the most elemental particles, the simple building blocks, even though they can do pretty well at explaining the makeup of a galaxy? To those truly interested in the interplay—the teasing, even—between simple and complex, a singular depth becomes apparent in each; each calls out for the other and neither one can be neglected. As for the arts, the simplicities of a Matisse line drawing or a Delta blues song contain their own questions: Why? How? Yet we cannot stop with the simplicities. Even though they defy explanation, they are not enough. Just as deep cries out to deep, so complexity cries out for complexity, and we must participate in the cry.

Strange to familiar. Despite the vivid contrast between these two words, they too comprise a continuum. Something may be vaguely familiar or somewhat strange. Even the most familiar things—a wife's kiss or a rose's fragrance—are at once near and far, expected and mystifying. Likewise with art. For a Westerner, Tibetan chant is strange. For the Tibetan, a Bach fugue is strange. For that matter, a Bach fugue might be strange to a twenty-first-century German raised on heavy metal. For some people, abstract art is strange and representational art is familiar, yet for someone for whom art is a tangible way of seeing unseen things, abstraction is familiar and representation, if not strange in one sense, is estranging in another. A sonnet can be strange and a limerick familiar, or the reverse. The King James Version of the Bible now seems strange to a vast majority of Westerners, and the Living Bible familiar, yet the more familiar might be a stranger approach to translation.

To a person who lives by faith, the strange and the familiar can freely exchange places. Something repeated hundreds of times in worship may suddenly take on a holy strangeness, as if it had never been said or sung before. A completely new thing may appear as familiar and normal as a noonday sun because the circumstance of faith puts it at ease.

Ornamental/variational to developmental. This is an interesting continuum because it easily links with shallowness and depth, especially in the intellectual sense. Most popular, primitive and folk art is ornamental or variational. Jazz, for example, subsists on the act of improvising a certain number of variations on a set theme, or tune, almost always in a set form. The soloist ornaments and decorates the harmonic changes and the tune with as much imagination as possible while the rhythm section and other instrumentalists lay out the common boundaries of the tune and chord changes. The form is left rigidly intact throughout the performance. By contrast, much of classical music and art, while certainly employing variational and ornamental processes, goes further into the actual development of primary and subsidiary material, even to the extent that it may undergo complete change or metamorphosis. Motivic snippets and germinal ideas are often all that the composer needs to construct a complex shape, whereas popular and folk forms almost always demand a closed form and a complete tune. In the visual arts the developmental frame of reference in a Rembrandt or Monet is amazingly complex and structurally organic, whereas much of so-called folk or primitive art concerns itself more with pattern, ornamentation, variation and repeated design.

The more developmental and metamorphic the artistic process, the more intellectual work it takes both to create and to understand the work. In fact, it can be argued that the more extensive art and musical works in Western classicism are equivalent in intellectual complexity and overall structural precision and delicacy to the most sophisticated architectural and engineering efforts, say, the Golden Gate Bridge or the Chrysler Building.

Entertaining to engaging. It is here that I come to the defense of entertainment. Rather than being something in itself, decried by some and defended by others, it too is part of a continuum. I can take a deep piece of music, say, Prokofiev's Piano Concerto No. III, and simply let it wash over me—entertain me with its sensuous colors, its vivifying rhythms and instrumental virtuosity. I need know or think little about its complexities to thoroughly enjoy it. Or I can engage with it at a high intellectual level, tackling its parts and processes and, in a real sense, putting it together for myself as it makes its way, note by note, into my mind. On the other hand, I can take "Yesterday" and, as simple as it is, engage with it at a deep socio-musical level, making connections between it and Rachmaninoff, English folk music and analysis of contemporaneous British popular music. In this sense it no longer entertains but engages.

Entertainment is dangerous only when it becomes the exclusive thing, cutting itself away from any linkage with active engagement. However, popular art forms are meant more to entertain (in the most legitimate sense) than engage. The information pool in them is not as great as in the classical arts. Consequently the consumer can take them in and hold them close with minimum intellectual or technical knowledge. This is why they are popular. Do not forget that in the beginning of these remarks I noted that the various components of a given continuum are value-neutral. Thus for me to say that less intellectual effort is needed in one instance than another is not to say that one is a downgraded version of the other. To put it another way, popular art can be good or bad, just as classical art can. Intellectual content may be deep but ethically flawed, while popular wisdom can turn a heart and mind in exactly the right direction.

THE COMPLETE ARTISTIC DIET

One final matter deserves mention. The first pairing—shallow to deep—can be used as a master key to the remaining pairings, as follows. Shallow, simple, familiar, ornamental/variational and entertaining are all inherently linked, as are their companions at the other end of the spectrum. And here is where we need to make a qualitative distinction without undoing the original idea of neutrality among the various components of the pairings. All along I have avoided saying that shallow, for instance, is bad and depth, good. Avoiding this, however, does not mean that we duck the idea of progression or increasing value. So while we can say that shallowness can truly be good, we can say that increasing depth (or complexity or strangeness or development or engagement) is better. This follows the scriptural model of milk and meat. Each is good, each is necessary, each is wholesome and life giving, but one is the necessary outgrowth of the other. In this way we can insist that depth is to be eventually preferred over shallowness, strangeness over familiarity, complexity over simplicity and the like. Now here is where a full understanding of the entire group of pairings brings balance and relief: just because I am eventually urged and able to engage with depth does not mean that I must avoid or should no longer enjoy shallowness. On the contrary, each remains a part of my "diet" in the same sense that I can drink milk even as I chew meat. Paradoxically, I will then be able to drink my milk and chew it too, because my eating meat brings new depth to drinking milk. That is, if I delve into the complex meat of Romans 7 and 8 or Hebrews 11 and 12, I will find that the simple milk of "Jesus Loves Me" will begin to taste like meat.

Finally, here is the most crucial aspect to the entire concept. *Those who claim to be followers of Jesus Christ are intellectually and artistically incomplete until they engage as fully as possible in every combination represented in the spectrum.* We must explore the full range of human creativity, avoiding perpetual shallowness, not so that we can say we are cultured but because we are fully human and desire to be linked with the breadth and extent of human creativity. Remember, I am not just talking about artistic engagement in the context of corporate worship, for this context has a legitimate constraint that may prevent certain kinds of complexity or depth or strangeness to be presented. Rather, I am talking about what it means to live and move as continuous outpourers, throughout the entire range of human work, human creativity and human achievement.

Being completely and authentically Christian is a profound undertaking, a discipline of magnificent proportion and complexity. It takes every second of redeemed time and every ounce of redeemed strength. It is a welcome and winsome mix of work, rest and celebration. It is a God-authored consortium of things believed and things made. And in God's plan it is a life of continuous worship and perpetual offering.

13

THE CULTURAL EXPANSE, PART 2

ISSUES

In the last chapter I attempted to dissolve the question of cultural boundaries in the arts into a more useful matrix of procedural and perceptual connections. We can now deal with two aspects of general culture that superficially appear to be linked but in reality are quite separate: popular culture and mass culture. The distinction between the two is far greater than the older ones of popular and classical culture or low and high culture. It is important for the church to understand this distinction in that its present perspectives and practices may be more directly linked to those of mass culture than to the particularities of any one subset.[1]

It is no new thing to speak of popular culture as the predominant culture. Nor is it especially surprising to say that popular culture is influencing ecclesiastical culture as much or more than at any other time in church history. Furthermore, the *things* of popular culture should not be particularly troublesome in themselves. It is not enough to condemn these for their tendencies to gratify quickly and to entertain or for passing into and out of fashion. As we have already seen, shallowness, ornamentation, simplicity, familiarity and entertainment—as parts of the creative spectrum—are both useful and necessary.

Historically, popular, ethnic and classical cultures, along with the elements in the creative spectrum, have made use of and influenced each other's practices and in many respects comfortably exchanged places. But these connections may no longer exist. Something disruptive and unhealthy is at work. I call this mass culture, or better yet, the massification of culture.

What is mass culture? More than a body of interconnected techniques and things, mass culture is an overriding spirit, an ethos, that overcomes and subsumes this body of work, suppressing both distinctions and relationships and imposing a false unity that derives out of a combination of at least the following: experientialism, self-enclosed shallowness, massive relativism and the degradation of language. I want to deal with these as they relate to the burden of this book.

MASS CULTURE AND EXPERIENTIALISM

We live in an experience-driven culture. What do I mean by that?

A true experience can be described in multiple ways and from different perspectives. For example, to have a culinary experience in the fullest sense is to experience something beyond the aesthetic and sensory pleasure of an expertly prepared and presented meal. It means participating in the manifold history, richness and diversity of the higher things that a culture offers. But we could forgo this and simply experience a short-lived and self-enclosed sensation. This too is an experience, but it is not nearly as complete. It is merely a feeling that comes of having eaten and enjoyed the taste.

If we extend this example into all the experiences we have, and if each is short-lived and self-enclosed, we are coming close to the idea of what it means to live in an experience-driven culture. But there is one more step that closes the gap: short-lived and self-enclosed experiences are described exclusively in exaggerated feelings and emotions—awesome, miraculous, great, outstanding, unique, hellish, the pits. This is what I call *experientialism*: short-lived, self-enclosed, hyperbolized immediacies and satisfactions that fuel a worldview.

In the world of commerce, experientialism is transposed into the mechanisms of consumerism—advertising and selling by creating immediacies and promising satisfaction. In our church life, we often talk of providing worship "experiences," reduced further into descriptions of worship moods or worship attitudes. If we are not careful, we can divert doctrine into expressivism and meeting "felt needs."

This issue of experientialism brings us back once again to the subject of the arts and arts-related environments. In an experientialist culture the usefulness of the arts is posited far more on how they feel than on what they substantively are. This is not limited to the popular art forms. It does not matter whether there is a significant intellectual expenditure on the part of the artist or performer, for there is no desire on the part of the consumer to engage that way. After all, art is feeling; its ability to bring emotional satisfaction becomes its sole justification. We can end up saying something like this: "Art makes me feel a certain way, and if it doesn't, then it's not a part of my experience." The upshot is that "experience," in its shallowness, preempts experience in its depth and fullness.

Mass Culture and Self-Enclosed Shallowness

Self-enclosed shallowness and experientialism go hand in hand. This kind of shallowness is markedly different from the shallowness of a bona fide popular culture or, for that matter, classical and ethnic cultures. In the previous chapter I said that shallowness (or simplicity or ornamentation and so on) is fine in itself, but I went on to say that, given the rich spectrum of human creativity, it is not enough. A culture that goes deep welcomes the kinship that simple and complex, ornamental and developmental have with each other. But the shallowness of contemporary mass culture is another matter. This kind becomes and remains its own self-enclosed singularity. Transiency, trendiness and fast change become their own ends; they serve as stand-ins for wholeness, excursions into depth and maturity. They lead nowhere and turn back on themselves.

As implied earlier, mass culture does not limit itself to popular art forms. The classics are taken in, but only in a way that accords with the dictates of experientialism and self-enclosed satisfaction. Pachelbel's Canon or Bach's "Jesu, Joy of Man's Desiring," for instance, join the parade without leading to any inquiry into all of Pachelbel's or Bach's work and their connections to the rich weave of Baroque music and their influence on later music. The Three Tenors, for instance, thrive more on the attractiveness of personal charisma and vocal skill than on stimulating a continuing engagement at the deepest level with classical music. The so-called Mozart effect on human intelligence lends a side-door legitimacy to classical music, but it is more about increasing learning skills and getting better grades than deepening musical intelligence. Periodic and highly advertised art exhibits—the Monet Exhibit Syndrome—do little to return the culture to a serious and continued engagement with fine art. It is an experience with high art, yes, but only a passing one, with long lines of people whisked past a lifetime of magnificent artworks, each one deserving extended periods of deep engagement. These are examples of so-called cultural experiences without any change in the culture, any reopening of the wonderful conversations and deepening engagement with all art forms. It is in this sense that mass culture is neither highbrow nor lowbrow but, in the words of a current author, "nobrow."[2] What we end up with is an embarrassingly kitschy seriousness and self-remarkability existing at catchword depth and subsisting on a personality-ridden, almost cultic sacramentalism. Hence the tragedy lies not only in the exile of depth but also in the absence of an intellectual, aesthetic and moral highway between it and the massive, self-enhancing and self-congratulating culture.

MASS CULTURE AND MASSIVE RELATIVISM

Mass culture no longer acknowledges a moral or truth center. It may be aware of it, thanks to the Judeo-Christian witness that still survives in the church and here and there in society. But knowing *of* truth and *knowing* it as culture's operating center are two different things. Even where moral causes are articulated, they are most often unrelated to other moral causes. We live among a bewildering mix of single-issue moral groups, few of which articulate their cause out of an integrated worldview in which morality is a comprehensive reality. Thus it is no longer noteworthy that a majority of the culture is more interested in saving whales or spotted owls than saving babies in the womb. Even among right-to-life Christians there is little emphasis on articulating a comprehensive worldview that not only takes in the right-to-life issue but encloses it within a grand scheme that imprints its ethical wholeness on the whole of culture. Thus conservative Christians are known more for being right-to-lifers than for being followers of a risen Christ who embrace a totality of goodness while rejecting a totality of wrongdoing.

I do not want to get caught up in the usual catchwords for the condition we are in, dismissing the whole as "postmodernist" and "deconstructionist." I am not sufficiently skilled to probe these two phenomena to map out a scheme that separates chicken from egg and impression from fact. And while I do not wish to evade the subtleties of postmodernism and deconstruction, and while I understand that there are useful elements in each, I believe I can safely say that massive relativism finds safe haven in their systems.

It is one thing to question massive relativism philosophically; it is another to acquire the intellectual stamina and prophetic outspokenness to do so Christianly. For the Christian, intellectual stamina is truth guided and faith related. It is that which is responsible for the careful construction and living out of a worldview that, at every turn, reflects moral judgment and spiritual insight. It is the kind of stamina that is virtually absent in the culture of experientialism and self-enclosed shallowness. But it is this very stamina that should mark the life of the church and force the question that Romans 12:1-2 raises: To what extent are living sacrifices transformed or conformed? Everyone in leadership in the church must examine the entire construct of corporate and personal living to find out where massive relativism, self-enclosed shallowness and experientialism have become normal enough to be spiritualized. As to relativism, we all know that it will not be found in what I called policy theology in an earlier chapter but instead in operational theology—the workaday schemes and constructs that drive the week-to-week life of the church. It will be found in the presence or absence of a distinction between what the citizens of mass culture want and what they need. The question to artists and ministers of worship is directly related to the extent to which they discern the difference between experience and experientialism, between shallowness and depth, including the neglect of depth and the kind of relativism that backs away from making artistic value judgments for fear of insulting or losing someone.

THE DEGRADATION OF LANGUAGE

We are all guilty of degrading language to one degree or another. This could not take place in our culture to the extent that it does unless other degradations accompanied it, for language usage should carry with it the profound moral imperatives of temperance, precision, eloquence, clarity and, above all, truth telling. If a moral imperative is absent, then our speech, including propositional truth-speech, will be degraded, if not trashed.

I was watching one of the educational channels and happened upon a documentary about a detachment of British soldiers who were captured by the Germans in World War II and subjected to the worst possible torture and deprivation. As a part of this documentary, several survivors, now old men, were interviewed. The typical question, "How did it feel to be liberated?" was asked of one of them. I was moved by the answer. Instead of the usual "It felt awesome/incredible/unbelievable," this quiet and wearied veteran simply said, "I had a pleasant feeling." That was it. I heard a common man, a good man, hold the magnificence of the English language in reserve for things that would transcend even his extraordinary situation. Some people would call this typical British understatement. I would call it wisdom coupled to temperance and humility. I would also call it clarifying truthfulness, the kind that rides free of superlatives and exaggeration, keeping the one for transcendence and refusing the other in the name of accuracy.

Mass culture is a culture that has lost this kind of love and respect for its language. It is a culture marked by the demise of a reverence for words and for their careful placement within an idea and its articulation. This demise cannot be fully understood without the recognition that the loss of a truth center allows us to use words not only untruthfully but also with carelessness and little thought of accountability. Between politics (for which language is situationally adjusted), the advertising industry (for which language is the instrument of exaggeration) and moral relativism (for which language is its deconstructed lackey), there is virtually no forum in which a consistent working respect for this fragile but central medium is in evidence. Everything that rises above a mere scratch on the experiential surface—everything from a pizza to an orgasm to God—is awesome, incredible, unique, spectacular, excellent, great. No words are left to express magnificence without resorting to the same words with which we have described the commonplace. On the other end of the spectrum, virtually everything from striking out in a Little League game to not getting

into Yale is the pits, a bummer, horrible, it sucks, I went through hell yesterday. These verbal toss-aways are pimpled with as many "O my gods" as
can be worked into the rest of the words.

There is a direct connection between an experientialist culture and the
degradation of language. In addition to using superlative language to describe ordinary experiences, we are just as liable to say that there are no
words to describe them. The problem is not with the insufficiency of language but with insufficient attention to its expressive potential. We have
become linguistically lazy and experientially overworked. This degradation is furthered by those who say that language can be bettered at its own
task through nonverbal languages and other forms of expressions that "express what words cannot." The irony of this is that the proponents must
always resort to words to show what the nonverbal languages are "saying."
This is not only arrogant but also intellectually silly. Even though it is true
that every kind of nonverbal expression possesses uniqueness, it is likewise true that no form of nonverbal expression can do what words can do.
A jazz riff can no more articulate a methodology for day trading than a
Bach fugue can explain substitutionary atonement. So every form of nonverbal expression, instead of going beyond what words can do, simply
goes its own way, just as words go their way in doing what no other form
of expression can do. And since truth is the most important thing that we
can articulate, and since words are a better vehicle for this than any other
existing form of expression, the word remains preeminent among all other
forms.

I believe there is a form of profanity that goes beyond our everyday definitions of it. It is taking language itself in vain, which is second only to taking
the Lord's name in vain. Empty speech is vain repetition; exaggerated speech
is vain repetition; imprecise and sloppily crafted speech is vain repetition.
The words that God emptied his truth into are also my daily words for my
daily affairs. Do I value them so intently that his Word is not robbed of its
richness because of my tawdry appropriation and vain use of words?

To what extent do we Christians pledge ourselves to forsake verbal
worldliness—taking language in vain—and discipline ourselves so thoroughly as to be able to go into every catechetical and creedal corner and
every societal setting to articulate, eloquently and precisely, what it means

to explore the full counsel of God and articulate this to a culture that has lost itself in meaninglessness? With what quality of thought and speech do we craft and deliver our public prayers, our sermons, teachings and public witness? To what degree has the "old tradition of the fullness of prose," as George Steiner puts it, been forsaken in preaching, teaching, mentoring and praying?[3] This need not mean inflated, complicated or out-of-date rhetoric as much as richness, range, comprehension, and temperate and timely word choices. It means emulating the styles of the great prayer books, the great sermon writers and religious thinkers. This of course means reading and absorbing them, so as to emulate and add to their richness. It means learning to think and speak in these ways, however stumbling they may at first be. It means the careful and continual nurture of this fragile treasure called language, beautiful in its stewardship and sickly in its neglect. For language is only as eloquent and meaning-full as its users can make it, and the users who have committed themselves to the deepest and most passionate continuous outpouring may be the last bastion for excellence in this culture.

Language can be turned toward truth only by truthful people. It can be treasured only by treasuring people. There is a deep-rooted reason why we are assigned the privilege of cherishing language and keeping it aligned with every possible dimension of truth. The fundamental reason is *imago Dei*. There are those two words again, reminding us in yet another way of our uniqueness and our God-infused responsibilities. Just as God, in revealing himself in words through the prophets, took poetry, wisdom and proposition to its fullness, so must we. Just as God saw to it that the incarnate Word, in the full eloquence of his life, fulfilled every jot and tittle of the written Word, so must we. We are living epistles, responsible to match deed and word. The richness and eloquence of the one must be matched by the other.

I cannot insist enough on the strategic importance of a speech-rich church to a speech-degraded culture. The church is, after all, a rich cross section of civilization: mothers, fathers, farmers, technicians, scientists, teachers, lawyers and artisans. No one is excused from the responsibility to speak carefully, temperately, accurately, even poetically. For the authentic worshiper, nothing but God is awesome. Only Christ went through hell last week. Only the most holy moment (for the Christian this can mean any moment) justifies the honor of saying, "My God."

As we make our way through these dilemmas—experientialism, self-enclosed shallowness, the forsaking of a truth center and the degradation of language—it is not difficult to see how one feeds another. Nor is it difficult to see how they can steal into the body of Christ and ever so subtly rob the gospel of its pointedness, its sufficiency for every human condition and its need for precise, temperate and rich speech.

To conclude, I would ask that all leaders examine these four issues in an attempt to ascertain the extent to which they may be affecting their various ministries. Has the fullness of what it means to experience God in Christ been turned into short-lived and self-enclosed experiences? Or does experiencing God mean taking in his fullness, learning the full extent of his gospel and, through it, summoning all of life's circumstances into its scrutiny? Is the spiritual and intellectual depth to which all Christians are called turning into self-enclosed shallowness? Is the loss of a truth center in culture in some way, however subtly, drawing us into a thinning out or obfuscation of the ruthless glory of gospel truth? And are we doing everything in our power to rescue our language and to see rich, precise, authoritative and temperate use of it, not for linguistic or aesthetic reasons, but because the magnificent reach of the gospel demands it?

Excellence

14

WHAT OF QUALITY?

Any serious discussion of the arts inevitably turns to the subject of quality. When quality is perceived to be present, both art and artist are vindicated. When it is thought absent, agitation and scorn darken the discussion. Furthermore, quality questions do not exist just between artist and laypersons. Some of the bitterest invective about quality has been generated by artists about other artists. In fact, since questions of quality about great art, good art and bad art are raised within artistic practice itself, this might suggest that art itself has no inherent quality control system. That is, art itself does not necessarily provide its own aesthetic salvation. This suggests that questions about quality transcend art itself and reach out into all of life. Thus, beyond the narrow question of art and aesthetics, there is the more pressing issue of life itself and living aesthetically, living qualitatively.

For the Christian, the issue of quality turns out to be not merely artistic but theological. I want to believe that just as there are specific qualitative acts called the arts, so there is a qualitative dimension to the whole of living that transcends the word *art*. I want to insist that making art and doing everything as artistically as possible are literally one with each other. Here is a simple way to state this: Excellence, the lifelong process of becoming better than I was yesterday, must be the normal condition for the exercise of stewardship. Good stewardship comprises the entirety, not just parts, of my living. I am called to a life of continuous outpouring; therefore excellence, good stewardship and authentic worship are bonded in such a way as to bring everything I do under common scrutiny and, if need be, judgment. Only then can the arts be brought under similar scrutiny.

So what do we do? How do we go about the pursuit of quality when there are so many conflicting opinions about its necessity or irrelevance? How can we combine sincere aesthetic thought with biblical thought? Better yet, is there a Christian aesthetic that goes beyond Christianizing classical aesthetics? Is there a way to view the wide range of artistic practice with something more than art in mind? I believe there is, and I want to make a beginning attempt at it. Above all, I continue to insist that the issue of quality cannot be lightly treated by the Christian. And I must say that within my own life—an ordinary life as far as intellect, creativity and artistry go—the issue of quality burns brighter and brighter. If continuous outpouring and authentic worship are to remain the primary themes, and if they are the essence of what it means to be alive, then the issue of quality must take root in them long before it becomes an exclusive artistic issue. I want, therefore, to turn to that essential triad of love, faith and hope and make a case for quality within their conditions.

LOVE AND QUALITY

Love is unconditional. Love loves everything except evil. The love of neighbor takes in everything about that neighbor. The only kind of selective love that has any sanctity is marital love. But selective love of this kind only goes so far—only as far as the beginning fact of courtship and the continuing circumstances of marriage. It applies to two people at a time as they continue to choose each other, ethically and lovingly, for as long as they have life. But even in the best possible marriage, this turns out to be insufficient. My love for my wife and hers for me are brought to their highest heights by the transformation of selective love into neighborly love. Selectivity is metamorphosed into all-preceding love by which I am to conduct all of my affairs on this earth. This all-preceding love is love of neighbor. My wife, beyond being one with me, becomes my neighbor. This both remakes my love for her and elevates my concept of my neighbor, both of whom I now select comprehensively and unconditionally.[1]

What am I getting at? This fact comes immediately to mind: 99.99 percent of humankind honestly loves what we call the arts. Forget for a while artistic types, quality and functions, and just think widely of the arts as human actions deriving out of aesthetic imagination. Think next of responses to the arts. Do not allow yourself to qualify this thought with any aesthetic paraphernalia, personal bias or cultural criticism. Just let the fact remain that people love art, make art and respond to all kinds of it because they love it. It is this kind of love that we as trained artists must recognize and preserve no matter how much we believe and teach that this love can be deepened and enriched. This common love of art may also be absent in trained artists, many of whom have been made unsure of what to love for fear of being criticized or have been taught to loathe what others love. Neighbor love of art has been reduced to and overcome by selective love. It is difficult for these artists to love what they do not like, to like people who do not love what they like and to love art simply because it is art, even if it is, by the most compassionate standards, bad art.

Here is an analogous mystery: Not all people are physically beautiful. Some of us are downright ugly, but people fall in love with us anyway, don't they? We may whisper over our coffee that we cannot figure out what this person sees in that person, yet they are giddy with love, blinded to what we think we have the eyes for. But is it the other way around? Have their eyes been opened to what we are blind to? Is there something at work that has emptied them of certain prerogatives, only to fill them with deeper ones? It seems so. Does worth transcend beauty, and is love grounded in worth? Yes. And if this is so in the higher realm of human interaction, can it not also be so in the lower realm of artifactual action? Yes, it must.

Could it be that our approach to the arts should manifest this same kind of love—a love for the very fact and existence of artistic action itself, a love that loves those who love what we cannot love, a love for art that goes deeper than the art we fervently know to be good or even better? Do I love artistic creativity at its *imago Dei* level, so much that I can love what I outspokenly dislike? If so, I have earned the right to undertake three crucial tasks.

First, at a lower level, I want to love the fact of art so much that I will press for its fullest flower even in the so-called average person and in the most humble or misguided artistic circumstance. The love of beauty has no meaning if it hates ugliness, for who can find the middling gradation between the two? Likewise, the love of excellence has no meaning if it distances itself from, and ridicules, mediocrity. Again, who can find the middling gradation between them? If I am truly artistic—that is, if I truly love the primary fact of art—I must company with the aesthetic equivalent of the unwashed, the poverty-stricken and the handicapped. I must participate in its rescue and healing, knowing that my work may not be far removed from it, when it is compared to truly great art. This way, both my art and that of a lesser quality are healed that much more, because it is *art* that is being served, not just a special kind, not just my kind.

Second, at a much higher level, I want to love people so much that I work myself to the bone for their qualitative betterment. I should be interested in raising people up, not just their standards. The first being done, the second can surely come. I want to serve all people by enriching them, by taking them higher. And I want to take what they already have, honoring it because they made it. I want to take what they are—my loved neighbors—and give them the best of what I know and have. I also want them to know that my artistic journey is nowhere near complete and that I too must be taken higher by those above me who continue to teach me. I no longer want to give myself to the aesthetic Pharisees, trying to meet every one of their jots and tittles and separating myself from the unclean who cannot meet their demands. I would rather be with the gluttons and winebibbers, loving them, showing them how they can truly eat and drink at a more richly furnished table.

Third, at the highest level of love, I want to love God and his ways of thinking and his show of quality so much that in my art and in the teaching of it to others I pursue the highest possible quality *so as to be like him*. Here is where aesthetic doctrines and canons of taste must surrender themselves to an entirely different order. Here is where the pursuit of quality goes through exponential change. Here is where I make art as well as I can because seeking out, doing and wisely teaching everything as well as I can is a godly thing to do. Paul calls it pressing on (Phil 3:14), being living epistles (2 Cor 3:2), doing everything as if God were making his appeal through us (2 Cor 5:20) and seeking out the mind of Christ, in whom rest all the treasures of wisdom and knowledge (Phil 2:5; Col 2:3).

In summary, I must love art as a comprehensive fact. I must love people who love the art they make and use. I must love their love for Jesus while they sing what they love to sing. I must love art so much and them so much that, without ever taking their song from them, I add to it wisely and re-demptively. I must love God so much that, for his sake, and with the qual-itative supremacy of his work constantly before me, I cannot avoid the pursuit of quality whatever my present condition.

Faith and Quality

The exercise of faith and the seeking of quality also have more than one level. At a lower level, gifted and trained artists must trust and have faith in the proven work of fellow artists down through the years. We must not forget that time itself has a way of sifting and sorting. The cream does, if ever so slowly, rise to the top. Quality inevitably wins, and in any artistic field, a body of work emerges that we call the classics: classical jazz, swing, art music, rock. Artistically sensitive people commonly trust in artistically sensitive work. There is no mechanical explanation for this except that quality has faith in quality and, out of this, a quality-seeking community emerges, is nourished and enriched. Despite all the historical debates about quality—who outshone whom, who was first-rate or second-rate— the truth finally comes out: quality stands on its own and is finally notice-able. I unswervingly trust the fact that Mozart was among the greatest of composers in Western civilization. This faith about the quality of his work urges me, at whatever level I am, to emulate him as best I can. And Mozart had a faith about Haydn and, later in his life, Bach, that drew him to use their work as a way of changing his. As the generations of artists multiply, the community of quality likewise enlarges. All serious artists look to and trust in this carefully established community for qualitative guidance.

But this faith is not useful until it is coupled with the faith I must have in my own artistic instincts and urges. I am drawn to the quality of a Mozart or a Duke Ellington because of a gift, a "nose" within myself that draws me to them more than to lesser lights. There is something at work in me, even though it may be the artistic equivalent of a mustard seed or a smoking flax, that is alive and real. It is alert and hungry. It seeks out the ones with the richest wine and the finest meat. If this is not true of me in my artistic practices, I am a hypocrite. I should cease and desist. This kind of faith, even though it is obviously different from saving faith, is still analogous to it and at the heart of a love for quality. Quality is out there; I have an instinct for quality within me; I seek and I find, struggle and achieve. In this faith-and-seeking sense, quality remains an upward goal within a community, in which the less-than-great can learn from the truly great.

A second level of artistic faith is that of upward sojourn toward a finality. And here is where we can join with biblical instruction about faith. Faith is a walk, a sojourn into new, even strange country. Faith cannot stand still; if it does, it is no faith. Furthermore, the sojourn is toward a better place. Growth in faith can mean only one thing: growth within excelling, growth as betterment and increased fruit bearing. The implications of this for the arts are obvious. If faith is an upward sojourn in which increasing excellence is not the exception but the norm, and if a life of faith encompasses all of living, then no quarter of it is exempt from the mandate to upward excellence. Preachers must become better preachers; parents must become better parents; plumbers must become better plumbers; artists must become better artists. Furthermore, for the laity, this means following the lead of the artists who are upwardly excelling. Again, the strictly aesthetic side of the quality question is subordinated to a wider, more complete dimension. We should not pursue quality for quality's sake; this is legalism. But when we pursue quality because our upward sojourn demands it, we then have placed faith and works in the proper order. Only then can quality be described as a function of faith.

Notice the introduction of the word "excellence" a few sentences ago. Contrary to the false ideas we get about excellence from the world (excellence as winning, excellence as success, excellence as perfection, excellence as being number one, excellence as being better than someone else or as good as someone we think is excellent), the biblical concept of excellence is coupled to upward sojourn—pressing on, becoming better than I was yesterday, making sure that one kind of excelling in my life calls for all kinds of excelling.

Thinking of excellence as a sojourn is not only restful but challenging. I can rest in my individual capabilities and potentials, knowing that I do not have to become, or win out over, someone else in order to show that I am excelling. I can rest in my excelling while knowing that perfection is no longer the issue, for how can I press on to an upward goal if I am already perfect? My earthly task is to be sure that when I am taken home to the Lord I will literally be caught in the act of excelling. What else is continuous outpouring but continuous excelling?

The quality-sojourn question that we must ask of ourselves is short and plain: what is my next step, and of what quality will it be? The next person and the church down the road, if both are alive to the fact of excelling, cannot be examples, because they are not standing still. Simply keeping up might mean that we are always behind. Keeping up might also be driven by envy dressed up in that good old American virtue called *competition*. This does not mean that other churches cannot be models but that Christ in them should be the primary focal point of our emulation.

But at the highest level, we face the ultimate aspect of faith and therefore the ultimate aspect of quality. Just as loving God means loving everything about God and striving to imitate him in his comprehensive excellence, so having faith in God means trusting in everything about him, everything that he does and the way he does it, as well as everything that he says and the way his Son lived it. It is impossible to think of this kind of ultimate trust without thinking of quality in a completely new way, not as limited to our specialty, but as pertaining to our every breath. Then our artistry is placed under the comprehensive scrutiny of faith.

Altogether, then, these three aspects of faith and quality are in complete concord: temporal faith in the existence of quality both around me and within me; faith as upward sojourn into increasing excellence; and final and preeminent faith in the only One who does all things well. Or they can just as easily be seen in reverse order: my ultimate faith in Christ presses me on to upward sojourn. I have no alternative. My upward sojourn provides both hunger for the upward sojourn of others and a hunger to join them. Thus, when I look around me and discover the ways in which civilization has been graced with artistic magnificence, and when I look within myself and discover the curious love that God has put within me and the emerging desire to exercise it, it would be the artistic death of me as well as of those for whom I am ministerially responsible.

HOPE AND QUALITY

How do we couple artistic quality to hope? We often talk about how much we hope our art is good or acceptable or mistake-free. This is not hope but wishful thinking or lack of confidence, like saying I hope I did well on a test. Biblical hope is not about something already done, nor is it impractical or beyond reach. Biblical hope is as real and substance giving as faith is. It is, as I said in chapter two, the long-range architecture of faith. It is the future contour of the substance and evidence that faith alone is. Thus artistic and qualitative hope have little to do with artistic and qualitative dreaming ("I hope my art is good") and everything to do with the secure sense that what I do in my sojourn brings more than artistic satisfaction in what I have done or am doing, for hope that is seen is not hope. Rather, this true hope brings further hope, further architecture to my faith, hence more upward growth and more pressing on. It is no longer "I hope *that* . . ." but "I hope *toward* even as I work toward." Quality, seen in this light, is dynamic and fosters growth.

I realize that in putting the case for quality this way, I might end up with something too soft and warm, too spiritualized and aesthetically noncommittal. I have provided you with no hit lists, no agenda of masterpieces to emulate. There are no methods or standards, no "Here's what you do to achieve quality" slogans.

We Christians often misinterpret love as smarmy tolerance, a curious combination of exaggerating the commonplace and overlooking things, even while forgiving endlessly and turning the other cheek. We are often influenced by a mass culture that defines love in a way that plays into the hands of sloppiness, sentimentalism, passing relationships and massive relativism. Some might say, "Well and good. I'm already living a life of love, faith and hope. My art is the way it is because I live the way I do. I can assume that my striving for quality meets all the criteria. So, back to work." Fine. I have no way to challenge or verify this, because I have no way of knowing what goes on between them and the Lord. I simply hope that something strong and winsome emerges out of this concept, something that goes beyond the highest aesthetic dream and yet includes it as a normal thing.

I want to trust God in his ways of working within artists. And I want to trust artists themselves, hoping that, of all people, they are the most inquisitive and hungry, the most sensitive to how far they must go and how ardently they must pursue what lies before them. I hope that sensitive Christian artists will discover that the world of artistic action is larger than they are, that within the grand diversity of worldwide and history-long creativity, they will wake up to the need to sharpen their skills, widen their borders and repair their tastes. For, as too many of us already know, mass culture has done great damage to the human spirit, and the body of Christ must do much better in fulfilling the upward call to excellence. It does no earthly good for us to hide behind the skirts of spiritualization, spiritualized styles, measurable results, soft-fleshed ministry, feeling versus reason and quantity versus quality. Many of us have hidden there far too long and need desperately to let the light of excellence break in on us.

I can think of no better way to conclude this section than to ask a question based on the spirit of the closing verse of Psalm 139: Do we ask God to search our artistry as only he can search it and to show us how much we fall short? Are we ready to start from zero, if need be, only to build toward quality upon quality, whatever it costs? And as harsh as it may sound, are some of us ready to admit that we have made the mistake of turning our private liking for the arts into a public calling? Should we confess this, forsake our public work and return to the simple joy of making art privately for Jesus, unknown to any but him? After all, final authorship before him is the only thing that counts anyway.

Popular or Classical? A Personal Note

Musical creativity brings virtually endless options and as many opinions about them. How can I compare a Keith Jarrett improvisation to a Zulu harvest song or a praise chorus to a Lutheran chorale to Stravinsky's "Symphony of Psalms"? The postmodernists tell me that I need no longer do this because everything is equal to everything and what I decide is good is a private, unverifiable and untransmittable module in a sea of similarities. Certain multiculturalists tell me that qualitative comparisons are not only useless but also chauvinistic, if not racist. The conservatives tell me that there must be some single center point for determining such things, but the only centering point that they seem to come up with is a Western aesthetic. The experientialists tell me that value lies in feeling and personal choice, so how can anyone change my mind when it is wrapped around what feels good? Ministers of worship and the arts are likely to say that diversity is not only a secondary matter but also a local one: what works in parish A might not work in parish B. Or they might say that ministerial effectiveness is its own definition of quality.

Permit, then, these personal remarks. My own artistic sojourn, until just a few years ago, alternated between a kind of aesthetic absolutism and free relativity. I was educated, through the doctorate, to assume the superiority of Western classicism. An introduction to ethnomusicology, along with the musical upheavals of the 1960s and 1970s, caused me to question the classics-only idea. My love for popular music, especially blues and jazz (allegedly America's "classical music"), brought me to yet another aesthetic point of reference. In forty-plus years of work in Christian higher education, I have been regularly faced with the intellectual debate, not only about all of the above, but also about the difference between concept and practice. Finally, my fifty-plus years in church music kept me busy with the issue of the arts as aids to or acts of worship. Now, in the beginning of my eighth decade of life, I have come to a set of convictions that I want to write about. I know that I cannot impose them, as much as I might like to, but I hope you will consider and apply them as carefully as possible. Early on in this book, I pledged not to take stylistic sides, especially in a spirit of polemicism. I am remaining true to this promise, but with one permissible caveat: all honest artists should not only be widely eclectic but should lean heavily in one stylistic direction or another and should be able to say why this is so. I too lean in a direction in the midst of a joyful—at times hilarious—eclecticism.

After all these years of practicing music and attempting to think it through, I have concluded that the art and music of *any* high culture, not just Western, is the *qualitative* model toward which all other artistic actions in that culture should strive.[2] What makes this kind of music so preeminently worthwhile? As best as I can figure out, it is technically, intellectually, architecturally and aesthetically the most complete body of music we have. Its makers have made endless inquiry into virtually every procedure and component available to them. Spiritually, no corner of the human con dition is left unexplored and each is taken to the depths, whether of joy, of suffering, of mystery, of hope, of faith, of love, and not just in tunes, lyrics and accompaniments, but in vast constructions of great length and complexity. Intellectually, the work of a Bach or a Bartók reaches the same heights as that of a Barth or a Planck. And as with all high human achievement, classical music is polylateral. It does not lock itself into one way or one mode or subsist on self-enclosure. While complete in itself, it points to things beyond itself.

In the course of a single composition we can be taken through any number of events that can be highlighted or merely implied. They can slip into or out of prominence, yet they always count. There is flux, change, development, transformation, foregrounding and backgrounding, thinning and thickening, and contouring, all settled, balanced and worked through into one unique shape after another. It is out of the development and synthesis of all these parts that such shapes are created, one after another. And to a massified culture obsessed with rhythmic *quantity*, the ever-present beat and its limited ornamentations, classical music offers rhythmic *quality* and complexity of an entirely different and higher order. No single beat dominates. Rhythm and meter contribute integratively to the final architecture.

Now that I have committed myself so fully in this way, how can I incorporate selective love and all my other loves? Is there room in a Christian aesthetic for some kind of hierarchy? I believe so, as long as the mandates of faith, love and hope win out and rule my ministry, teaching and creativity. Here are two principles and two analogies to help make the point.

The first principle is that there is a world of difference between intrinsic worth and relative value. And here is the first analogy: A nickel and a dollar each have intrinsic worth, but a dollar has more value than a nickel. Not even a massive relativist can deny this. He or she would be foolish go to a taco stand, two for a dollar, and try to pull the purchase off with a nickel, saying that everything is relative. Try the other way around. I can buy bubble gum for a nickel a chew. But if I confuse worth and equality, I might lay down a dollar for my one chew and walk contentedly off, this time to buy a new convertible. Somewhere I will run out of money while my brother Joe, who knows the difference between worth and value, having both his bubble gum and his convertible, will have money left over for a summer vacation with his family.

We can now intersect the first principle with another one: differences in kind allow room for differences in quality *among* kinds. Here's the second analogy. Let's say I run a fresh fruit drink stand, having bought my brother Joe out. I find a way to make better lemonade than he did and my sales charts show it. In fact, I make the best lemonade in the neighborhood, perhaps anywhere. But someone comes by and says that all lemonades are, after all, equal, so isn't it unfair and demeaning to say that my lemonade is better? I have a choice: continue to make the best lemonade and live with the whining, or succumb to the guilt, start producing mediocre lemonade, then watch my sales drop precipitously and try to live off the happy feeling it gives my critic (who, meanwhile, may clandestinely look out for a better lemonade).

But let's say that I stick with making the best lemonade and turn so successful that I am able to purchase a vineyard and go into the winemaking business. Again, quality wins and I make an award-winning merlot and another coequalist comes around with the same message. But I stick to my guns, making the best lemonade *and* the best merlot, and I am now able to buy a custom furniture business. And my success continues.

Excelling in everything I make—lemonade, wine, furniture—I come upon two truths. First, making great wine is a higher achievement than making the best lemonade, hands down. Second, I still enjoy both, each for its own worth and each in its place. In both cases I am driven by a desire to take something as far as it will allow me to go. Making lemonade goes so far, and making wine even further, but the making of each is a completed journey.

Now I realize that this analogy can be turned in other directions. You might want to say that classical art is really the lemonade and jazz the merlot, or that there is a lemonade kind of classical and a merlot kind. I will not argue with either contention, especially the second one, given the earlier comments in chapter twelve about shallow and deep. I also realize that I might perform a merlot kind of music with a lemonade capability, and so on. Nevertheless, I would like to believe that the original analogy is valid. In short, the art of *any* high culture will go deeper and wider than its popular and folk counterparts.

I want desperately to teach and share these insights with everybody, not as an exclusivist, not once taking their many musics away from them, never demeaning them for what they love and what they ascribe to, never holding to a position of superiority. I want to talk about the fullest extent to which anything and any person can be taken. I want to talk about connections, not just the surface ones, not about how something feels or how it can keep me settled in what I already enjoy or know. I want a world of neighbors to understand that they have been created in God's image, created capable of enormous stretches, capable of intellectual probing and pleasure. I want to take them into territory that lies far outside of the poll-driven drivel that tells me how limited and superficial my neighbors are. I want to show them that it is possible to like one thing more than another while loving both. I want to show them that laying hold of a mystery is a wondrous paradox, that while the greatest things are attainable by a very few, they can be offered to all. I want to show them that they are more alone by staying the same or moving with the crowd than by being stretched within their minds and spirits. I want, above all, to show them that going beyond, instead of just looking or being around, is what authentic diversity is truly about.

I am a husband, a father and a grandfather, and professionally I was privileged to be a teacher. One question haunts me continually: what shades of beauty and nuances of spirit have we taken from our children, our young people, our fellow outpourers in the name of the idiocies of massified culture and easy Christianity? What are they missing that the art to which they have naively grown accustomed claims to offer but cannot grant? It is their forced ignorance, not their present choices, that grieves me so. We may have many reasons for fussing over this or that monstrosity or lapse in their artistic diets, but fussing can in no way compare to the reconstructive teaching we must do to bring them to fuller aesthetic, spiritual and intellectual measure.

QUALITY AND LOCAL AUTHENTICITY

I want to conclude this chapter and bring the entire burden of continuous outpouring down to an irreducible corporate entity: the local assembly of believers. In all the diversity with which the church and culture are faced; in all the pressure to be relevant, to reach out and grow; with all the conferences and symposia given over to seeker sensitivity, evangelism, cultural issues, worship and the arts; with the enervating debate about worship styles and artistic content; with ministers of worship and the arts often holding on to their jobs by the skin of their choices; with small churches wondering what to do to match the megachurches; with megachurches wondering what outgrowing growth means; in a culture in which ornamented sameness is worldwide, what about the local assemblies in Dubuque, Punxsutawney, Temecula, Bonners Ferry and Provo?

Just this: continuous outpouring is above all a personal responsibility and only then a corporate one. It is therefore of fundamental importance that all authentic worshipers be sure that they are so firmly rooted in Christ that their individuality is never lost in the rush of spiritualized sameness. It is further important that every authentically worshiping assembly find its local and unique place in the kingdom, not glancing over its shoulder, looking here and there for an outside stimulus to inspire and steer it. Authentic Christianity, both personal and corporate, is sorely needed. It is through personal credibility that servanthood is manifest. The same is true of the local assembly. This kind of Christ-centered integrity is what I like to call *local authenticity* (and what I earlier on called *the creative signature*).

This is as good a time as any to broach what to me is one of the most overlooked issues in the life of the church. We live in a world of renewed interest in underrepresented groups. We are continually challenged to honor all kinds: societal stations, races, ethnicities and colors. So far, so good. But if underrepresentation of *all* kinds is at issue, why is it that so few churches reach out to one of the most overlooked minorities in present-day culture: the intellectually and artistically sophisticated? When will a cadre of Spirit-filled churches and humbled leaders come to the honorable decision of taking the full intellectual and aesthetic burden of the good news on their shoulders? When will such a group take strength in *not* growing as much, because a neglected body of culture's citizens needs the gospel? Even the most socially descriptive kind of seeker sensitivity should join in agreement.

We constantly chafe about the dangers of the secular and godless intellect. But an intellect is neither godless nor godly by itself. It needs to be filled to the full, challenged and evangelized to the maximum. If meeting people where they are is more than a majorities-tinged, growth-by-leaps-and-bounds dimension, it will certainly take in the solemn responsibility of meeting everybody where they are, person by person, group by group, station by station. Only then can our consciousness about the unreached be more fully and honestly implemented.

I pray that all local assemblies, all continuous outpourers, will come to understand that however poverty stricken or richly appointed they may seem in comparison with others, they will remain poor in their richness, uniquely rich in their poverty and authentic in their outpouring. For this we have an exemplar, the Christ. In the midst of poverty and struggle, affluence and triumph, a high calling is being fulfilled: continuous outpouring, borne along by love, faith and hope. And within that magnificent intertwining condition (Christ in God; God in Christ; the Spirit, the Father and the Son eternally in each other; Christ in us; the Spirit in us; the Father in us; we in each other, even as the Son is in the Father), we the outpourers can be both locally authentic and eternally verified. In the midst of this singular glory, we can understand the prophet Zephaniah lining it out in poetry:

> The LORD, your God, is in your midst,
>   a warrior who gives victory;
> he will rejoice over you with gladness,
>   he will renew you in his love. (Zeph 3:17)

And as the great Sebastian Bach often initialed in Latin at the head of so many of his compositions: *JJ—Jesu juva.* Jesus, help.

EPILOGUE

I want to repeat the definition of worship from the opening pages: *Worship is the continuous outpouring of all that I am, all that I do and all that I can ever become in light of a chosen or choosing god.* I hope that I have been faithful to the many ramifications of this statement. More importantly, I pray that I have been faithful to the Scriptures as I have sought to explore the fullness of authentic worship and continuous outpouring. And most important of all, I pray that God alone has been honored throughout and that other gods have been cast away.

Here, in summary, is what I have tried to develop in the two major divisions of the book.

God is the eternal Outpourer. Within and toward his triune Self, he outpours himself in endless love and unapproachable holiness. This outpouring continues uninterruptedly with nothing outside of itself to support it, increase it or satisfy it. God chose to extend his outpouring beyond himself. He created in a gracious outpouring of imagination and skill, culminating his handiwork with a race of beings made in his own image. Thus, we were created outpouring, not to satisfy the idea that God needed to be worshiped, but as evidence that we were *imago Dei*—created to act the way God acts. What we call worship is the finite side of outpouring, just as lordship is the infinite side, and communion is the natural and uninterrupted intercourse between Creator and *imago Dei*.

When Adam fell (and we in him), we exchanged gods but continued our outpouring. This turning away meant turning toward; it meant the complex and deluded invention of any number of religious systems and idolatries. The statement that nobody does not worship holds true for as long as this world and all of its systems, artifacts and institutions endure. The only solution to fallen worship is Jesus Christ, who takes our twisted and inverted worship and sets it right. The call to salvation is a call to redeemed worship. It is offered in the continuum of God's acceptable time, accepted in the regenerative work of the Spirit and once for all settled in Christ. All subsequent calls to worship, then, are subordinate to, and reflections of, this one call.

The Scriptures bear this out in the broadest manner possible. The Old Testament, while emphasizing time and place more than the New Testament, contains everything that is later fulfilled and summed up in Christ. There is no contradiction between the Testaments but rather a gradual, inevitable unfolding, preparation, and peering ahead that finds fulfillment and satisfaction in every precept that gathers around Christ. In him, continuous outpouring is complete. Time and place, while continuously important, even commanded, are folded into a comprehensive spiritual dimension. We are continuous living sacrifices who undertake everything in the beauty of holiness, in Spirit and truth, as living epistles, as permanent ambassadors. Physical sanctuaries and specific times of worship remain but are now swept up in a transcendent spiritual reality: mutual indwelling, stretched to the full and immensely deepened by the realities of Christ in us; and we in each other, even as we—one body—are in Christ, who is in the Father and in the Spirit, even as each is in the other. Because worship is a continuum, we can now understand that we do not sing or pray or preach in order to worship. Rather, we do these things because we are already at worship. Worship and witness are now inseparably linked: witness is overheard worship, and continuous worship cannot but witness. The sum of all of this is the singular fact that authentic worship is a life of action, of acts of worship, undertaken by faith, gladdened by love and set firm in hope.

Art is but one of countless actions to which continuing worshipers are called, and to call them to account under the singular and comprehensive wonder of continuous outpouring. Hence the making of all art, for all believers everywhere, is an act of worship. We sing, we dance, sculpt, paint, act as living sacrifices because we worship. Our art, offered by faith, goes to God through the merits of the Savior and is accepted on this account. Within the constraints of the gathered assembly, art and artists serve the liturgy and the Word. Outside the gathered assembly—in the world—art is made to the full in numerous contexts, serving one purpose after another, invading one context after another and contributing to the aesthetic nurture of the many cultures in which it is made.

God is the uncreated Creator and the unimagined Imaginer. No one can outstep him or outimagine him. His handiwork is replete with examples, models, architectural wisdom and sheer variety from which all of us should learn. It is not the artist's task to imitate God's creation nearly as much as to join him in the first days of creation, to peer into every detail of his handiwork, to be humbled by what is learned and to exhaust his or her imagination in the shaping of things that bear the stamp of individual authenticity and far-reaching insight.

Among all the arts used within the corporate assembly, music has a unique role, not because it is superior to the other art forms, but because of its native peculiarity. Each of us has a God-created instrument within us: the voice. We are commanded to use this instrument in singing the praise of God. A congregation of untrained voices singing mightily to the Lord has a beauty that immediately sets it apart. In addition, music carries text with little effort, especially in chant, simple melody and wisely crafted harmony. Thus congregational song, while being the center of all church music, is both truth carrier and melodic offering. The power of music is readily admitted but kept under close scrutiny because it can easily become equated with the power that comes only from the Lord.

Meanwhile, the other art forms have their own intrinsic significance to communicate. Each has its unique way of communicating things that no other art form can quite communicate. It is important for Christian artists, ministerial leadership and the laity to understand that every art form is weakened in direct proportion to the way it is expected to communicate what it cannot, to act outside itself. The arts must be allowed to remain in vivid and dignified contrast to each other and to be placed in the liturgy for what they are.

In the practice of the arts, idolatry is subtle. It can creep in whenever we place artistic action between us and the Lord as if it mediates his presence or substitutes for the work and power of the Spirit. The warnings in the Bible (especially in Deuteronomy) against worshiping God in displeasing ways indicate that there is such a thing as worshiping God *while* using idols. In addition, we must also guard against making idols of beauty, quality, style or results.

In the last three chapters, two comprehensive issues were discussed: culture and quality. With respect to the former, I tried to show how so-called high (or classical) and low (or popular) are ideally a reciprocating continuum. I presented another way of looking at the arts by creating pairings through which any of them could be seen. I wanted us to understand that there is nothing pejorative about art that is shallow, ornamental, simple, familiar or entertaining. Rather, I argued that it is important for all of us to take in all of artistic thought (for that matter, all kinds of thought) and to move back and forth easily between shallow and deep, ornamental and developmental, simple and complex, familiar and strange, entertaining and engaging. This way, we are filling out the potential of what it means to be created in the image of God, whose creation and plans mysteriously take in all of the foregoing.

Contemporary culture is not just a culture filled with popular things. It is a complex ethos in which the best of human creative action has been absorbed in what many are calling *massification*. Massification is a noxious ethos in which experientialism, self-enclosed shallowness, massive relativity, the loss of a truth center and the consequent degradation of human speech have become subversive partners. Thus it is not the things of culture that are nearly as dangerous as the worldview with which this mass culture puts them to use. And it is this worldview that can so insidiously be at work in the body of Christ and its worship.

We can approach the subject of artistic quality from the viewpoint of love, faith and hope and local authenticity. I did this, not because the strict aesthetic approaches to art are to be avoided, but because they often lead us too quickly to the subject of quality and taste and often cause us to pursue quality for its own sake rather than see it as a symptom or result of acting lovingly, faithfully, hopingly and worshipfully. It is the worth of Jesus that should lead us to the search for quality rather than mere artistic standards for their own sake.

In all of this, I have attempted to recognize and honor all who teach, preach and pray the Word as well as those who make art in obedience to their calling. None of us has it all put together; each of us is in a particular place in the call to work out our salvation. No one but God knows the relationship of where we are to where he longs for us to be, and only God is able to provide us with the spiritual strength to get there, whether we mount up as eagles or simply walk. In any case, as we press on, we can say with the psalmist, "By my God I can leap over a wall" (Ps 18:29). For some, the leap will be a mere centimeter or two; for others, a country mile. But the glory is in the leaping itself and not its size, and the strength we have is his strength only made perfect in our weakness. Thus, the amount of our talent, the size of our ministries, the quality with which they are undertaken and the changes wrought within the whole, whether large or small, are of less account than the faithful, fixed-on-Jesus stewardship that informs our every action.

I would like to conclude with some comments on three stories from the book of John. They are history, to be sure, but I would like you also to see them as simple, uncomplicated parables for the responsibilities that all Christians have in the discharge of their daily tasks. The first (already cited several times in the previous pages) is found in John 12:1-3—Mary pouring perfume on Jesus' feet. The second is in John 13:1-5—Jesus washing the disciples' feet. And the third is in John 21:1-13—Jesus making breakfast for his disciples.

Continuous Outpouring and the Worth of Jesus

The story of Mary bathing Jesus' feet with costly perfume has a private innocence to it that ever so easily unites with its public testimony. But I am quite sure that Mary had no idea of making a universal example out of her worship. She simply loved Jesus so much that she could do no other. In so doing she turned the prose of everyday life into poetry, making Jesus the center of her action and her gift the symbol of her worship.

We would be mistaken if we saw her action only as an isolated or a cli-
mactic, once-for-all enactment. As lavish and expensive as her action was,
it would make no sense for us to assume that she had set such a singular
precedent for herself that nothing subsequent to it would have any significance. Rather, it must have been one of countless varied expressions of adoration and worship, each of which was costly in its own way. Without a
connection to a life of continuous outpouring, Mary's action could tempt
us to work ourselves and our resources up to one grand summation, one
explosion of adoration, instead of living steadily and seeking to do everything to the fullest.

I believe the secret behind the mention of costliness in this story does
not lie in the works-driven ideas that costly perfume is "perfect perfume,"
that pouring better perfume than others pour is what counts and that
spending extravagantly by itself impresses God. Instead three truths go beyond the idea of costliness as a hyperabundant quantity or a grand climax.

The first has to do with the supreme worth of Jesus. His value, not the
cost of the perfume, is central to this story. Why must my outpouring be
costly? The answer is simple: because of the infinite worth of Jesus. It is his
worth that summons me to costliness: how I work, with what quality and
intensity I work, and with what consistency and steady growth I do my
work. We have to remember that costliness is first of all a description of
the work of God in Christ. He redeemed us at great cost, with the precious
blood of his Son. Therefore our work is to be costly, not to impress him,
but because we are to be like him.

The second truth, as strange as it may first sound, lies in the relativity of
costliness. That is, a conviction of costliness is revealed to me on the basis
of my capabilities, the full surrender of these to God's enablement and the
exhaustion of these in ardent stewardship. Thus costliness is not a measurably fixed maximum, a static ideal, to which all believers everywhere are
equally accountable. We are not clones of each other, spiritually, ministerially, aesthetically or in any other way. Some have been given a greater measure of talent than others. Each of us is growing up into a measure of
Christ's stature differently.

Only God knows the identity of the most talented person ever created,
and he also knows who is the least among us. Knowing these things is not

for us, nor are we to make them any of our business. It is not up to us to look over our shoulders to see who is spiritually creeping up on us, staying abreast or falling behind. It is our business to ask God to search us as only he can, reveal to us that which impedes us and, through his Spirit, enable us to forsake every besetting sin and keep our attention fixed on Jesus, the supreme Gift and the only Gift Giver. As I said in an earlier chapter, excelling is the process of becoming better than I was yesterday, and this process cannot be separated out from a life of authentic worship. Every action to which I have committed myself is thus costly in its own way. In this sense costliness does not so much mean scrambling for the best there is, as it means working toward, and then beyond, the best I can personally achieve at that time, time after time.

I think of the gracious way the Lord recognized this scale of costliness way back in Leviticus 5:5-13 (and time after time throughout Leviticus, Numbers and Deuteronomy). Instead of expecting an identical sin offering from each person, he asks for two lambs from those who can bear the cost, two turtledoves or pigeons from those who cannot and a simple measure of fine flour from those who cannot bear the cost even of two doves or pigeons. But whatever the gift, God demands that it be unblemished, not tainted with sickness or lameness (Deut 15:21), at least as far as the one who offers can know. (This is what Numbers 28:19 seems to imply by saying, "They shall be *unto you* without blemish," KJV, italics mine.) And in making costly offerings, unblemished as far as we can know, we will fill the "room" of our daily outpouring with a fragrance that pleases the Lord. Above all, whether those around us are thankful for our excelling or indignant because of their perception of waste, the aroma goes up to God through Christ and is pleasant, sweet and satisfying.

The third truth reaffirms the union of worship and witness. The aroma of Mary's offering filled the room. What she offered to Jesus in worship could not be kept to itself. It wafted. It "witnessed" immediately, both in blessing and offense. This oneness of worship and witness cannot be avoided. What I offer to God in the totality of my worship will immediately be communicated to those around me. We are, after all, living epistles who cannot avoid being known and read. The worth of Jesus demands costly offerings— this is first and foremost. But the inestimable worth of each human being, each image of God, condition notwithstanding, likewise demands costly, unblemished offerings.

There will be those who are refreshed, even turned right side up, in the midst of our outpouring. But there will also be those who cannot abide the abandonment with which we pour perfume, and they may chastise us for our waste. "This money could have been put to better use" often indicates a misunderstanding of the worth of Jesus and the comprehensive expenditure that a response to him demands. It is easy to spiritualize our priorities falsely—foreign mission is more important than local witness, spending money on the arts will take away from taking care of the hungry, and the like. But if our conviction about the worth of the Savior takes in the fullness of his desire for the redemption and nurture of every whole person, and if our outpouring reflects these, then we need not worry about artificial priorities. That is, if we keep the infinite worth of Christ as the only focus of our outpouring, that which is "wasted" will in no way drain away from that which is "important," and waste, want or profligacy will be replaced by abundance.

So then, we are, above all, perfume pourers. The feet of Jesus, beautiful in their journey toward us and toward the Father, are our altar.

CONTINUOUS OUTPOURING AND SERVANTHOOD

But outpouring cannot be limited to private transactions between us and the Savior. Perfume pourers are servants, after the manner of the One over whose feet we lavish our offerings. We are to become like the One whom we worship. In this lovely encounter between the disciples and the Savior, Christ is again the focus, but in a completely different way. The One whom we worship reveals himself as the quintessential Servant. Just as worship and witness join up with each other, so do worship and serving.

We cannot fully understand the foot-washing story without the perfume story. This means that before we can make our way into the mystery of Christ's emptied servitude, we must elevate the image of perfume even higher than John 12 implies. We must, in a sense, start over and understand that Jesus, from the eternities, is the most costly Perfume imaginable. Even before he took flesh upon himself, he and the Spirit and the Father were pouring out their infinite richness over each other in endless generosity and abounding love.

Then, in the fullness of time, Jesus came to earth and here poured himself out over the feet of his Father as the only perfect offering, such that the world itself is still filled with his fragrance. As the One in whom no beauty can be seen, marred beyond mere ugliness, he became both a life-giving and a fatal perfume. The perfume of the Savior is the fragrance of life for those who turn to him and the stench of death for those who turn away. If, in Paul's words (2 Cor 2:15-16), "we are the aroma of Christ to God among those who are being saved and among those who are perishing," and if we are to some "a fragrance from death to death" and to others "a fragrance from life to life," then we can take for granted that we are joined with the Savior in the fullness of his work as long as we understand how expensive the perfume of continuous outpouring is.

If we put the two stories together, then, we have this: worship as witness can only be effected in servanthood, and servanthood is of no use unless it is bathed in worship, for it is the pouring of perfume that validates and lends credence to our service. Service, as its own proof of the worship of God, is dangerous, whereas authentic worship can only issue in service.

Further, we need to remember that, just in the case of Peter's reaction to Jesus, there will be those who will not understand what we do when we serve them. Likewise, as ministers, we too may slide into a mistaken concept of our relationship to our brothers and sisters by confusing such things as service and leadership or authority and power. And they too might want to suggest to us what form our service should take so as to satisfy their concepts of service rather than our call to it. But Jesus' response to Peter was exactly what he needed and what all of us need, church leaders and laity alike, when we try to undo or reverse the call to servanthood.

We are, then, perfume pourers who wash feet. But we must be sure that we choose the right feet for the right action. We must not pour perfume over our brothers' and sisters' feet—this is misdirected worship, maybe even idolatry. This is easy to do because, way down inside each of us, there is a desire to be liked, to please and to placate. And every so often these desires, having limited good in themselves, overtake and rule out the real force of our calling. If we are not careful, we will end up with only water to pour out on Jesus' feet because our perfume has gone in the wrong direction.

Another aspect to servanthood lies in its variety. The prophet cries out against wrong and lapse as a servant of the Word. The preacher builds, edifies, teaches and warns as a servant of the Word. The artist imagines and crafts a servant path within the liturgy, even as the liturgy in its totality serves the Word. The body of Christ serves itself and the world, member by member, group by group, need by need and triumph by triumph, through the mystery and responsibility of mutual indwelling. The outpouring God, the outpouring Christ, the outpouring Holy Spirit and the outpouring bride, an outpouring world of believers, history-long and cultures-wide, temples within temples within Temple, are sworn to the loveliness, the emptiedness and the relentlessness of washing feet, but only if the perfume comes first. Just as Jesus once turned water into wine, so he alone can turn the water of outpouring service into perfume. If we get the order right—perfume first and water second—he will make a Cana out of the two. No one else is able.

CONTINUOUS OUTPOURING, SEEKING AND FEEDING

Authentic worshipers are seekers. It might not be too much to say that they continue the great hunting story begun when God walked in the garden looking for Adam and Eve, who were now worshiping falsely, now stripped of glory and hiding. Hunting means finding, and finding means nurturing. The story of Jesus making breakfast, the final one in this great Gospel, is not just about the kind of breakfast we have come to treasure—breaking bread with friends and family on a frosty, fire-lit Saturday morning. This story is more comprehensive, for it takes in the richness of perfume and the clarity of water and turns them in the direction of a world of estrangement, uneasy friendships, hurt, doubt, confusion, dimly burning wicks and broken reeds. The beauty of this story rests in the solitary wonder of Jesus always looking for people and, whatever their opinion of him, making breakfast and calling them (really, recalling them) into the warmth of his company and the search of his questions. It is not so easy to think of inviting people to breakfast who harbor doubt about us, who recently may have cursed and denied us or forsaken us. They may or may not have repented, and we are not sure of their surety. But for Jesus, breakfast was a combination of redemptive love, incisive questions and unswerving fidelity to his sworn purposes. The four Gospels present a remarkably varied picture of reactions among the friends and disciples of Jesus after the Resurrection: joy, wonder, fear, confusion, doubt, repentance and emerging trust. We have no sure way of knowing how unified the disciples were after the Resurrection, of knowing exactly where Peter was in his sojourn, nor whether, for instance, Thomas continued to be plagued with doubt throughout his life, even after his remarkable confession (Jn 20:28). What we must understand is that just as you and I were responsible for nailing Jesus to the cross, so we are also represented in the varied behaviors of the eleven after the Resurrection. We are the ones for whom Jesus makes breakfast, whatever our condition, whatever our opinion of him.

Without haranguing us, he opens his table. He provides the fire and the food but also asks us to bring some of our own, even as he asked the eleven to share their catch at the fire. And as soon as we see his provision and respond to his invitation to bring something as well, we sit down to eat, sharing each other's bounty, filling out what lacks and basking in the growing realization that, indeed, we are eating with the very Son of God, who—as has often been said—is at once Guest and Host. This kind of breakfast making is community at its best; it is the body of Christ in its commissioned work of participating in God's reconciliation of the entire world to himself, for this kind of seeking and feeding rebukes no one, omits no one, favors no one and is driven by the redemptive love that brought the Savior from the skies to the dust.

Are we breakfast makers? Do we unconditionally seek, feed and nurture? Do we do these things without worrying who is for us and who is against us? I pray so, and we must pray so for each other. The Paraclete joins in, voicing our emptied-out praying in groans that cannot be uttered. Jesus hears. He is the grand Chef. He is the glorious crucified, resurrected, ascended Lord with whom one day we will be seated at a feast beyond all earthly breakfasts: the marriage supper of the Lamb.

Perfume, water, breakfast. Worship, witness, service. Seeking, feeding, continuous outpouring. These are our duty and our delight. God be with you. God grant you the faith to understand your commission, the love to bathe its every act and the hope to see through to the end.

I pray that the Lord will regularly increase the force of his indwelling company with each of you and that, with St. Paul, you will keep forgetting what is behind and press on within the increasing richness of what lies ahead. I hope that all of us together will come to understand how innocently shortsighted yet prophetically hungry the Wesley brothers were when they prayed for only a thousand tongues to sing. God being with us, the thousand will not be enough, yet any single one, sung by faith, and in hungering abandonment to the wind of the Spirit, will point to, and then beyond, the Pentecost to which each of us is called. Amen.

NOTES

Chapter 1: Nobody Does Not Worship

[1]I distinguish between lostness and fallenness here in this respect: fallenness is every person's lot, whereas lostness is the lot of those who are fallen and choose to stay that way by rejecting the only Savior of the fallen. Even in the redeemed, fallenness continues in a way fully admitted by Scripture and proven continuously in our lives.

[2]I admit to a poverty of thought and word here. But the sheer joy of trying to talk about God in his infinite reach is such that everyone who names Christ as Savior should spend time thinking, writing and speaking of these glories. As John says of his witness to Christ, "The world itself could not contain the books that would be written" (Jn 21:25).

Chapter 2: What Is Authentic Worship?

[1]Karl Barth, *The Epistle to the Romans* (London: Oxford University Press, 1968), p. 110.

[2]Every Christian should read Søren Kierkegaard's *Works of Love* (New York: Harper & Row, 1962). It is an extraordinary book, based on 1 Corinthians 13 and the commandment to love one's neighbor. Kierkegaard takes the reader through the complex territories of selective and unconditional love, inch by inch, with enormous inventiveness and nuance. The reader should not grow weary, even though in the best sense *Works of Love* is a wearying book. Furthermore, no one should ignore Jonathan Edwards's impeccably lyrical sermon "Heaven Is a World of Love." It can be found in *The Sermons of Jonathan Edwards,* ed. Wilson H. Kimnach, Kenneth P. Minkema and Douglas Sweeney (New Haven: Yale University Press, 1999).

[3]The exemplary exegetical work of David Peterson is the foundation for what I am attempting (*Engaging with God* [Downers Grove, Ill.: InterVarsity Press, 2002], especially pp. 64-68).

[4]David Peterson renders "spiritual worship" as "understanding worship." See ibid., pp. 174-79 for a thorough treatment of the passage in question.

[5]Because of this grand synthesis, it makes little sense for us to separate theology as story from theology as proposition, as if truth could be held tightly in one at the expense of the other. It seems to me that the best preaching and teaching will always keep the two at work with each other.

Chapter 3: Mutual Indwelling: The Final Geography of Worship

[1]Brother Lawrence, *The Practice of the Presence of God* (Westwood, N.J.: Revell, 1958), p. 64.

[2]The term "mutual indwelling" is not my invention; I am quite sure of that. But I cannot remember

how I came upon it. I have tried to locate its source and have come up empty. If I am using it without duly crediting its originator, I sincerely apologize.

Although there is no definitional relationship between the concept of mutual indwelling and *koinonia*, I feel that there is a theological one that surrounds and perhaps intensifies it. Please refer to David Peterson's comments on *koinonia* in *Engaging with God* (Downers Grove, Ill.: InterVarsity Press, 2002), pp. 154-55. In those pages, in which he includes a significant quotation from D. P. Seccombe, he develops the definitional ideas of *koinonia* as "common participation" and "partnership" (which seem to create a bridge into the idea of mutual indwelling).

[3]Peterson, *Engaging with God*, pp. 95-97.

[4]G. Campbell Morgan, "The Vine," in *The Westminster Pulpit* (Westwood, N.J.: Revell), 7:265.

[5]The hymn is "My Song Is Love Unknown," by Samuel Crossman (1624-1683).

[6]J. Ernest Rattenbury, *The Eucharistic Hymns of John and Charles Wesley* (London: Epworth, 1948), p. 179.

Chapter 4: The Corporate Gathering and Authentic Worship

[1]I first heard witness expressed this way some years ago in a conversation with Richard Stanislaw, former president of King College, Bristol, Tennessee. At the time, I had not yet come to notice the deep unity of worship and witness, nor had I come upon the discussion of other leaders who think in these terms. Even so, something began to work in my mind that, even to this day, gains continued luster.

[2]I heard this (or words to this effect) in several of Professor Miller's sermons in Common Ground Worship Conferences, sponsored by the Baptist Sunday School Board, in which I was a participant.

[3]The hymn is William Williams's "Guide Me, O Thou Great Jehovah."

Chapter 6: Worship, Praying and Preaching

[1]*The Book of Common Prayer* (New York: The Church Hymnal Corporation, 1979), p. 279.

[2]*The Private Devotions of Lancelot Andrewes,* trans. F. E. Brightman (New York: Meridian, 1961). This version also contains a remarkable essay, "Lancelot Andrewes," by T. S. Eliot. Andrewes was one of the translators of the King James Version.

Chapter 7: Continuous Outpouring and Artistic Action

[1]I received a copy of a letter from a country preacher who truly believes that the Lord gives him songs. At the bottom of each copy of music he says words to this effect: "Because the Lord gave me this song, it is not really mine; it is everybody's. Feel free to make as many copies as you wish." He had it right.

[2]Paul says it so well: "What is the conclusion then? I will pray with the spirit, and I will also pray with the understanding. I will sing with the spirit, and I will also sing with the understanding" (1 Cor 14:15 NKJV).

Chapter 8: What Creative People Can Learn from God's Creation

[1]Some of the concepts found here also appear as part of chapters one, three and four of my book *Music Through the Eyes of Faith* (San Francisco: HarperSanFrancisco, 1993). I have included and expanded on them here because of my desire to speak as comprehensively as I can in the same work.

[2]For starters, see James Gleick, *Chaos* (New York: Viking Penguin, 1987); and Nina Hall, ed., *Exploring Chaos* (New York: Norton, 1994).

[3]We should be thankful for the hymnic work of contemporaries like Bishop Timothy Dudley-Smith, Fred Kaan, Fred Pratt Green, Brian Wren, Margaret Clarkson, Bryen Jeffery Leech and Carl P. Daw Jr. The best of their work is fresh and culturally insightful yet theologically aware and scripturally substantiated.

Chapter 9: The Peculiarity of Music and Its Unique Role

[1]Since, when it comes to truth telling, music is the most ambiguous of all art forms and words are the least ambiguous, perhaps in texted music we have a near-perfect metaphor for a union of tongues and prophecy and an interesting parallel to the Ephesians and Colossians passages. This may be so especially when we couple them to this statement, again from Paul (my editorial insertions in brackets): "He who speaks in a tongue [he who sings and makes melody in his heart] does not speak [sing] to men but to God. . . . But he who prophesies [he who teaches and admonishes with text] speaks edification and exhortation and comfort . . . [and] . . . edifies the church" (1 Cor 14:2-4 NKJV). It might even be argued that all the arts, even those containing specific words and deeds, are to varying degrees related more to tongues than to prophecy. Assuming this to be true would relieve many artists of the onerous task of trying to make their art do what only speaking and living the truth can do.

[2]See, for instance, Andy Park, *To Know You More* (Downers Grove, Ill.: InterVarsity Press), pp.163-67.

[3]Ibid., p. 156.

[4]Ibid.

[5]Ibid.

Chapter 10: The Arts in Contrast: Allowing Art to Be Art

[1]Karl Barth, *The Epistle to the Romans* (London: Oxford University Press, 1968), p. 278.

[2]When I mention music, I do not mean lyrics and music. I mean music all by itself. Words and music together constitute a unique union, as was discussed in the last chapter.

Chapter 12: The Cultural Expanse, Part 1: Realities and Unities

[1]I beg the indulgence of those readers who may have read *Music Through the Eyes of Faith*, particularly chapter one, in that a portion of the material in the present section is found there as well, albeit in less detailed form.

[2]I make use of the word *community* along with *culture* because I believe that what we call culture is often described more scientifically and anthropocentrically than theologically. Even though we are a fallen race, and even though beauty and gentility, hurt and ravage, saturate the cultural story, we have to begin with the knowledge that "having in common"—being in community—is what first of all marks the foundation of human intercourse, just as disrupting community is what marks its demise. Theologically, "having in common" begins with the doctrine of creation and its human consequent, *imago Dei*. As we have seen, the triune Godhead is "in common" not only with itself but also with humanity.

[3]If there is a foundational weakness in the culture of liberal education, it is that too much time is spent thinking *about*, and too little thinking *in*, the various disciplines. It is far easier to think about the arts than to think in them, because doing the latter would mean learning the various discursive mechanisms they employ. Yet, for most, mere thinking about seems to suffice. This of course means that without the ability to think in the arts, individuals are not liberally educated in the way educational institutions claim them to be.

[4]I use the word *artifact(ual)* here and elsewhere in its widest and best sense. Just as culture is not just art but comprehensive human action, so an artifact is not just a piece of pottery but comprehensive evidence of our ability to think up and make all kinds of things from pottery to complex mechanisms and institutions.

[5]Nicholas Wolterstorff makes this point splendidly in *Art in Action: Toward a Christian Aesthetic* (Grand Rapids, Mich.: Eerdmans, 1980), in which he speaks of art in service of the liturgy. By "liturgy," he (as well as I) means any order or sequence in public or private worship. This is closer to the earlier meaning of the word signifying service and work—in this case, the service and work of the people of God in public worship or private devotion.

Chapter 13: The Cultural Expanse, Part 2: Issues

[1]Certain parts of this chapter have appeared elsewhere in a more extended form and with a different readership in mind. See my two-part article "Art, Words, Intellect, Education," *Arts Education Policy Review* 101, no. 6 (2000): 3-11, and "Art, Words, Intellect, Education," *Arts Education Policy Review* 102, no. 1 (2000): 3-10.

[2]John Seabrook, *Nobrow: The Culture of Marketing and the Marketing of Culture* (New York: Knopf, 2002).

[3]George Steiner, *A Reader* (New York: Oxford University Press, 1984), p. 303.

Chapter 14: What of Quality?

[1]This I should have learned from Scripture, but it took Kierkegaard to bring it fully to my heart (Søren Kierkegaard, *Works of Love* [New York: Harper & Row, 1962]).

[2]Certain of these thoughts can also be found in my article "Lemonade or Merlot: Authentic Multiculturalism and High Culture," *Arts Education Policy Review* 104, no.1 (2002), pp. 3-10.